MODELING FOR
RELIABILITY ANALYSIS

MODELING FOR RELIABILITY ANALYSIS

Markov Modeling for Reliability, Maintainability, Safety, and Supportability Analyses of Complex Computer Systems

Jan Pukite
DAINA

Paul Pukite
United Defense

IEEE Press Series on Engineering of Complex Computer Systems
Phillip A. Laplante and Alexander D. Stoyen, *Series Editors*

The Institute of Electrical and Electronics Engineers, Inc., New York

This book and other books may be purchased at a discount
from the publisher when ordered in bulk quantities. Contact:

IEEE Press Marketing
Attn: Special Sales
Piscataway, NJ 08855-1331
Fax: (732) 981-9334

For more information about IEEE PRESS products,
Visit the IEEE Home Page: http://www.ieee.org/

IEEE Order No. PP5738

Library of Congress Cataloging-in-Publication Data

Pukite, Paul.
    Modeling for reliability analysis: Markov modeling for
reliability, maintainability, safety, and supportability analyses of
complex systems / Paul Pukite, Jan Pukite.
        p.   cm. -- (IEEE Press series on engineering of complex
computer systems)
    Includes bibliographical references and index.
    ISBN 978-0-7803-3482-3
    1. Computer engineering.   2. Reliability (Engineering) --
Mathematical models.   I. Pukite, Jan, 1928-   .   II. Title.
III. Series.
TK7885.P85   1998   97-46570
004.2'1'01176—dc21   CIP

IEEE Press
445 Hoes Lane, P.O. Box 1331
Piscataway, NJ 08855-1331

Books of Related Interest from IEEE Press . . .

ONES AND ZEROS: Understanding Boolean Algebra, Digital Circuits, and the Logic of Sets
John Gregg
1998   Softcover   296 pp   IEEE Order No. PP5388   ISBN 0-7803-3426-4

INTRODUCTION TO REAL-TIME IMAGING: A Guide for Engineers and Scientists
Dougherty and Laplante
1995   Softcover   256 pp   IEEE Order No. PP5368   ISBN 0-8194-1789-0

REAL-TIME IMAGING. Theory, Techniques, and Applications
Laplante and Stoyenko
1996   Hardcover   328 pp   IEEE Order No. PC4242   ISBN 0-7803-1068-3

PROBABILISTIC RISK ASSESSMENT AND MANAGEMENT FOR ENGINEERS AND SCIENTISTS, Second edition
Kumamoto and Henley
1996   Hardcover   616 pp   IEEE Order No. PC3533   ISBN 0-7803-1004-7

Contents

Series Introduction

Complex computer systems are computer applications or environments for which simplifying assumptions for design and implementation fail significantly. They are typically characterized by intricacies in hardware platform, interaction of software modules, use of shared resources, interaction with the external world, or criteria for correctness and improved performance. There are real-time, fault-tolerance, and security constraints, among others, whose failure could have serious economic and safety consequences. Complex computer systems are becoming common in many sectors, such as manufacturing, communications, defense, transportation, aerospace, hazardous environments, energy, and health care.

Engineering of Complex Computer Systems (ECCS) is a rapidly growing area in which traditional CS/CE core, systems, and applications professionals converge to address what are perhaps the most challenging tasks and problems of today. There is a significant interest in the area, as illustrated by the recent emergence of the IEEE Technical Committee on Complexity in Computing (previously, IEEE Technical Segment Committee on ECCS), its annual International Conference (ICECCS), a stream of special issues of IEEE and non-IEEE journals, and scores of meetings and other activities in the IEEE and non-IEEE spheres.

In this book, *Modeling for Reliability Analysis,* P. Pukite and J. Pukite show how Markov modeling through finite state machines and Petri nets can be used to tackle the problems of balancing reliability, fault-tolerance, system effectiveness, maintainability, and availability. The authors demonstrate both the theoretical foundations and the practical applications of their approach in real-world systems. They also introduce their unique methodology and tool, CARMS (computer-aided rate modeling and simulation). We think you will appreciate the approach of this book, which is extremely practical without sacrificing rigor. This is exactly the kind of text we envisioned when we developed this series.

We call your attention to other upcoming books in the series: *Mathematical Design* by J. Paul Roth and *Foundations of Complex Systems Design and Analysis* by Alexander Stoyen, Phillip Laplante, Mike Hinchey, and Tom Marlowe, and we encourage interested authors to request a book proposal form.

We know you will enjoy this book; we certainly did.

Phillip A. Laplante
Alexander D. Stoyen

Preface

This book is written for the practicing systems and reliability engineers engaged in designing complex redundant systems. It contains the necessary background material for probability theory and Markov analysis. It also contains an interactive Windows-based computer program suitable for solving small to medium-sized problems. The program is available from the Internet at the Web site location http://umn.edu/~puk/carms.html.

Chapter 1 contains an introduction to the field of fault-tolerant systems reliability modeling.

Chapter 2 defines the concept of system and identifies the analysis and modeling framework required to design a fault-tolerant system.

Chapter 3 discusses the foundations of probability theory and needed probability definitions.

Chapter 4 relates the concepts of probabilistic faults and failures to a state-based reliability model.

Chapter 5 reviews the basic probabilistic reliability models, including reliability block diagrams, fault trees, stochastic Petri nets, and Markov models.

Chapter 6 introduces the state-based Markov model through matrix evaluation, a state diagram mapping, and approximate solutions.

Chapter 7 applies the state diagram Markov modeling approach to various nonredundant and redundant hardware configurations to evaluate reliability.

Chapter 8 applies the state diagram Markov modeling approach to various redundant software configurations that can experience failure.

Chapter 9 applies the state diagram Markov modeling approach to combined hardware and software configurations.

Chapter 10 discusses approaches to reducing large and complex Markov models to a manageable size through system state partitioning and mapping.

Chapter 11 applies Markov modeling to the evaluation of maintainability for systems that can undergo failure and repair.

Chapter 12 defines the concepts of availability of systems and the distinction between dynamic and static availability.

Chapter 13 introduces the field of safety analysis.

Chapter 14 details the important factors in Markov model evaluation, in particular computer-aided solutions.

Chapter 15 discusses the current approaches to system effectiveness modeling, including availability, dependability, and capability.

Chapter 16 lists the important support analyses to reliability evaluation, including mission definition, failure mode analysis, and tradeoff evaluation.

Chapter 17 presents an extended system effectiveness evaluation example and other applications.

Chapter 18 gives practical advice for dealing with fault-tolerant system and software design and future directions that implementations will take.

Chapter 19 is the user's guide to the CARMS reliability evaluation program.

Chapter 20 is a model library of common redundant system configurations that can be evaluated through the CARMS program.

Chapter 21 is the reference manual for CARMS, listing all of the commands and keyboard functions.

J. Pukite
P. Pukite

Acknowledgments

Thanks to the Pukite family and Zelma Bititis for their continuous support. We also wish to thank S. Bhimani, A. Stoyen, and P. Laplante for their help in getting this book into print.

Jan Pukite
DAINA

Paul Pukite
United Defense

1

Introduction

This book addresses the problems associated with the practical design of complex, yet reliable systems. These systems are used in many applications, including avionics and banking. Designers of such systems have to be methodical and careful to meet all specifications and requirements, many of which have origins in safety or mission-critical applications. Criticality has several meanings in this context; *safety-critical* systems are those where loss of life must be avoided, *mission-critical* systems stress mission completion, and *business-critical* (often also called mission critical) are those that are needed to keep a business operating.

The design of these systems is a lengthy and time-consuming process. Thus, from a designer's standpoint, a major problem is the lack of an established integrated approach that considers overall design concurrently with reliability optimization. Throughout the text, we stress the *Markov model* approach as a means of providing a unified approach to reliability, performability, and system- and cost-effectiveness evaluation.

1.1 SYSTEM COMPLEXITY

The complexity of a fault-tolerant system is one of the major problems facing the system designer. This complexity is due partly to the addition of redundant components and partly to the interaction between the components. Correspondingly, the complexity of the fault-tolerant system directly mirrors the reliability model.

As the number of system components and their failure modes increase, there is an exponential increase in system states, making the resulting reliability model more difficult to analyze. For example, if the system consists of n different components, then the resulting number of system states is 2^n (without considering the fault sequence), or approximately $e \times n!$ states (when considering the fault sequence, where e is the natural logarithm base). Thus, even for a relatively simple system the resulting Markov model may contain an extremely large number of states.

The large number of system states makes it difficult to solve the resulting model, to interpret state probabilities, and to conduct sensitivity analyses. In particular, it is difficult to identify the critical components. The basic issue to address here is how and when to use techniques for both *largeness tolerance* and *largeness avoidance*. Largeness tolerance is dependent on automated design tools with adequate computer resources, whereas largeness avoidance requires designer ingenuity and experience.

1.2 DESIGN METHODS AND TOOLS

During the design of fault-tolerant systems, the system analyst and the designer must understand the details of the process: what options are available to meet the objectives, which parameters are approximate, and which parameters are secondary (can be neglected). Software-based system designers, in particular, need methods to handle the overwhelming state-space complexity.

Knowledge of the design process determines the need for specific design tools. Tools (or a toolkit) supported by an interactive and integrated environment should be capable of providing reasonably fast answers to design problems. Support tool designers must also realize that the information and data available during the early design phase will be approximate. Thus, even in the best case, the computed answers to the design problems will also be only approximate and will not require the computing process to achieve ultra-high accuracy.

In the latter part of this book, we will describe and illustrate the application of the CARMS reliability program. This tool has been developed for fault-tolerant system reliability and effectiveness analyses. To give an idea of the most basic type of analysis that the CARMS program can provide, we give a short example of a problem application.

EXAMPLE—TRIP RELIABILITY

One of the most common and tangible examples of a fault-tolerant system is the automobile with spare tire. As a practical matter, it makes good common sense to take a spare tire along on a long trip. The reason? To improve the reliability or the probability of reaching the destination without delay.

As an example, consider a jeep with a single spare tire (see Figure 1.1). From thousands of similar vehicles on the road, one can estimate the failure rate of a tire (that is, a flat) per mile traveled by taking the total number of flats encountered and dividing by the miles driven. This number takes into account unexpected road hazards as well as wearout. Since we are using computed average failure rate, an exponential distribution should be used to provide an unbiased estimate for the probability of successfully completing a trip.

Figure 1.1 Jeep with Spare Tire.

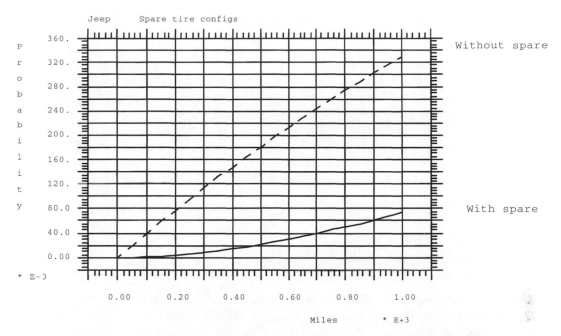

Figure 1.2 Probability of a Failed Trip versus Mileage without and with Spare Tire.

After creating the model with CARMS (see Chapter 19), we can evaluate it. Assuming that the failure rate for the tire is one flat per 1000 miles, we obtain the trip reliability for the situations with and without a spare, as shown in Figure 1.2.[1]

As one can see, the probability of becoming stranded is much higher without a spare tire. However, as the trip becomes longer, the curves tend to merge.

Although the example analysis may be intuitively obvious, the methods and tools on which it, as well as this book, are based give a foundation on which to formulate a quantitative analysis.

1.3 SYSTEM EFFECTIVENESS

System effectiveness analysis is part of the overall system design process. It specifically deals with the definition and evaluation of system figure-of-merit (FOM) measures.

In general, a figure of merit is any index that indicates the quality of a system. In the simplest case, it may be a measured physical quantity, such as range or payload. In other cases, it may be a calculated quantity based on measurement, such as the mean down time or the mean time between maintenance actions. Lastly, it may be a predicted quantity based on measurement or simulation. For example, *"the probability that a system can meet an operational demand at a random point in time,"* will require prediction since there will be some uncertainty about the operational environment.

[1]As a followup question: assuming that we have a jeep and a motorcycle with the same failure rates for a tire, which vehicle will have the highest probability of completing the trip?

Figures of merit indicate what can be expected from the system. They must be in an operationally oriented form that can be readily understood and used in planning. Where the number of significantly different mission outcomes is small, the probabilities of each of these outcomes can be useful figures of merit. When the number of mission outcomes is large or when a continuous range of outcomes requires consideration, a measure of relative "adequacy" may be assigned to each possible outcome, and the expected "adequacy" may be used as a figure of merit.

System Effectiveness Definition. System effectiveness measures the extent to which a system may be expected to achieve a set of specific mission requirements. System effectiveness is usually defined as a function of availability, dependability, and capability:

MISSION.   The mission definition is a precise statement of the intended purpose(s) of the system and of the environmental conditions (natural and synthetic) under which it is required to operate.

AVAILABILITY.   Availability is a measure of the system condition at the start of the mission and is a function of the relationships among hardware, personnel, and procedures.

DEPENDABILITY.   Dependability is a measure of the system condition(s) at one or more points during the mission, given the system condition at the start of the mission. It may be stated as the probability(ies) (or other suitable mission-oriented measure) that the system

1. Will enter and/or occupy any one of its significant states during a specified mission and,
2. Will perform the functions associated with those states.

CAPABILITY.   Capability measures the ability of the system to achieve the mission objectives, given the system condition(s) during the mission, and specifically accounts for the performance of a system.

Thus, system effectivness is a compound measure combining availability, dependability (reliability), and capability (performance). Details of the system effectiveness model derivation and evaluation are discussed in Chapter 15.

1.4 PRACTICAL DESIGN FOR RELIABILITY

The design of a real system involves the following steps:

1. *Define the key components of the system.* To simplify the design process, the key components of the system must be identified. These should be selected on the basis of their functions and independence.
2. *Estimate base component reliability.* For each of these components we need to obtain the associated failure rates. These failure rates may be based on MIL-HDBK (Military Handbook) 217 data or may be obtained through available commercial programs. It is important to remember that these failure rate estimates are only approximate, instead of being highly accurate. Once the failure rates are

known, the next step is to perform a first-cut reliability estimation. This will provide a nonredundant, single-thread, system reliability estimate, which will also help to identify those subsystems where redundancy will be required.

3. *Select a number of redundancy approaches.* In the beginning, only the desired reliability goal will be known. If a nonredundant single-thread system is unable to meet this goal, then redundancy will have to be introduced. The initial redundancy configuration considered should be the simplest that will have the potential of meeting the specified reliability goal.

4. *Develop simplified models for these components.* At the start of the design process, the designer should work with a simplified redundancy model to gain a better understanding of the potential gains of redundancy and to be able to select an acceptable redundancy level. For example, the designer may consider using different numbers of active components, passive spares, hot standby units, and so on. Each of these configurations will have a different model. A simplified model will allow testing of more options and more time to select the viable one. The initial reliability model should be based on ideal conditions (perfect recovery, no interaction between subsystems, etc.) for simplicity reasons.

5. *Select a simple system model and expand it as necessary.* Repeat the previous step at the system level. Since the initial model was chosen to be a simple one, the next step will introduce additional factors. These additions will include modifications for recovery, standby failure rates, and the like. Again, these model expansions should be introduced gradually, and their effect on the model noted. The main objective is to work with a minimum complexity model.

6. *Identify the critical design areas.* The simplest way of identifying the critical areas is to examine the shortest transition paths and determine which specific failure or recovery rates affect these transition paths. The critical components are the least reliable and as such form the weakest link in the proposed design. Then, one can develop more detailed reliability models for the critical subsystems and derive simple parametric equations relating component failure rates to the probability of failure.

7. *Determine the key factors affecting failure probability.* Once the critical factors have been identified, available options for further improvement should be identified. These options may include the use of higher reliability parts or additional levels of redundancy. For each of these options, reliability and performance models should be developed and evaluated.

8. *Determine the level of the required redundancy.* Once the desired reliability goal has been reached in the preliminary stage, a more detailed reliability model is developed to determine if all of the goals have been met.

9. *Select fault recovery process.* Since the fault-tolerant system is vulnerable during the recovery process, a dependable recovery scheme must be implemented. To achieve the desired reliability improvement, the interaction between the components must be controlled to avoid fault propagation to adjacent components or to other subsystems.

2

System Requirements
and Design

Future systems will have to meet a wide range of customer- or market-imposed design constraints, such as reliability, safety, weight, volume, power, cost, and maintainability. These requirements become more stringent with time, and, thus, there will be an ever increasing need to meet higher reliability and safety requirements. Particularly severe safety requirements will be imposed on those systems that operate in critical environments, where many of the system failures could result in loss of life or valuable resources.

Fault-tolerant designs will be needed to meet these requirements and will play a major role in the development and successful operation of future high-performance systems. However, the level of fault-tolerance will have to be carefully balanced against the available resources. For example, increasing the fault-tolerance will not be achieved without expenditures in other areas. One can expect the redundant system acquisition and maintenance costs to increase because of the additional equipment needed and the increased complexity.

Since many of these constraints are interrelated, the redundant system design is often difficult. Even more difficult will be the task of assuring that the chosen configuration is optimal.

2.1 PROBLEM IDENTIFICATION

Problem identification is an important task. It will start at the beginning of the system analysis process. At this early stage, we need an approximate qualitative identification of the system boundaries and a rough formulation of the stated and implied requirements both internal and external to the system.

Functional Requirements. Functional requirements will be obtained from the user requirement specification document.

Constraints. Any real system is subject to numerous constraints. These constraints will specify minimum performance parameters, as well as other physical and operational parameters. Constraints and their influence on redundant system operation should be considered concurrently during the design phase.

2.2 ANALYSES IN SYSTEMS ENGINEERING

Systems engineering, as we know it today, encompasses a variety of analyses that will be performed sequentially during the system design cycle. A discussion of the more important ones follows.

2.2.1 Application Analysis

Application (or mission) analysis is performed during the early feasibility phase. It is important to develop a basic and sound understanding of the application objectives and the ultimate operational use of the system. This analysis will play a part in selecting the final system for accomplishing the stated application objectives. Application analysis includes a thorough study of the various functions to be performed, their alternatives, gross operational requirements, and detailed objectives for the selected system.

2.2.2 Functional Analysis

Functional analysis is closely related to problem identification in the early stage and to hardware and software definition at a later stage. It comprises a study of what functions are to be performed and how they relate to each other. This requires the development of a coarse conceptual model of the system describing the process by which the system performs its functions. As the system slowly develops, the adequacy of the problem identification and functional analysis is reevaluated and the necessary changes and additions are made.

To define the functions performed by the system and to identify the hardware and software needed to perform these functions, the system mission (purpose) must be expanded to lower level functional blocks. At this level, it should be possible to correlate these function blocks (or subsystems) to specific hardware and software requirements.

An important factor during the functional analysis is the minimization of interactions or interfaces between the functions. This helps in two respects. First, by having functional independence we indirectly improve the overall system effectiveness, since we can depend on more than one way of accomplishing a required task. This approach is called functional redundancy and is very common in real-world situations. Its importance in the system design has not yet received the proper attention. Second, by having functional independence we can often simplify equipment design, since we can reduce the number of interconnections and use a higher percentage of standard modules.

Functional Blocks. Functional blocks may represent either hardware or software functions, or both. They are always related to the functional specifications established by customer requirements and are normally presented in a formal specification document.

2.2.3 Operations Analysis

Operations analysis is a detailed study of the proposed system to select the best operating methods. This task is accomplished by determining the operational requirements to achieve a system that has the highest effectiveness, where system effectiveness includes performance, operation, and the accomplishment of application objectives.

2.2.4 Design Analysis

Design analysis uses the results of application and operations analyses to establish system and subsystem design requirements, specifications, and design evaluation criteria. Note that often the system analyst tends to stop after completing the application and operation analysis. However, during the design analysis, the results of the application and operations analyses should be continuously reviewed to ascertain that the selected configurations meet the minimum requirements.

2.2.5 System Synthesis

System synthesis is the translation of system requirements and functions into hardware specifications. System synthesis usually involves the development of conceptual designs that undergo feasibility studies. Here reliability and maintainability must be approached as part of the overall design process. System synthesis continues until each of the stated system functions is resolved and the performance requirements are met. Achievement of the final solution requires a number of iterations that are reflected in changes of the configuration. Furthermore, as the system analysis progresses we can define the system in more detail, and this requires some changes or adjustments to the system boundaries or functions.

System synthesis will usually yield several potential candidates that satisfy the application requirements. Selection of the best system among competing alternatives is called system optimization. Optimization is a difficult task because there are several criteria in addition to given system resource constraints. This topic is important but beyond the scope of this text.

System analysis can also be viewed from another perspective, involving analytical, economical, and management aspects. Trading off these involves some compromises and changes before the final system is selected.

2.3 SYSTEM DEFINITION

Many of the steps in redundant system design modeling have counterparts in conventional system design. For example, the initial step in system definition is the same in both. This involves a detailed development of the functional specifications and establishment of a functional flow diagram. The required functions are then correlated with elements of specific hardware and software functional blocks.

2.3.1 System Characteristics

To describe a given system quantitatively, it must be characterized and expressed in numerical terms. System characterization is not unique, with many different characterizations each having certain advantages and disadvantages. For effectiveness evaluation, we would like to obtain a characterization of the system with relatively independent individual elements. One suitable representation would be to define the system in terms of its hardware, software, and support facilities.

System hardware characteristics can be further subdivided as static and dynamic. Static characteristics describe the basic design parameters such as cost, size, weight, and power. Dynamic characteristics include those that describe performance as functions of time. Included are not only performance, but also reliability, survivability, and the like.

System facility characteristics also follow the same pattern. Static characteristics include area and initial cost, whereas dynamic characteristics consist of operating costs, maintainability, and so on.

Static software characteristics include the number of people required to operate, maintain, and support the system. Dynamic characteristics include utilization of people and performance.

2.3.2 Definition of a Single-Thread System

The initial starting point in redundant system design is the single-thread system. The single thread is capable of meeting all of the functional performance requirements, but since it does not contain any redundancy it will not be able to meet the reliability and safety requirements (i.e., the requirement that single failures cannot cause system failure).

The single-thread system plays an important role in redundant system design because it provides the baseline against which future improvements are measured. The single-thread subsystem is lacking in any internal redundancy and usually represents a subsystem with the lowest reliability. A subsequent subsystem in the same family may contain some redundancy above the single-thread member.

By definition, all of the functions performed by the single-thread assembly of a family can be performed by any alternate subsystem in that family.

2.3.3 Independent Subsystems

A system is often assumed to consist of families of independent subsystems (assemblies). An independent subsystem is a portion of a system (functional grouping of hardware) that can in general perform its assigned function independently of the rest of the system. The functions of each subsystem can be performed by one or more different groupings of the hardware (for example, one or more independent assemblies in different redundancy configurations). In a typical system, there will be many independent subsystems.

2.3.4 System Optimization

To optimize the design with respect to system redundancy, it is necessary to establish a hardware level at which a configuration can be uniquely and conveniently described. This is an evolutionary process. At one extreme are parts, with their individual failure modes and failure rates. At the other extreme is the hardware associated with major application functions. The part level information cannot be used in the early design phase because detailed implementation data of the subsystem are not available. Similarly, designing entirely at the application function level needs careful consideration, since it must be correlated with many hardware assemblies, some of which may also perform other application functions.

During redundancy optimization, the common approach requires working simultaneously upward from the part level and downward from the application functions. This approach results in the definition of independent assemblies as the common denominator.

We can also distinguish the concept of a family. Members of the same family can perform the same functions. A subsystem can be replaced in its entirety by another subsystem from the same family of independent assemblies.

2.4 SYSTEMS APPROACH TO REDUNDANT SYSTEM DESIGN

When designing a new system, we must start with the overall view of the proposed system and the operating environment because the process must consider the entire design and all of the associated disciplines.

Redundancy analysis is an integral part of the system design process. It begins with the system analysis and continues throughout the design and manufacturing phases. This implies that the designers must be familiar with the redundancy analysis tools and must use them properly to achieve the desired reliability goals. Thus, the present approach, in which reliability analysis is performed after the system has been designed, must be modified.

Since the design of a redundant system seldom follows a well-defined sequence of steps, an adaptive approach to reliability analysis is needed. For example, in the more complex situations, prototyping may be needed to investigate the feasibility of a new redundancy concept.

Problem Definition. A clear and concise problem definition is needed before a detailed design is attempted. To accomplish this, we must ask the following questions:

1. *What is the problem?* The problem definition must be complete. Since the desired solution is a system that must meet a specific user's or customer's requirements, we must work backwards from this goal and find a feasible design solution.
2. *What are the alternatives?* In almost every design situation, there will be many design alternatives, including different redundancy configurations and different components. These alternatives must be defined and ranked.
3. *Which alternative is best?* The best selection should be based on some cost-effectiveness criteria that will be acceptable to the customer and is a feasible goal.

Goal, Objective, and Design Criteria Definition. System design goals must be based on mission goals and customer needs. Once the system goals have been identified, a full set of system design objectives must be developed. These design objectives will typically define the minimum acceptable design parameter values, such as performance, reliability, and safety. After the design objectives have been defined, they must be expressed as quantitative design criteria.

Fault-tolerant systems have to satisfy stringent reliability, availability, safety, performability (performance and reliability), system effectiveness (performance, availability, and reliability), maintainability, and testability requirements. These systems must be designed to achieve the required goals within the specified system constraints (cost, weight, size, and power).

Choosing the best system design is determined through multiparameter optimization. Since these parameters can affect system design in unknown ways, it is often desirable to evaluate design changes with respect to a single parameter. Evaluating the various controlling factors, also known as sensitivity coefficients, will allow comparison in terms of reliability, weight, volume, or power consumption increase.

If the specified systems constraints cannot be met, then knowledge of the unsatisfied constraints may be helpful in finding an alternative approach.

System Partitioning.   The partition of the system into logical subsystems is the first step in redundant system design. Next, the key functional blocks are identified. These blocks normally perform some well-identified function (e.g., we may see a natural breakdown by considering the functional requirements). Each of the selected functional blocks is then examined in detail, and its subfunctions are identified. This approach is used because partitioning at the functional levels normally results in minimum cuts (minimum number of interconnections) and has less chance of undesirable interactions. There is also the extra benefit of obtaining a better organized design. Furthermore, the functional partitioning also permits easier access to specific system functions from other system components. The physical partitioning of the system is normally done after sufficient design information becomes available.

Hardware and Software Identification.   The initial functional partitioning and the development of functional flow diagrams are done at an abstract level, without considering the actual physical implementation. In the next step, the key hardware and software blocks required for system operation are identified.

Fault-Tolerant System Design.   There are three aspects to redundant system complexity: reconfiguration, redundancy management, and handling system operation in degraded modes.

1. *Reconfigurable systems.* Although fault-tolerant systems have historically used fixed configurations, the current approach is to use dynamic reconfiguration of components to enable the continuation of mission operation after equipment failures are experienced. This approach is feasible because of the commonality of many functional blocks and the development of highly reliable data buses.

   The reliability of reconfigurable systems cannot be analyzed with conventional reliability block diagrams because a failure at a random time will change the resulting system configuration. Detailed reliability analysis of these systems will require development of a Markov reliability model that can represent changes in the system configuration, while the system experiences failures.

2. *Redundancy management.* Redundancy management is closely related to reconfiguration. Its objective is to best assign spares to optimize the mission effectiveness and goal achievement. Optimum redundancy management requires knowl-

edge of equipment status and the expected probabilities for the various system states that can be reached from the current state. Again, a Markov model can be used to compute the needed state probabilities.

3. *Degraded modes of operation.* Often, equipment will fail in a degraded mode that is still functional but will not perform at full effectiveness for all of the needed system functions. In these situations it is still possible to achieve a safe return or use the equipment in a diminished capacity mode.

Evaluating the degraded equipment and how it will affect system reliability and safety requires use of a model that can represent more than just two equipment states: good and failed. Thus, for reconfigurable systems permitting degraded operation, there is a need to represent a variety of degraded states that the conventional reliability block diagram cannot handle.

Redundant System Synthesis. Because of the complexity of fault-tolerant systems, fully automatic synthesis of a new system is not feasible. Instead, we must select an initial starting point, usually based on experience with similar systems. Once the initial systems configuration has been chosen, detailed analyses of this configuration can begin. These analyses will cover the various design and design-related disciplines, such as design, reliability, maintainability, logistics, and cost estimation. The actual process will be directed to a goal and will iterate over the feasible solutions, until an acceptable configuration is found.

2.5 SYSTEM MODELS

General system theory is a theory of models. These models encompass the specific theories concerned with the various systems disciplines and at the same time providing the necessary inputs to the overall systems model.

A mathematical model is a set of equations (algebraic or differential) in which the state of the system is described by certain variables and the interaction and specific characteristics by others. Often these equations are presented in a functional form, where the state of a given system is expressed as a function of time.

In addition to the mathematical model, a number of other models are employed in systems work. Some of these models are simply illustrative, whereas, others contain partial mathematical representations. Usually, these models are not complete enough to permit numerical evaluation with sufficient accuracy.

Some of these models are: program schedule, functional diagram, procedural diagram, and material flow chart. These models are often the only sources of information available in a particular area and as such should not be ignored during the system analysis phase.

A given mathematical model can usually be classified as either linear or nonlinear. The linear model may be either algebraic or differential. Both of these are important in system effectiveness evaluation. However, the nonlinear models are usually very difficult to solve.

The linear model is important for several reasons:

1. It is the only model for which a reasonably complete analytical theory is available.

2. Many physical systems are such that their behavior can be reasonably approximated by a linear model.

3. If the differential equations describing the behavior of a nonlinear dynamical model for a particular set of operating conditions are expanded in Taylor series, an equivalent linear model may be obtained which will represent the behavior of the original system for small-amplitude variations in the system variables.

4. The results of the linear analysis often can be extended to deal with certain simple nonlinear systems in a straightforward way.

The wide availability of computers provides capabilities to numerically solve some of the nonlinear models. However, there are other difficulties in working with the nonlinear model. Scaling is not possible, thus requiring the investigation of a wider range of conditions. System stability is also dependent on the amplitude and the specific nonlinearities. Furthermore, in the nonlinear case it is usually not possible to apply superposition, resulting in a complicated solution.

2.5.1 Basic Characteristics of Mathematical Models

The general mathematical model has two key aspects: one is concerned with the structure or form of the graph underlying the model, and the other is associated with the algebraic quantities superimposed on the graph.

For example, the electronic circuit diagram has these characteristics:

1. The *geometrical* structure that consists of the various electronic part symbols and their interconnections, and

2. The *algebraic* structure that gives information about the component parameters (values and tolerances).

Similarly, for a system state diagram, we can distinguish the same characteristics:

1. The *geometrical* structure consisting of the state symbols, together with the transition arrows, and

2. The *algebraic* structure provided by the superimposed transition rates.

In the following, we will proceed with a detailed derivation and description of the state-space mathematical model.

2.5.2 Concept of State

In any system characterization, we should seek the minimum mathematical description that leads to an understanding of the system. The state of the system can be considered to be this minimal amount of information that will completely characterize any possible future behavior of the system. The state variable approach has been shown to be capable of placing our physical intuition on a more precise basis. The power of the state variable approach lies not nearly so much in its role in helping our intuition, but rather in its ability to carry us beyond the intuitive boundaries of our minds.

Fundamentally, the concept of state is associated with the mathematical characterization of a system. It was formulated in a mathematically precise form by H. Poincaré in his description of the theory of dynamical systems. The concept was further developed by G. Birkhoff, A. Markov, V. Nemitskii, and L. Pontryagin, and more extensions are still taking place.

The systems that can be analyzed using the state concept form a majority of the known systems. The concept of state plays a particularly important role in the physical sciences, particularly in the field of thermodynamics, mechanics, and physics. In these fields, the state of the system is defined in a heuristic manner as a set of numbers that collectively contain all of the information about the past of the system that is relevant to determining its future behavior. In recent years, it has been employed in such new fields as information theory, decision theory, and optimal control. The growing complexity and the wide diversity of present-day systems have led to a more general formulation of a state, a formulation that is not limited in its applicability to systems or to a particular physical or mathematical form.[1]

One property that all physical systems have in common is causality. This means that the output of a causal system at any given time can depend only on the input up to and including that time, but not beyond that time. This property is considered so basic that physical and causal systems are often equated, and noncausal systems are considered only mathematical abstractions.

Thus, any physical system can be said to be subjected to laws that will govern its future. For example, a particle in a gravitational field is subject to Newton's laws of motion, and its position, velocity, and acceleration at any given time describe the states that we can observe. Similarly, physical systems are subject to the laws of deterioration and failure and these states can also be observed. While the laws of motion are deterministic in the sense that given the present state of the particle, all future states are determined, system probability of survival is stochastic in the sense that we can only estimate the probabilities of a future state. Yet, both systems are nonhereditary in the sense that their future is determined only by the last observed state—that is, the present.

Since most engineers are quite familiar with the analysis of deterministic systems, we will proceed to the next area of investigation—connecting the state approach with the theory of stochastic processes, leading to Markov analysis.

2.5.3 Mathematical Formulation of State-Space Model

The solution of a large set of differential equations describing the dynamics of a physical system presents two difficulties:

1. It is not always easy to express equations in a form that can be conveniently solved by a computer.
2. Some representations do not provide an insight into the physical behavior of the system because results are difficult to interpret.

The state-space representation and solution provide a useful approach to overcom-

---

[1]The definition of state in a form that would make it applicable to all known systems is a very difficult or, perhaps, impossible task. The current approach is to develop a specific definition tailored to the particular field in which it is being applied. The effort to find some general principles in this area which apply to both conceptual and concrete systems is probably one of the most interesting and most promising aspects of system science. These concepts could close the gap between formal and nonformal sciences.

ing both difficulties. It gives a simple and systematic format into which the individual equations may be fitted, and it is well suited for computer solution. The insight is at a different level from that given by individual equation or a transfer function. The individual features of certain parts of a problem may be ignored, and the attention may be focused on the major variables determining the system performance. We can also approximate the nonlinearities by changing the coefficients of the linear equations for different operating points or by inserting nonlinear components between the linear parts of the equations.

Let us proceed with a general description of the state-space method of system characterization. Consider a physical system in which the adjective "physical" is used in a sense that is sufficiently broad to cover any process occurring in the real world. Let us idealize this system to be able to describe it at any given time t by a set of finite quantities:

$$x_1(t), x_2(t) \ldots, x_n(t) \tag{2.1}$$

These quantities are called state variables and are components of the system state vector $x(t)$.

The formulation of the state variable of a physical process in analytical terms is a difficult task and requires utmost care and attention. It is also important to realize that often many alternative approaches to the formulation are possible and that the same problem can be expressed in different ways.

When constructing a descriptive model of the behavior of a physical system, we need to relate the time changes of the system to the state of the system. As an example, assume that we are dealing with a physical process in which time is measured continuously, not discretely. The derivative of the state vector, $x(t)$, then represents the change in the system. A simple and useful assumption to make is that the rate of change depends only on the current state of the system and not at all on the history. This assumption is the foundation for Markov processes, which will be discussed in detail later in this book. This assumption implies that the system is nonhereditary or memoryless.

On the basis of the above assumptions, we can formulate a mathematical description of the system in terms of ordinary differential equations as

$$x'_i = f_i(x_1, x_2, \ldots, x_n, c) \tag{2.2}$$

$$x_i(0) = c_i \tag{2.3}$$

for states $i = 1 \ldots n$, where the quantities c_i specify the initial state of the system. Normally, it is more convenient to employ the standard vector notation and to write the set of the state equations in a shorthand form as:

$$x'(t) = f(x, t)$$
$$x'(0) = c \tag{2.4}$$

When studying a physical system, the problem is to develop and solve the state equations in order to study the behavior of the system as a function in time.

2.5.4 System Life Models and State Diagrams

A state diagram is a mathematical model that can be used to represent system life characteristics of the system. The basic concept is old, but the applications are many. The original representation was probably borrowed from physical chemistry, where it was used to represent the chemical rate process. Similarly, the state diagrams used in reliability, maintainability, and availability analyses are rate diagrams. They represent the system evolution process from state to state, a process similar to radioactive breakdown or chemical reaction.

The state diagram approach was used in the past for reliability work on a less than widespread basis, mostly because of the lack of an adequate explanation and understanding. The initial work pointed out the almost universal applicability of state diagrams to reliability problems. In particular, almost all of the known redundancy configurations could be handled using the state diagram approach. From there various studies have demonstrated the application of the state diagram techniques to actual hardware configurations and led to the development of specialized simulation programs.

Thus, many of the mathematical models used in operations analysis can be based on a Markov process representation and expressed in a state diagram format.

2.5.5 Redundant System Modeling

Redundant systems are not only complex, but also very difficult to analyze and to evaluate. One approach to the system evaluation, short of building the actual system, is to build models representing the planned system. Although these models are also complex, they provide a lower cost reliability and performance evaluation option.

To perform a detailed redundant system analysis, we usually work with three key models:

1. *Reliability model.* The reliability model is used to estimate mission success probability and the probabilities associated with completing less than a perfect mission.
2. *Performance model.* The performance model is used to verify that the expected system performance is within the specified bounds.
3. *Optimization model.* The optimization model enables the selection of the most promising configuration from the list of feasible implementations.

Although it is sometimes possible to develop a single model for the whole system, such a model would be extremely large. Thus, it would be difficult to interpret and to evaluate.

2.5.6 Subsystem Models

As a rule, models for each subsystem are developed individually, assuming that the subsystems act independently in the system. This is often a good assumption in that having dependence leads to more complex models, as well as possible reliability degradation.

2.5.7 Subsystem Model Integration

Subsystem models are integrated on the system level using mapping. This mapping involves consideration of how the subsystem states will affect system operation.

2.6 SYSTEM SIMULATION OR EVALUATION

The available system simulation models can be classified as static (steady state) or dynamic (transient). Furthermore, each category can be either deterministic or probabilistic. Most designers are familiar with deterministic models of a static or dynamic nature. In developing reliability models, we can often merge deterministic with probabilistic models. Although reliability and effectiveness are usually expressed in static form, the dynamic model will be found to be of more value. It will provide a simpler representation and will assist in understanding the system operation.

In developing system models, one must make simplifying assumptions or be inundated by the large number of equations. Thus, one of the tasks will be the selection of the relevant aspects of system performance and their representation in the system model.

The general theory of systems consists of many, often unrelated, disciplines with their own theorems, models, and expressions. Each area also has many approximate techniques developed for specific applications. The reasons are:

1. The basic difficulty of solving problems containing many variables.
2. The absence of a generalized framework in which the problem can be stated and solved.
3. The lack of emphasis on the symmetry and combinatorial aspects of the problems.

Although most physical systems are highly symmetric, considerable skill is needed to recognize this symmetry and to take advantage of it. Similarly, randomness does not mean that the system is not predictable, but that the system operation should be described by the use of probability theory.

Thus, we find that the same differential equations that are used to describe the physical behavior of the system can also be used to describe the system life and operational characteristics. In the latter case, these equations will govern the flow or the change in probabilities associated with the system instead of the time/motion behavior of the system.

For effectiveness evaluation, our model must be general, it must emphasize the common features of all systems, and it must be applicable to a wide range of systems. It must have the scientific character in the sense that it is uniquely defined. The conclusions derived must also have meaning for real systems.

2.7 SYSTEMS SELECTION

The task of system design normally involves new systems or major modifications of existing ones. The challenge of system design is to develop new systems that surpass the existing goals and yield higher performance, higher reliability, and safer systems. To reach this level requires the development of new redundancy implementation schemes, as well as new redundancy evaluation techniques.

The final system selection will be based on the previously established goals and requirements and will involve several tradeoff decisions.

2.8 SYSTEMS IMPLEMENTATION

Before the final system implementation, approximations and assumptions used in the earlier analyses must be reviewed and verified. These may include functional block independence, limits of fault propagation, monitor fault detection capabilities, and design limitations. Many of these factors may not have been included in the initial analysis because the design details were not then available.

The verification process requires a good understanding of not only the design details, but also the redundancy analysis techniques and assumptions that are made.

3

Foundations of Probability Theory

3.1 HISTORICAL BACKGROUND

Like calculus, probability theory emerged during the renaissance era of applied mathematics. While Newton was formulating calculus in the seventeenth century, Fermat and Pascal originated many of the concepts of probability. Whereas most of the other mathematical disciplines were concerned with applications dealing with practical problems, such as surveying land, probability theory started in an area dealing with recreation (i.e., gambling). Much later, as the areas covered by natural sciences became more demanding, probability theory was extended to cover these areas, at the same time becoming more sophisticated. The modern period in probability theory dates back to the nineteenth century. Most of the basic work during this period was performed by the Russian mathematicians Tchebychev, Markov, and Liaponov. These scientists introduced the concept of the random variable and also established the basic mathematical techniques for dealing with this concept.

During the nineteenth century, the field covered by the theory of probability expanded to the point that probability concepts are now used in every branch of science. Many of the newer branches of physics, such as statistical mechanics, thermodynamics, and quantum theory cannot even be described unless one employs the concepts of probability.

3.2 APPROACHES TO THE DEFINITION OF PROBABILITY

Most mathematical disciplines are characterized by exact and accepted definitions. Unfortunately, various definitions have been proposed and new ones are still being added (for example, the fuzzy logic extensions). Instead of discussing the different approaches in detail, we will concentrate on the most general approach.

Gnedenko [Gnedenko 63] classifies probability definitions as follows:

- Definitions dealing with the quantitative measure of the degree of certainty of the observer.
- Definitions dealing with the concept of equal likelihood (the classical definition).
- Definitions dealing with the relative frequency of occurrence of an event in a large number of trials (the modern definition).

Our areas of concern are the last two categories. Normally, definitions in the first group are highly subjective and sometimes cannot be reduced to numerical expressions.

3.3 THE CONCEPT OF PROBABILITY

Let us assume that we conduct an experiment and note what happens when a certain set of conditions occur. In this case, we will observe a cause and associated effect. In some cases, the output will depend precisely on the input. For an example, if a certain voltage is applied to an accurate amplifier, its output can be predicted with a high degree of certainty. As a counter-example, flipping a coin is an experiment where the outcome cannot be predicted unless one uses a trick or biased coin. Hence, this experiment is probabilistic. When considering the probabilistic experiments, we are more interested in the general characteristics. This includes the long-run outcome or the most likely event.

On the basis of these experimental observations, it is possible to formulate the following laws:

- Deterministic case

  Whenever a certain set of conditions S is realized, the event A occurs. The above law is self-explanatory, with an example given by the amplifier output.
- Probabilistic case

  Here we find that we actually have a range of cases. First, we may have an event that is inevitable whenever the set of conditions is realized. Second, we may have an event that may or may not occur whenever the set of conditions is realized. This event is called random and occurs within the range of the two cases.

Suppose, now, that we perform a particular experiment N times and observe a particular event A a total of M times. One then may say that the probability of event A is M/N, if N is assumed to be large. Or, statistically, we may write:

$$P(A) = \lim_{N \to \infty} M/N \qquad (3.1)$$

Now we can formulate the law for the probabilistic case: Whenever the set of conditions S is realized, the probability that the event A will occur is equal to $P(A)$. The different modifications of this law are referred to as probabilistic or stochastic definitions, where stochastic typically refers to a process [Cox 65].

3.4 THE FIELD OF EVENTS

Let us consider a set of conditions S and a family of events $A, B, C, \ldots$. These events are assumed either to occur or not to occur whenever the set of conditions is realized. A number of relations can exist between these variables. These can be listed as follows:

- If A implies B and at the same time B implies A, then these events are equivalent and we denote this relation by $A = B$.
- The simultaneous occurrence of A and B is called the product and is denoted by AB.
- The occurrence of at least one of the events A or B is called the sum, or union, of events A and B and is denoted by $A + B$.
- The occurrence of A and the nonoccurrence of B is called the difference and is denoted by $A - B$.
- The occurrence of A given that B already occurred is $A|B$.

These cases can be represented graphically. Examples are shown in Figure 3.1.

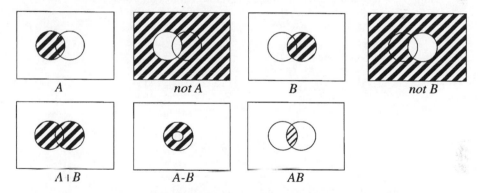

Figure 3.1 Boolean Operations on Events.

Other relations include the following.

- The concept of the impossible and the sure event is used so often that it is desirable to denote these two events by special symbols. The impossible event is denoted by $\varnothing$; the sure event is denoted by Ω, using the conventional notation.
- Two events are called complementary if the following relations exist:

$$A + \overline{A} = \Omega \qquad A\overline{A} = \varnothing \tag{3.2}$$

and hold simultaneously. These can be read, respectively, as A or *not A* always occurs, while A and *not A* cannot occur simultaneously.

- Two events are called mutually exclusive if their joint occurrence is impossible:

$$AB = \varnothing \tag{3.3}$$

3.5 CLASSICAL DEFINITION OF PROBABILITY

The classical definition of probability is based on the concept of equiprobability (or equal likelihood) of events [Feller 57]. This concept is a basic one. For example, tossing a coin results in either tails or heads. Using the classical definition, we can assume that these two events are equiprobable if the coin can be considered uniform in all respects.

Under these conditions, the classical definition of probability may be formulated as follows:

If an event A is decomposable into the sum of M events belonging to a complete group of N pairwise mutually exclusive and equally likely events, then the probability $P(A)$ is equal to

$$P(A) = M/N \tag{3.4}$$

3.6 RANDOM VARIABLES

Suppose that we are investigating a variable x that can take on only the values

$$x_1, x_2, \ldots, x_n \tag{3.5}$$

with the respective probabilities

$$P(x_1), P(x_2), \ldots, P(x_n) \tag{3.6}$$

Since we are investigating the variable x over its complete range of values

$$\sum_{i=1}^{n} P(x_i) = 1 \tag{3.7}$$

Under these conditions, x is called a random (or stochastic) variable. The function $P(x)$ which takes on the discrete values at the given points is called the probability frequency or probability density function. In shorthand notation

$$P(x_i) = \text{Prob } (x = x_i) \tag{3.8}$$

Similarly, we can define another important function, the distribution function, as follows:

$$P(x) = \text{Prob } (X \le x) = \sum_{x_i \le x} P(x_i) \tag{3.9}$$

where X refers to the set of all x_i. In effect, this is a cumulative function.

To differentiate the two functions, we use the following convention: the probability frequency function will be denoted by lower case $-$ $p(x)$, while the probability distribution function will be denoted by the capital letter $-$ $P(x)$. The functions can be discrete or continuous. Often, x will refer to time, for example, in a reliability application, a random distribution of the failure times.

3.7 NUMERICAL CHARACTERISTICS OF RANDOM VARIABLES

For reliability applications, we will be using certain simple numerical characteristics to describe random variables. Besides the probability frequency and distribution functions, the most important and probably the most useful one in practical work is the expected value of a random variable. This term has the same meaning as the mean value or the average value and is often used to denote the same concept.

$$E(x) = \sum_{i=1}^{n} x_i \cdot p(x_i) \tag{3.10}$$

In the general case, we can define the expected value of a deterministic function of x by the equation

$$E[f(x)] = \sum_{i=1}^{n} f(x_i) \cdot p(x_i) \tag{3.11}$$

If $f(x) = x^2$, we obtain the so-called second moment of the random variable. Also, if the second moment is defined with respect to the mean:

$$\text{Var}(x) = D(x) = E[x - E(x)]^2 \tag{3.12}$$

the resulting quantity is called the dispersion or variance of the random variable.

The square root of the variance is called the standard deviation or RMS (Root-Mean-Square) value of the random variable.

3.8 BASIC RULES OF OPERATION

Ordinary arithmetic is based on addition and multiplication. In probability theory, the basic rules are called sum and product rules, corresponding in many respects to the usual arithmetic operations. Before discussing these rules in detail, it is necessary to define some of the basic events considered earlier in this section.

- The probability of the impossible event is zero. In mathematical notation

$$P(\varnothing) = 0 \tag{3.13}$$

- The probability of the certain (or sure) event is unity.

$$P(\Omega) = 1 \tag{3.14}$$

- The probability of the event, $\overline{A}$, complementary to the event A, is given by the expression:

$$P(\overline{A}) = 1 - P(A) \tag{3.15}$$

Given these basic definitions, we can now proceed with the task of stating basic rules. Let us first consider the sum rule.

■ The probability of the sum (or union) of two mutually exclusive events is given by the sum of their probabilities. In mathematical terms

$$P(A + B) = P(A) + P(B) \qquad (3.16)$$

If the events are not mutually exclusive, we need a modification. For any two events that are inclusive, the probability of the sum is given by

$$P(A + B) = P(A) + P(B) - P(AB) \qquad (3.17)$$

Similarly, the product rule can be stated as follows:

■ If two events are independent, the probability for their joint occurrence is given by

$$P(AB) = P(A) \cdot P(B) \qquad (3.18)$$

If two events are not independent, the probability of the product of the two events is equal to the probability of one of the events by the conditional probability of the other event, given that the first has occurred. In mathematical notation:

$$P(AB) = P(A) \cdot P(B|A) = P(B) \cdot P(A|B) \qquad (3.19)$$

In the above definition, we used the concept of independence. This means that event A is independent of event B if the relation

$$P(A|B) = P(A) \qquad (3.20)$$

holds; that is, the occurrence of the event B does not affect the probability of the event A.

It is possible to extend the above rules to the cases where there are more than two variables by simply applying the stated rules repeatedly until all variables are accounted for.

3.9 COMPUTING CONDITIONAL PROBABILITY— AN EXAMPLE

Consider the results of two experiments. Assume that each experiment is as likely to result in a failure as in success (flipping a coin). Then we can ask: What is the conditional probability that both experiments are successful, given that

1. the first experiment is a success, and
2. at least one of the experiments is success?

SOLUTION

Let A represent the event that the first experiment is a success, and let B represent the event that the second is a success. Then $A + B$ is the event that at least one of the experiments is a success, and AB is the event that both experiments succeed. The probability that both experiments are a success, given that the first one is a success, is equal to

$$P(AB|A) = P(AB)/P(A) = \frac{1}{4} / \frac{1}{2} = \frac{1}{2} \qquad (3.21)$$

The probability that both experiments are a success, given that at least one of them is a success, is equal to

$$P(AB|A+B) = P(AB)/P(A+B) = \frac{1}{4} / \frac{3}{4} = \frac{1}{3} \tag{3.22}$$

3.10 MARKOV CHAINS AND PROCESSES

A problem of major interest in applied probability is that of time-resolved evaluation of the state of random phenomena. The theory of Markov chains plays an important role in these investigations and, in particular, for the prediction approach described in this book. Markov chain theory derives its name from the Russian mathematician A. A. Markov (1856–1922), who pioneered a systematic investigation of mathematically describing random processes.

Let us imagine that we perform a sequence of trials, in each of which one of k mutually exclusive events may be realized. We say that the sequence forms a Markov chain, if the conditional probability of occurrence of a certain event in the $(s + 1)$ trial, given that a known event has occurred in the sth trial, depends only on which event has occurred in the sth trial. This is contingent on not being affected by the events that have occurred in the earlier trials (such as $s - 1$). In other words, the next trial depends only on the present state and ignores everything that has happened in the past. One may say that the trials have no memory.

Markov chains are random processes in which changes occur only at fixed times (trials). On the other hand, many of the physical phenomena observed in everyday life are based on changes that occur continuously over time. Examples of these processes are equipment breakdowns, arrival of telephone calls, and radioactive decay. It is possible again to define a random process where the future will depend only on the present state and will be independent of history. Processes with this property are called Markov *processes* and form the basic framework in investigations of system reliability analysis.

Basic Reliability Concepts

This section presents a brief review of the basic concepts of probability that will be needed to develop suitable reliability models. As the system becomes larger, corresponding to the introduction of redundant components, our reliability model development will be based on the system state model introduced in Chapter 2.

4.1 MEASURES OF RELIABILITY

For reliability evaluation, we will be using several functions for describing the failure process (or the repair/renewal process) [Cox 62]. The key functions are:

1. *Probability density* of failures, $p(t)$
2. Cumulative failure probability, $P(t)$
3. Failure rate, $\lambda(t)$

The equations relating these functions are:

$$P(t) = \int_0^t p(x)dx \qquad \overline{P}(t) = 1 - P(t)$$

$$\overline{P}(t) = \exp\left[-\int_0^t \lambda(x)dx\right] = R(t) \qquad (4.1)$$

The reliability, $R(t)$, of a component is defined as the probability that the component will operate correctly until time t, given that it was operational at time 0 (i.e., the survival probability). The failure density of the component, $p(t)$, can also be expressed in terms of reliability as

$$p(t) = -\frac{d}{dt}R(t) \qquad (4.2)$$

The instantaneous failure rate function, $\lambda(t)$, is given by

$$\lambda(t) = \frac{p(t)}{1 - \int_0^t p(\tau)\,d\tau} = \frac{p(t)}{R(t)} \tag{4.3}$$

A well-known example of a probability density of failures is the exponential:

$$p(t) = \lambda \cdot e^{-\lambda t} \qquad \lambda > 0, \quad t \geq 0 \tag{4.4}$$

The choice of this density leads to a constant failure rate (or hazard rate) function $\lambda(t) = \lambda$, which provides a memoryless or independence of age approximation. Note that this will be used in the Markov analysis.

The unreliability of the system, $Q(t)$, is the probability that the component will fail in the time interval from zero to t. This is given by:

$$Q(t) = \int_0^t p(\tau)\,d\tau = 1 - R(t) \tag{4.5}$$

Note that the unreliability of the system, $Q(t)$, is identical to the earlier defined cumulative failure probability, $P(t)$.

Of particular importance is the mean time to failure (MTTF), given by

$$MTTF = \int_0^\infty t\,p(t)\,dt \tag{4.6}$$

Often, the reliability of redundant systems is expressed in terms of the mean time between failures (MTBF) or the mean time between critical failures (MTBCF). However, these measures are poor for redundant system reliability requirement specification, unless the mission time and operational conditions are clearly indicated.

In particular, MTBF and MTBCF are meaningful only for redundant systems that will be operated without repair until they experience system failure. In a real situation, this is not true because most of the mission-critical systems undergo a complete checkout before the next mission is undertaken. If a redundant component is found, it is normally replaced at this time and the system is returned to a fully operational status. Fortunately, more useful measures are available.

4.2 SPECIFICATION OF RELIABILITY

There are many ways of specifying reliability requirements. These may range from specifications expressed in terms of the number of failures per time interval to more specific requirements related to a particular mission, environment, and mission time.

Critical Mission Factors.   First, all of the critical mission factors should be identified. This identification considers mission phases, timing, functional blocks, and function priority. These factors will be needed for the development of detailed reliability models.

Function Criticality.   If the redundant system is designed to operate in degraded modes, then criticality factors must be assigned to all system functions. In most situations, these criticality factors depend on the specific mission phase. Once these factors are established, a mission outcome tree can be developed which relates the functions to specific mission outcomes.

Quantitative Mission Reliability.   A quantitative measure of reliability must be established. For fault-tolerant systems, this measure should be specified as a probability instead of a mean-time measure, such as MTBF. For most mission-critical systems, minimum acceptable critical failure probability must also be established.

Mission Profile and Time Specification.   Since reliability is a function of time, a mission profile should be developed that clearly shows when specific functions are needed.

Importance of Mission Time.   When evaluating the actual mission reliability, mission time and maintenance philosophy play an important role. Depending on the specific situation, the measured MTBCF may differ greatly from that predicted (because of short mission times, repair strategies, etc.). Thus, in any practical situation, reliability evaluation should be based on mission policies.

4.3 FAULTS AND FAILURES

Definitions.   In our evaluation, we will use the following definitions:

1. *Failure*. A failure causes the system performance to deviate from the specified performance.
2. *Fault*. A fault is an erroneous state of system hardware or software.
3. *Error*. An error is the manifestation of a fault.

Failure Classification.   Failures are commonly classified as either fail-safe, fail operational, or catastrophic. These classifications relate to the system behavior in terms of operational capabilities:

1. A *fail-operational* state represents the condition in which a system component has failed but the system is still fully operational. These modes are used to identify and classify system states in the reliability model.
2. A *fail-safe* state represents the condition in which a component has failed, resulting in the loss of major operational capabilities, but retaining sufficient capability for the safe recovery of personnel and equipment.

In practice, the faults leading to failures can be further categorized as permanent or intermittent. Faults may be assignable to a specific cause or unassignable, if the source is indetermine.

Failure Independence.   When a fault occurs in the system, it may cause secondary faults. Fault independence is often assumed to simplify reliability model development and to obtain first-cut reliability predictions. Since fault dependency reduces reliability, design changes should be considered to reduce this dependency.

      Fault Isolation or Containment.   Fault isolation is needed to prevent the fault in one area of the system from affecting the operation of other system components.

4.4 STATE-BASED RELIABILITY MODEL

Any given system may operate in several states. These states may be classified as operational or failed, depending on the available system functionality. Note that the transitions between the states may be caused by changes in operational requirements *or* by component failures.

      The state diagram for each subsystem defines the unique states in which the equipment may exist when subjected to all significant element failure combinations. Associated with each state is a state probability that expresses the probability that the subsystem will be found operating in this state. This probability depends on mission time, spare component availability, and failure and repair rates for the components.

      Ultimately, all subsystem equipment failure states should be further interpreted and resolved into one or more assigned system states. This operation involves a mapping from the subsystem states to the system states. There is also a corresponding mapping for the physical and other system parameters.

      For example, consider an aircraft system. The specific parameters or sensitivity coefficients (such as volume, weight, cost, power, and failure rate) can be thought of as penalties of ownership of a system. The consequences of control system failure are dependent on a particular aircraft, the control system, the pilot, and the circumstances at the time of the failure. As detrimental consequences, they may also be considered penalties of ownership. They may vary from a simple nuisance of manually assuming control for the failed system to a safety-critical scenario. It is necessary to select the most representative outcomes for the given vehicle and to assign them as the universal system states to which other equipment failure states are resolved.

      In an aircraft, the pertinent consequences of equipment failure can be failure of a complete mission or loss of the aircraft. These may be assigned as the terminal states (mission outcome) on all state diagrams. Other states may represent degraded modes of operation and can be associated with a weighting function representing the relative value of operating in that state with respect to the mission outcome.

4.4.1 Model

Since our reliability measures include not only the basic reliability computation, but also other measures, such as availability and effectiveness, a unified formulation of a general model will be developed. In the derivation of this model, we follow the notation introduced by Barlow [Barlow 65].

      A system state at time t is specified by a vector-valued random variable or tuple:

$$X(t) = (X_1, \ldots, X_n) \tag{4.7}$$

In the simplest case of a single component, $X(t)$ will be a one-dimensional variable, $X_1(t)$, with value 1 representing the operational system state and 0 the failed system state. When dealing with redundant systems, there will be other states, with the possibility of values between 0 and 1 representing modes of degraded operation. For example, in a four-component state system.

	X_1	X_2	X_3	X_4
operational	1	1	1	1
failed	0	0	0	0

Since $X(t)$ is a random variable, there will be a cumulative probability distribution function for an operational system given by

$$P[X(t)] \qquad 0 \le \tau \le t \tag{4.8}$$

From a statistical basis, the probability functions can be thought of as a histogram of data collected from a large number of experimental trials. How they are derived assuming a state-based Markov process is the basis of Chapter 6.

Regardless of how the function is obtained, however, we can assign a gain (reward or payoff) function specified by $g[X(t)]$. In the case of reliability, the gain from operating in the operational state (all $X_i = 1$) will be *one*, and that of operating in the failed state (all $X_i = 0$) will be *zero*. Expressed in an equation form:

$$g(\mathbf{1}) = 1 \qquad g(\mathbf{0}) = 0 \tag{4.9}$$

In the more general case the gain, $G(t)$, will be given by

$$G(t) = \mathrm{E}[g(X(t))] = \sum g[X(t)]P[X(t)] \tag{4.10}$$

In computing the gain for a given system, Eq. (4.10) will be incorporated in a general effectiveness model for the system (Chapter 15).

4.4.2 Performance Specification

Since redundant systems are often designed to support operation in a degraded mode, performance specification should cover the fully operational and the degraded operational regions.

A performance specification corresponding to fully operational will often be expressed in terms of the availability of specific functions. Degraded performance specifications describe the minimum operations needed to complete or meet certain objectives. Should the system performance fall below these limits, the system will be classified as failed. Often several levels of degraded operation levels will be identified.

5

Basic Reliability Models

To perform reliability modeling, we must be familiar with the system, its failure modes and their effect on the system; we also need to know the failure rates of the individual components. In this chapter, we provide a brief overview of the different models used in reliability analysis. In later chapters, we will be considering reliability model development for hardware, software, and the total system.

5.1 WHAT IS A RELIABILITY MODEL?

A reliability model is an abstract mathematical and graphical representation of the system reliability characteristics. The evaluated model can then be used for predicting mission reliability and so on. Although specialized model description languages have been used for evaluating reliable systems [Butler 86; Palumbo 92], this approach is usually not necessary because of the flexibility of the diagram representation techniques.

To both set up and evaluate the models, software tools are frequently used. A list of reliability analysis programs can be found in [Caroli 92] and [Johnson 88].

5.2 RELIABILITY MODEL USE

Reliability models support system design and are used to:

1. *Set and interpret requirements*. A preliminary reliability model is developed and evaluated during the initial conceptual design phase to help determine reliability requirements for the proposed system.
2. *Predict reliability of different configurations*. Alternative design configurations

require development of specific reliability models. These models are developed and evaluated during the initial design phase to select the most promising (optimal) configuration.

3. *Identify weak points in the system.* If the selected system configuration does not meet the stated reliability requirements, then reliability models are evaluated to find those components that are the least reliable and need reliability improvement.

4. *Support cost-effectiveness tradeoffs.* Reliability of the equipment will greatly affect the system life-cycle cost (LCC). Reliability models are used in support of this task to estimate the expected number of component failures.

Documentation. Documentation should be an integral part of the modeling task. A standard file output, such as a spreadsheet or database, can be used and the data transferred to other programs.

Standard Model Libraries. A library of standard reliability models (such as different redundancy configurations) can be used with different base rates and other parameters to represent the actual cases being analyzed. The stored model information should include numeric data and their graphical representation. The availability of such a model library will help in simulating and evaluating alternative system implementations. For example, we can envision specific models developed for a certain service facility or for analyzing a particular fault-tolerant system.

5.3 PARTS-COUNT MODELS

A parts-count reliability model is used to estimate the reliability of a nonredundant component or assembly. The basic assumption is that a single failure of a component or assembly will cause system failure. This reliability model is also known as the serial model. The parts-count model is also used in redundant system design to estimate failure rates for the individual system components. A good reference on parts-count modeling is [O'Connor 91].

This method requires the following steps:

1. Obtain the parts list.
2. Determine or estimate stresses for each part.
3. Select the failure rate source (such as MIL-HDBK-217, or commercial equivalent).
4. Look up the appropriate failure rate for each part.
5. Determine the component failure rate by adding individual failure rates.
6. Compute reliability for the given mission time.

Note that steps 4 through 6 can be computerized using the available reliability prediction programs.

5.4 COMPUTING SERIAL SYSTEM RELIABILITY

The reliability of a system, consisting of N series components, in which the failure of a component will cause system failure, is given by

$$R(t) = R_1(t) \cdot R_2(t) \cdot R_3(t) \ldots \cdot R_N(t) \tag{5.1}$$

where $R(t)$ is the system reliability and $R_i(t)$, $i = 1, 2, \ldots, N$, are the component reliabilities.

If the components have exponential failure densities, then

$$R(t) = \exp\left(-\sum_{i=1}^{n} \lambda_i t\right) = e^{-\lambda t} \tag{5.2}$$

where

$$\lambda = \lambda_1 + \lambda_2 + \lambda_3 + \ldots \ldots + \lambda_N \tag{5.3}$$

The computation of redundant system reliability is more complex and will be considered as we progress.

5.5 COMBINATORIAL MODELS

Combinatorial reliability models include reliability block diagrams, fault trees, and success trees. These models are applicable to simple systems and are based on perfect spare-component switching assumptions.

Combinatorial reliability models have serious limitations because they cannot be used to model system repairs or dynamic reconfiguration of the system. Hence, non-standard extensions have been added to these models to increase their expressiveness in modeling fault time dependence. More recent additions to the reliability models include Petri net and Markov process representations. The advantages and limitations of these models are discussed later in this section.

5.5.1 Reliability Block Diagrams (RBDs)

The oldest and most common form of reliability model is the reliability block diagram. A major advantage of using the RBD approach is the ease of reliability evaluation. Typically, a reliability block diagram is used to show a highly abstract view of the system redundancy. For example, a system consisting of two parallel components, **A** and **B**, is represented as shown in Figure 5.1.

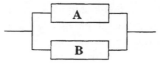

Figure 5.1 Reliability Block Diagram for Parallel Redundancy.

However, reliability block diagrams cannot always provide the required reliability and fail-safety information that is needed to design fault-tolerant systems. The problem arises because RBD's can only represent two states per component (i.e., good and failed), whereas redundancy analysis usually requires the representation of multiple states. For example, reliability block diagrams are incapable of handling time-dependent redundancy configurations, such as standby with switching, load sharing, and many others.

Advantages of Reliability Block Diagrams.   Reliability block diagrams are simple, well known, and usually easy to evaluate. They are widely used as an initial starting point in reliability analysis.

Limitations of Reliability Block Diagrams.   Reliability block diagrams can represent only a limited range of redundancy configurations, namely, those where all the individual components are energized during the mission. To represent other redundancy configurations, additional notational description is needed. Specific formulas for evaluating these blocks must be derived and added to the library.

5.5.2 Network Models

Network reliability models find application in representing communication networks, consisting of individual links. Most network applications are in the communication domain. The computation of network reliability is the primary application of network models.

A sample network diagram showing two parallel communication links, **A** and **B**, is illustrated in Figure 5.2 (numbers indicate nodes).

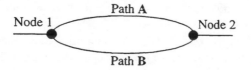

Figure 5.2 Network Diagram Representing Parallel Links.

In a network analysis, the individual communications links (channels) are assumed to be either operational or failed (open). This is a Boolean analysis. A link failure is assumed to have no secondary effects on remaining links.

Advantages of Network Models.   Because of the model's simplicity, computation is not very complex. Some efficient algorithms are available.

Limitations of Network Models.   The major disadvantage is the limited application domain.

5.5.3 Fault Tree Analysis (FTA)

Fault tree analysis is a basic tool in system safety analysis. More recently, fault tree analyses have been adapted for a range of reliability applications [Bavuso 87].

The fault tree diagram (FTD) is the underlying graphical model. Whereas the reliability block diagram is mission success oriented, the fault tree shows which combinations of the component failures will result in a system failure. An example of a fault tree diagram for a parallel system consisting of two components, A and B, is shown in Figure 5.3.

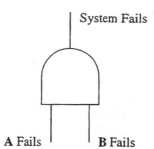

Figure 5.3 Fault Tree Representation of a Parallel System.

Advantages of Fault Tree Diagram.   A fault tree diagram can clarify fault processes and, in particular, fault propagation in the system.

Limitations of Fault Tree Diagram.   Although the fault tree approach is popular, it suffers from so many basic limitations that its use should be seriously questioned in redundant system design. Since the fault tree is used in many reliability programs, it is important to identify and understand the basic limitations of this approach.

1. *Time exposure.* Multiphase missions require different equipment configurations during different mission times. A fault tree representation does not allow an easy representation of this situation, where different exposure times apply to different functions. Furthermore, a fault tree representation does not lend itself to simple representation of specific time intervals (snapshots), which are needed for redundant system modeling.

2. *Severity of faults.* Complex systems exhibit complex fault behavior, including multiple fault modes. These faults will have different effects on the mission outcome. The severity of the faults may range from the loss of equipment or life to a nuisance fault that will have minimum effect on system operation. Thus, the reliability model should provide for inclusion or exclusion of specific faults. The basic fault tree model does not support this type of modeling.

3. *Fault sequence.* In a complex redundant system, the sequence of faults is important in determining their effect on the mission outcome. Thus, in a multiple fault situation, it may be important to distinguish the sequence of the specific faults because system monitors will respond differently depending on the sequence. Since a fault tree is a Boolean representation, it cannot represent these cases.

4. *Duplication of faults.* When a fault tree is used for reliability modeling, the same fault may appear in different parts of the fault tree diagram. Unless the fault tree evaluation program recognizes this and corrects for it, erroneous results will be obtained.

5. *Fault propagation in the system.* The occurrence of faults in a redundant system will change the configuration of the system. Since these changes will occur at a random time during the mission, a dynamic reliability model is needed to properly evaluate probabilities. The Boolean representation used in the fault tree formulation is not suitable for the representation of dynamic reconfiguration.

6. *Repair and maintenance.* Repair and maintenance are two important operations in redundant systems that cannot be expressed using the fault tree formulation.

5.6 MARKOV MODELS

The previously discussed reliability analysis techniques were based on combinatorial approaches such as RBD and fault trees. In these modeling schemes, we are assuming that the system components are limited to operational or failed states, that the system configuration does not change during the mission, and that the sequence of component failures does not affect system reliability. Many of the complex systems, however, cannot be modeled in a combinatorial manner.

The Markov model considers system states and the possible transitions between these states. The basic assumption in the Markov model process is that the system is memoryless; that is, the transition probabilities are determined only by the present state and not by the history. In reliability analysis, these conditions are satisfied by the Poisson process, which implies constant failure rates.

Markov modeling also finds wide application in many areas other than reliability because of its simplicity and applicability.

State Transition Diagram (STD).   A state transition diagram is a directed graph representation of system states, transitions between states, and transition rates. These diagrams contain sufficient information for developing the state equations. For example, in a parallel system consisting of two components, A and B, we can identify the following unique system states:

State	Description
S_1	Fully operational system
S_2	Component A has failed, B is still operational
S_3	Component B has failed, A is still operational
S_4	Both components have failed, system has failed

and the following failure rates:

Rate	Description
λ_A	Component A failure rate
λ_B	Component B failure rate

The corresponding Markov diagram is shown in Figure 5.4.

We will then assign a state probability $P_i(t)$ to each of the states S_i. To solve these equations, initial conditions for the state probabilities are also needed.

Since Markov models can be fairly large, we should be able to develop, extend,

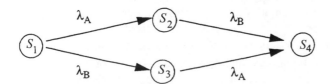

Figure 5.4 Markov State Transition Diagram for a Parallel System.

modify, and evaluate the model interactively. Thus, the effect of changes in the model parameters can be easily investigated. In particular, graphical representation of the state probabilities as functions of time helps to understand the model and the system behavior in terms of

1. *Change in state probabilities as a function of time.* In a detailed analysis, we need to examine the behavior of the various states. Although the probabilities associated with the initial system states (all components operational) will decrease and the system failure probabilities increase monotonically with time, the intermediate state probabilities may be increasing or decreasing, depending on the specific time range. Since the intermediate state probabilities are important in fail-safety evaluation and redundancy configuration management, detailed dynamic investigation of these state probabilities is needed to optimize the redundancy implementation.

2. *Effect of extended mission time.* Many analyses must evaluate the effect of extended mission time on the reliability and effectiveness. Displaying the state probabilities as functions of time will help to elucidate this relationship.

3. *Expected operation in degraded states.* Complex systems may not always fail completely. For example, a failure in aircraft navigation equipment may result in decreased navigation accuracy but otherwise operational performance. This capability could allow the aircraft to return to the home base safely. In this situation, a Markov model allows the user to model and to evaluate the probability of decreased performance and its effect on accomplishing the stated mission objectives.

Advantages of Using State Transition Diagrams. The basic Markov model is simple to formulate. If the Markov model evaluation is performed by computer, this simplicity is retained. These models also have wide applicability. For example, a Markov model can also be used in those situations where all the failure rate statistics are not available, but a first-order approximation is acceptable (e.g., the largest variance estimate). The results can then be used for many optimization tasks, where the initial information is not always accurate, but the ranking of results is critical.

A state diagram is more accurate than the reliability block diagram because it can represent more system states and component failure dependency. Understanding the system behavior is particularly important when different configuration schemes are evaluated. Alternatively, the use of Monte Carlo simulation will seldom provide the same level of understanding as a Markov model analysis. This is due mainly to the discreteness of the Monte Carlo simulation and the large number of replications needed to obtain results that are sufficiently accurate for design decisions. The latter is important in high-reliability systems, where the system failure probability is low and the discreteness of Monte Carlo simulation may mask the actual changes.

Limitations of State Transition Diagrams. We cannot and should not expect that the Markov model can solve all problems; it is not a universal problem-solving tool. However, if used with other design tools and models, it can improve analytical conclusions and result in a more optimal system performance.

Although the Markov model has been used in many applications, it does have several limitations. These limitations fall into two areas: basic assumptions about the model and numerical evaluation difficulties.

1. *Exponential failure rate assumption.* A basic assumption of the Markov model is that of a memoryless process. Although many physical processes are memoryless, in others this basic assumption fails, and a more complex model must be employed. However, physical processes occur, which can be approximated by the Markov model by introducing additional states.

    For example, a time-dependent transition rate may be approximated by a gamma-type distribution, which can be expressed in terms of a Markov model (i.e., the method of stages).

2. *Model approximations.* Besides the nonlinear problems discussed earlier, practical Markov models can easily become too complex if all of the possible system states are considered. Several approaches are available to reduce these difficulties. These include system partitioning, transition process truncation, and merging of states. For example, a complex model can be partitioned into several simpler models using realistic assumptions. These models are then solved separately and the results combined. Considerable work has been already accomplished, and research in this area is continuing.

3. *Stiff problems.* Stiff problems are particularly troublesome in Markov model evaluation. They are caused by roots in the model that are widely separated and thus require lengthy computations. For example, in a highly reliable system with very efficient maintenance, the failure rates are very low and the repair rates very high. Their ratio will be several orders of magnitude, which leads to loss of precision or poor choice of simulation time steps.

Stiff problems are not unique to Markov modeling but are also common in many design problems. For example, circuit analyses typically contain many stiff problems (where component values vary over a large range).

Within the last decade, this problem has been studied in detail and a number of approximations are now available. Some of these approximations involve splitting the model into slow and fast states. In addition to approximations, better numerical techniques for solving these equations are also becoming available. For stiff or difficult problems, improving the solution results will involve a combination of techniques including faster computers, better algorithms, and acceptable approximations.

5.7 PETRI NETS

Petri nets are useful in investigating state transitions in complex systems because they provide an easy to understand model of information flow. Stochastic Petri nets represent random transitions in a system. As such, they provide an alternative representation to state diagrams [Peterson 77].

To illustrate the Petri diagram, we will examine the development of a Petri net diagram for a two-component parallel system. The Markov diagram for this configuration is shown in Figure 5.5.

A Petri net (PN) consists of

1. Set of *places*. Places are represented by circles.
2. Set of *transitions*. These are represented by bars.

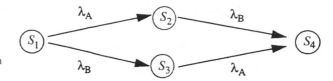

Figure 5.5 Markov State Transition Diagram for a Parallel System.

3. Set of *input arcs*. These are arrows entering a transition.
4. Set of *output arcs*. These are arrows leaving a transition.
5. Initial *markings*. Initial markings are represented by black dots (tokens) positioned within places.

Places in a Petri net correspond to discrete states and bars represent transitions. The execution of a Petri net is controlled by the position of the token. Tokens are moved by the firing of transitions. To fire, a transition must be enabled (by having the required number of tokens on the input side). During firing, the enabling tokens are removed from the input places, and new tokens are generated and placed in output places.

Stochastic Petri nets (SPN) are modifications of the conventional Petri nets, with the difference that they allow random sojourn times in markings with exponential waiting distribution.

Generalized Stochastic Petri nets (GSPN) provide the capability to model two types of transitions:

1. *Timed transitions*. These represent exponential firing delays. In Figure 5.6 they are represented by white vertical rectangular bars.
2. *Immediate transitions*. These fire in zero time and have higher priority than timed transitions. In the figure these are shown as shaded vertical bars.

Figure 5.6 shows a simple Petri net diagram representing the two-component parallel system. In the figure the initial markings (tokens) represent the system state where both of the system components (*A* and *B*) are operational.

Consider first that both of the initial transitions (*A failure* and *B failure*) are ready to be fired. The firing times in this case are determined by the transition probabilities. Then, for example, assuming that component A has failed, the corresponding Petri net diagram will be as shown in Figure 5.7.

After firing, the token has moved from the place marked *A operational* to the place marked *A failed*. The next expected failure will be that of component *B* failing.

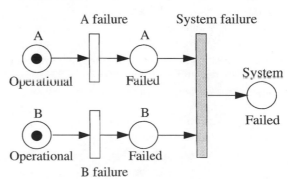

Figure 5.6 Petri Net for Two-Component Parallel Configuration (Initial State).

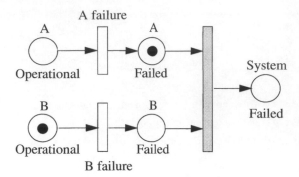

Figure 5.7 Petri Net for Two-Component Parallel Configuration (Component *A Failure*).

Once B fails, the respective token is moved from *B operational* to *B failed*, as shown in Figure 5.8.

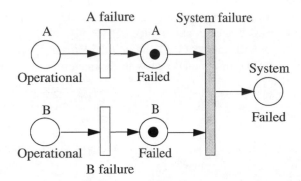

Figure 5.8 Petri Net Immediately After *B Failure*.

At this instant, however, the *system failure* transition is enabled and the instantaneous firing takes us to the next system state represented in Figure 5.9.

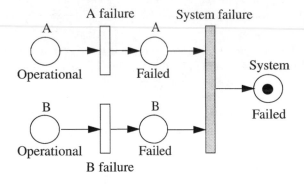

Figure 5.9 Petri Net for Two-Component Parallel Configuration (System Failure).

As another example, consider the same system with two repairmen present. Then the state diagram shown in Figure 5.10 applies.

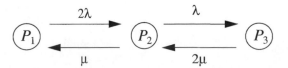

Figure 5.10 Two-Repairman Case.

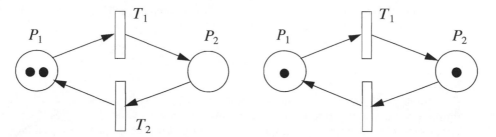

Figure 5.11 Petri Net for Two-Component Par-   **Figure 5.12** Petri Net after Component Failed.
allel Configuration with Repair.

The corresponding Petri net is shown in Figure 5.11. After a component has failed, the new marking is as shown in Figure 5.12.

   Advantages of Petri Nets.   Petri Nets have great expressive power and therefore can model a variety of situations.

   Limitations of Petri Nets.   The underlying model is difficult to solve. A larger model may lead to an explosion of states or may require a Monte Carlo solution.

5.8 MONTE CARLO SIMULATION MODELS

In a Monte Carlo simulation, a reliability model is evaluated repeatedly using parameter values drawn from random distributions [Lewis 89]. In particular, the Monte Carlo approach can be used in situations where the Markov process conditions do not apply (such as fixed or nonlinear failure and repair rates, fixed delays, etc.). Thus, it can provide insight when dealing with complex problems.

   The Monte Carlo simulation model is often used to evaluate the MTBF for complex systems. Here, the following steps apply:

1. Draw random numbers for each random variable needed in the simulation model.
2. Evaluate the desired function (MTBF, MTTFF, etc.).
3. Repeat Steps 1 and 2 a total of n times, to obtain n samples of the desired function. For example, the system failure times will be

$$T(1), T(2), T(3), \ldots, T(n) \tag{5.4}$$

4. Estimate the desired parameter. For example, the expected value of the system failure time can be obtained from

$$E(T) = \overline{MTBF} = \frac{1}{n} \left(\sum_{i=1}^{n} T(i) \right) \tag{5.5}$$

5. Obtain an estimate of the precision of the estimate, such as the sample standard deviation of the expected value:

$$S_{\text{T}} = \frac{1}{\sqrt{n}} \left[\sum_{i=1}^{n} \frac{(T(i) - \overline{T})^2}{n - 1} \right]^{1/2} \qquad (5.6)$$

As an example, consider simulating a redundant system consisting of two parallel components. For each iteration we have to draw failure times for each of the two components from an exponential or appropriate distribution with the given mean. The largest of these times will represent the system failure time. Once a large number of system failure times have been accumulated, we can compute the expected MTBF for the system. To judge when enough trials have been executed, it is necessary to compute the confidence limits associated with the expected value.

Advantages of Monte Carlo Modeling. Monte Carlo simulation can handle a variety of system configurations and failure rate models.

Limitations of Monte Carlo Modeling. Monte Carlo simulation usually requires the development of a custom program, unless the system redundancy configuration fits a standard model. It also requires lengthy computer runs if accurate and converging computations are desired.

5.9 RELIABILITY MODEL DEVELOPMENT

Reliability model development for a given system involves several considerations. Many of the important development steps apply to all models.

5.9.1 Definition of Subsystems

To reduce the complexity of a model, it is necessary to identify the independent components (subsystems or independent assemblies) of the system.

5.9.2 Operating Time Profile

A mission time profile must be developed for each subsystem. For cyclic or one-shot devices, the number of cycles occurring or expected to occur during the operation is also defined. The profile is segmented by mission phases corresponding to the different outcomes in a mission outcome tree. For each phase, the time profile shows whether the components are to be energized for the entire phase or just a part of it, or are operated for a specific number of cycles in each phase.

5.9.3 Derivation of Reliability Model

To conduct a quantitative reliability analysis, we need a mathematical model that abstracts and describes the failure process. In redundant system reliability analysis, the basic model we will use is the state diagram. Here, the states are defined by considering the operational components, with each state describing a list of remaining operational components.

For redundancy analysis, we have to draw an additional distinction in assuming failure modes. We may have two states that are identical as far as the operational equipment is concerned, but may differ in the sequence. Thus, these two states may have to be handled distinctly (e.g., component *A* fails before *B* fails versus *B* fails before *A* fails).

5.9.4 Outcome Tree

The outcome tree is commonly used to represent mission outcomes. It is particularly useful in showing outcomes of a multiphase mission.

An example of an outcome tree for a mission consisting of two phases, A and B, is shown in Figure 5.13

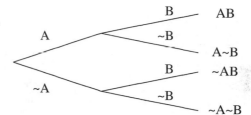

Figure 5.13 Outcome Tree of a Two-phase Mission.

where the symbol "~" (NOT) denotes failure of the phase.

5.9.5 System Map Matrix

A map matrix relates the operating states of the subsystems that comprise the system to the mission outcome tree. This map describes logically (using the success tree) the operating states that perform each system function per mission subphase. There is one map for each subphase. The individual phase maps may be part of a larger map matrix.

5.9.6 Fault Monitor Effects on Reliability

Often the fault monitor represents a major part of the subsystem. Since there are a limited number of monitor designs, only a few basic diagrams are needed to describe, say, all of the subsections using voting and median select monitors.

6

Markov Process Fundamentals

In this section we examine basic properties of Markov processes, with emphasis on practical applications. Detailed treatment of the Markov process is available in the books by Feller and Cox.

6.1 STOCHASTIC PROCESSES

Many processes observed in nature are stochastic or random. Whenever we examine the evolution of a process controlled by the laws of probability, we observe a *stochastic process*. These processes include growth and decay of living organisms, spread of epidemics, decay of radioactive materials, traffic on the freeway, and failure and repair of electronic systems. The study of stochastic processes can be defined as the "dynamic" part of probability theory in which we study a collection of random variables, their interdependence, their change in time, and limiting behavior.

Many topics that deal with stochastic processes were first developed in studying fluctuations and noise in physical systems. In this field, stochastic processes provide mathematical models for such physical phenomena as the thermal noise in electrical circuits, the Brownian motion of a small particle immersed in liquid or gas, the shot noise in a vacuum diode, and others. Stochastic processes also provide the required mathematical models for application to population studies, where the size and composition of population form random variables.

Types of Stochastic Processes. In the study of stochastic processes, it is useful to establish two distinct categories:

1. *Stationary*. A stationary process is one whose distribution remains the same as time progresses because the random mechanism producing the process is not changing in time.

2. *Nonstationary (evolutionary)*. An evolutionary process can be defined as one that is not stationary and where we can find changes, as the process evolves with time. For example, this process would be applicable in systems that change with time due to design modifications and other reasons.

6.2 SYSTEM DYNAMICS

Almost all systems are dynamic in nature. Even those that are normally considered static will exhibit changes, if observed at the proper time scale.

Surprisingly, many of the current analytical methods are static. For example, we often find reliability, maintainability, and even system effectiveness treated as static values, evaluated at some fixed time.

The static approach has serious limitations because it makes it more difficult to understand the behavior of the system and greatly complicates the analysis of dynamic systems. This is because most analyses must start with the dynamic environment and then make modifications to arrive at the static case.

One reason why the dynamic formulation was not used in the past was probably related to computational issues. Today, because of the wide availability of computers, this objection is no longer valid, since there is little time saving between the static versus dynamic approaches in setting up the problem.

6.2.1 Rate and State

The most important concepts in analyzing a dynamic process are those of *rate* and *state*. They appear in the most unexpected places and form the basic building block in almost every dynamic analysis problem. They apply to both living and nonliving systems. Thus, most of the modern data scientific studies involve the rate and state concepts in one form or another.

Since we will be dealing with rate processes in our analyses, we must select the proper type of mathematical abstraction to describe the model. The most natural way to describe the rate process is to use differential equations. Thus, we find that the fundamental equations will assume the simplest form when they are written relative to the rates of change of the system states rather than relative to the states themselves.

Thus, the expressions for the rate increase in mass, the speed of a particle, the growth of a biological colony, or the decay of radioactive material are simpler than the expressions that directly give the mass as a function of time or the speed of a particle as a function of time. Or, expressed in the language of calculus, the differential equations display a certain simplicity in form and can therefore be taken as the starting point in the analysis. Once the basic equations are found, the actual state behavior as a function of time can be derived by a simple integration.

In the systems studied in this chapter, there are various mutual interactions under the specific operating conditions, such as the available spare parts and personnel. Under these conditions, we will observe growth, decay, or equilibrium in our state variables. For example, we can examine how the state variables depend on the available spares.

6.2.2 Modeling of Dynamic Systems

The study of dynamic systems can be approached from two different perspectives. First, we can center our attention on the phenomena displayed by the system in bulk. Thus, we can speak of this as bulk mechanics or macromechanics of the evolving system. Second, the study of dynamic systems can be conducted with all of the attention centered on the phenomena displayed by the individuals of which the aggregate is composed. This branch of investigation is called the micromechanics of the evolving system.

In general, the two branches are closely related. The bulk effects observed are of the nature of statistical representation of the behavior of individuals; the study of this inherent connection is termed statistical mechanics.

In our study of reliability and system effectiveness, we employ both approaches. In other words, some models will represent the system at the macrolevel, and the others will be used to supply information on the microlevel.

6.3 MATRIX–VECTOR REPRESENTATION OF STATE-SPACE

Next, we will examine the details of the state equation formulation. Several notations have been used in the past to denote state-space equations. We will discuss one frequently used notation as a basis for further exploration.

1. *The Unreduced System.* A set of linear, first-order, state-space differential equations with constant coefficients can be expressed by the matrix equation:

$$Py = Qx + Ru \qquad (6.1)$$

2. *The Reduced System.* The reduced system leads to the standard state-space representation of the form:

$$x' = Ax + Bu \qquad (6.2)$$

$$v = Cx + Du \qquad (6.3)$$

where

Matrix	Description
A	Transition matrix
B	Input matrix
C	Output matrix
D	Transmission matrix

and

Vector	Description
x	State vector
u	Input vector
v	Output vector

Note: x' indicates a derivative of x.

By reduction, we refer to solving the unreduced matrix equations for the derivatives of the states and the outputs as linear combinations of system inputs and system states. The system states are the integrals of their derivatives. In the reduced system, there are no connections between the derivatives of the states and the outputs.

In a control system block diagram notation, the reduced system is represented as shown in Figure 6.1.

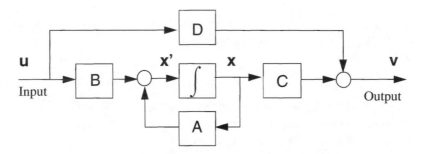

Figure 6.1 Block Diagram Representation of State Equations.

In practice, it is possible to use either the unreduced or reduced system of equations. Sometimes it is also possible to formulate the system as a set of independent subsystems and then to combine them on a system level. Through use of this approach, the state equations are simplified, and it is easier to gain an understanding about the behavior of the various parts of the system.

6.4 INTERPRETATION OF STATE-SPACE EQUATIONS

Up to this point, we have considered the state equations in a very general form without attaching any specific meaning to its components. Our next task is to examine the various vectors and matrices entering the state-space equations to assign specific meanings to these entities. Our analysis will begin with the interpretation of the reduced set of equations. We will repeat these for reference:

$$x' = Ax + Bu \tag{6.4}$$

$$v = Cx + Du \tag{6.5}$$

In Eqs. (6.4) and (6.5), the state variable vector, x, is a function of time. In engineering applications, this vector can represent different system variables depending on a particular application. For example, these variables may represent voltage, current, velocity, or acceleration. For system effectiveness (i.e., reliability analysis), we will be working with a different interpretation. Usually, the variables will be associated with state probabilities. It is also possible to associate other meaning, such as expected values, to some of the variables.

The specific system states represent different equipment operational states. Thus, a typical state may represent two operational units, or it may represent one operational unit, or even a failed system state. Normally, the selection of the states depends on the specific equipment configuration available and the operational rules.

6.4.1 A-Matrix

Examining the specific components of the formulation, we note that the matrix A, associated with the state variables, represents transitions between the given system states. For system effectiveness, we will deal with matrices that normally have constant coefficients. These coefficients are made up of failure and repair rates. It is also possible to further extend the model and include transitions that may be introduced due to external actions.

6.4.2 B-Matrix

The coefficient matrix B plays an important role in engineering as it represents the input signal matrix. For system effectiveness, this matrix will usually be set to zero, because the inputs are usually introduced via initial conditions. Using the expected value formulation, we can use matrix B to represent resupply or replacement parameters. To provide for future expansion, we will retain B matrix in the model formulation.

6.4.3 C-Matrix

The coefficient matrix C is the output matrix. In engineering analysis, it is associated with the output signal. In Markov analysis, this matrix denotes the relationship between the output vector, which is really the system effectiveness vector, and the state probabilities. In the current system effectiveness models, only one meaning is attached to this coefficient, and it is called either capability (the so-called WSEIAC model in Chapter 15) or performance. Under these conditions, the output equation assumes the simple form:

$$v = Cx \tag{6.6}$$

where the output vector will denote system effectiveness, and C − capability, and x − state probabilities evaluated at a particular time, usually the end of the mission.

The standard effectiveness model is really the expected capability of the system evaluated in terms of its performance, with unity value assigned to perfect operation. This interpretation is rather limited, because we may be interested in other payoff parameters such as the amount of data received and expected gain.

Since the state probabilities are obtained independently of the output equations, extension of the model is simple. In general, the C matrix represents the mapping from the state variable space to the system effectiveness space.

For this analysis, we will use two types of C coefficients: a sampling type and a continuous type. The first type will be used to evaluate system effectiveness parameters at a discrete point in time, and the second to obtain the average expected value. Here the average is summed over either the total mission time, or part of it.

6.4.4 D-Matrix

The D coefficient matrix in engineering work is related to transmission coefficients. It represents a direct relationship, or the direct transmittance between the input and the output. For system effectiveness, it will be used to account for the direct relationships between the input parameters and the system effectiveness vector. As an example, consider the following situation. At regularly scheduled times, we inspect the system and replace those components that have failed. Then, our replacements will enter via the input vector. Since replacement parts will carry an associated cost, the replaced parts will relate to the loss coefficient associated with the system effectiveness computations.

6.4.5 Connection to Markov Process

Let us summarize our accomplishment to this point. We started with the general model of the state-space equations used in engineering work, and we assigned new interpretations for the vectors and matrices appearing in the state-space equations. We found that we could assign definite meanings to each term and show how they will be used in applications. In other words, we have found a working model that can represent the system and that has the needed flexibility to support future model extensions.

We still need to establish a uniform system of notation. Although it may be desirable to retain the general formulation, this would create confusion with the existing established notation. To agree with the established convention, we will make the following changes:

1. We will change state variable vector x (equivalent to $X(t)$ in Chapter 4) to p to agree with the standard practice of using p to denote probability.
2. We will use uppercase P with an index i to denote specific probability associated with state i, that is, P_i. Thus, $P_i(t)$ will denote the probability of being in state i at time t. Therefore, from Chapter 4, $P(X_i(t))$ is equivalent to $P_i(t)$.

In the following section, we will derive the Markov process formulation to the state-space equations.

6.5 MARKOV MODELS

There are four distinct Markov processes, classified according to their state-space and time characteristics (see Table 6.1). These types are described individually in the following subsections.

TABLE 6.1   Markov Process Types

Type	Acronym	State Space	Time Space
1	DSMC	Discrete	Discrete
2	DSMP	Discrete	Continuous
3	CSMC	Continuous	Discrete
4	CSMP	Continuous	Continuous

6.5.1 Discrete Time, Discrete State

This model is represented by discrete transition matrices, specifying fixed transition probabilities.

When dealing with deterministic systems, each change usually leads to a unique outcome. In probabilistic systems, the situation is different. Here it is possible that as a result of a particular event we can expect several different outcomes. If we are dealing with a stationary process, then we can assign distinct transitional probabilities to each of the possible outcomes. The sum of these transitional probabilities will equal unity. (We also include the case where the system will not change state.)

The events resulting from a particular experiment can be thought of as further experiments. A sequence of these experiments is then a stochastic process that passes through a series of intermediate steps corresponding to these experiments. When the transitional probabilities to the next state are dependent only on the preceding experiment, this stochastic process is called the discrete Markov process or *Markov chain*.

Many statistical processes can be approximated by several discrete states and transitional probabilities of moving from one state to another. This is a convenient representation, because we can follow the system from state to state and formulate and solve for the various properties of the system.

Discrete Markov systems are defined by a set of states with a matrix of associated probabilities going from one state to another. These conditional probabilities are restricted to being functions of these two states. The mathematical model of the system is thus a collection of the system states and the conditional (transitional) probabilities between the states. Using an established convention, we do not show the zero conditional transitions. (Note that some texts do represent these as self-loops.)

Since we have fixed transition probabilities, the implication is that we are working with fixed time intervals and discrete events. Unfortunately, many redundancy configurations cannot be easily expressed and modeled using the fixed time interval scheme, because we may experience a random change of state during this time interval.

6.5.2 Continuous Time, Discrete State

Since this is the most important class of Markov models for reliability analysis, we will summarize the basic concept and its application.

In the previous case, we considered processes that were discrete in time. Now we will deal with an extension of the same concept and will allow time to assume a continuous range of values. Instead of letting transitions occur between discrete times T_n and T_{n+1}, we will consider transitions occurring in a very short time interval $h = [t, t+h]$.

An important concept in reliability modeling is the Poisson process. This process also finds wide application in other areas where it has been used to approximate such phenomena as the arrival of telephone calls at a telephone exchange, the emission of particles from a radioactive source, the number of people in a waiting line (queue), the occurrence of accidents, and many others. The Poisson process may appear in many combinations in reliability work. In the simplest case, it is used to model the time behavior of nonredundant systems that are not subject to wearout characteristics.

Let us now consider a simple model to illustrate the concept of a continuous Markov process. In this process, point (discrete) events occur singly in time and in a random fashion. We will assume that there is an interarrival constant, which is nonnegative and has the dimension of (time^{-1}). We will call this constant the rate of occurrence or the transition rate. In reliability modeling, these rates are represented by the component failure and repair rates.

If we let $K_{t,t+h}$ denote the number of events occurring in the time interval $(t, t+h)$, where h is a very small time interval, then we can assume that

$$P(K_{t,t+h} = 0) = 1 - \lambda h + o(h) \tag{6.7}$$

$$P(K_{t,t+h} = 1) = \lambda h + o(h) \tag{6.8}$$

It follows that

$$P(K_{t,t+h} > 1) = o(h) \tag{6.9}$$

where $o(h)$ denotes a function containing powers of h higher than the first. Under these conditions, $o(h)$ will approach zero as $h \rightarrow 0$. A process satisfying these conditions is called Poisson with rate λ. Since it is a constant, we do not expect any time trends or systematic variations in the rate of occurrence.

Assuming a Poisson process, the continuous-time Markov process mathematical model will be represented by a set of differential equations with constant rates. We will further assume that the system can exist in one of N states, numbered $1, 2, \ldots, N$. Then the probability that the system will be in state j at time t is given by $P_j(t)$.

On a system level, the state probabilities will be given by the state probability vector $P(t)$, which is defined as

$$P(t) \equiv [P_1(t)P_2(t) \ldots P_N(t)] \tag{6.10}$$

Then the state equation describing the system behavior is given by

$$\frac{d}{dt} P(t) = P(t) \times A \tag{6.11}$$

where A is the $N \times N$ state transition rate (failure and repair rate) matrix for the given system.

The elements of the A matrix are defined by

1. Off-diagonal elements $(i \neq j)$:

$$a_{ij} = \lim_{dt \to 0} \left\{ \frac{\text{Prob[StateChange}(i \rightarrow j) \text{ during } (t, t + dt)]}{dt} \right\} \tag{6.12}$$

2. Diagonal elements:

$$a_{ii} = - \sum_{j \neq i} a_{ij} \tag{6.13}$$

To solve Eq. (6.13), we also need to know the initial conditions, that is, the state probability vector at $t = 0$, given by $P(0)$. Then the state probabilities can be evaluated from

$$P(t) = P(0) \times \exp(-At) \tag{6.14}$$

Normally, Eq. (6.14) is not used directly; instead, numerical techniques are applied to the solution. This is because accurate evaluation of the exponential formulation is difficult.

EXAMPLE

To illustrate the state equation derivation, we will consider the simplest system consisting of only one component. This component may be in one of two states: *operational* (with probability of P_1) and *failed* (with probability of P_2). The state diagram for this component is shown in Figure 6.2.

Figure 6.2 Markov State Diagram Representing a Nonredundant Component.

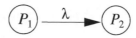

The probability $P_1(t+h)$ that the component is in *State 1* at time $(t+h)$ is the probability that it was in *State 1* at time t and that no change took place in the short time interval $(t, t+h)$. Thus

$$P_1(t + h) = P_1(t)[1 - \lambda h + o(h)] \tag{6.15}$$

Rewriting Eq. (6.15), we have

$$\frac{P_1(t + h) - P_1(t)}{h} = -\frac{\lambda h P_1(t)}{h} + \frac{o(h)}{h} \tag{6.16}$$

Taking the limit as $h \rightarrow 0$, we obtain

$$\lim_{h \to 0} \frac{P_1(t + h) - P_1(t)}{h} = \frac{d}{dt} P_1(t) = P'_1(t) \tag{6.17}$$

noting that

$$\lim_{h \to 0} \frac{o(h)}{h} = 0 \tag{6.18}$$

Then,

$$P'_1(t) = -\lambda P_1(t) \tag{6.19}$$

Correspondingly for *State 2*, the probability that the element is in this state at time $(t+h)$ is the sum of the following probabilities:

■ The probability that the element is in *State 2* at time t.
■ The probability that the element is in *State 1* at time t and that a change takes place during the time interval $(t, t+h)$.

Thus,

$$P_2(t + h) = P_2(t) + P_1(t)[\lambda h + o(h)] \tag{6.20}$$

Rewriting this equation as in the previous case and taking the limit as h approaches 0, we obtain

$$P'_2(t) = -\lambda P_1(t) \tag{6.21}$$

The two state equations derived in Eq. (6.21) together with the initial conditions are called the state equations of the system. In our case, the equations are

$$P'_1(t) = -\lambda P_1(t) \qquad P_1(0) = 1$$
$$P'_2(t) = \lambda P_1(t) \qquad P_2(0) = 0 \tag{6.22}$$

The solution to these equations is given by

$$P_1(t) = e^{-\lambda t}$$
$$P_2(t) = 1 - e^{-\lambda t} \tag{6.23}$$

This is the result for a basic Markov process analysis. For more complex systems, a similar derivation will apply, but of course we would like to use a more convenient notation (such as graphical) and let an automated problem solver do most of the work for us.

6.5.3 Discrete Time, Continuous State

This model is applicable if there are discrete changes in time in an environment where the states of the system are continuous over a specified range.

It is easy to see how the concept could be applied to the component parameter drift problem. Unfortunately, little work has been done in this area, and so multiparameter modeling and computation remain a difficult problem. There are two reasons: numerical data are seldom available, and the solution of the resulting partial differential equations is more complex.

6.5.4 Continuous Time, Continuous State

The conventional diffusion equations fall in this category. Usually when we talk about the system state space, we attempt to describe it in fixed terms. In reliability work, we talk about fully operational systems or failed systems. Once we introduce the concept of degraded operability, it is easy to imagine a continuum of physical states in which the system can exist. There could be some other advanced applications. However, the evaluation of these equations will be costly and more involved.

6.6 SEMI-MARKOV PROCESS

The semi-Markov process was introduced in 1954 by Paul Lévy to provide a more general model for probabilistic systems [Howard 64]. In a semi-Markov process, time between transitions is a random variable that depends on the transition. The discrete and the continuous-time Markov processes are special cases of the semi-Markov process.

6.7 STATE DIAGRAM

Now that the mathematical foundation has been established, the next step is to develop the associated graphical representation. A matrix representation is not as useful in practical work because it lacks visualization capabilities and as such is more difficult to interpret. The use of a state diagram also shifts the development of the state equations to the computer. In this respect, it is similar to circuit analysis, where the circuit is described in terms of component symbols and the circuit analysis program derives and solves the circuit equations.

A given system configuration is considered, at any instant in time, to exist in one of several possible states. A state diagram graphically represents these states and the possible transitions between them. In the state diagram, the states are shown as individual nodes and the transitions as arcs. Such a diagram can be developed to represent a single component or an entire complex system. For use in redundancy studies, state diagrams are developed for each alternate subsection (subsystem) and then combined as needed.

Alternatively, a state diagram can be thought of as a flow graph representation used in system analyses. It graphically represents the various system states and the rates associated with transitions between the system states. Thus, it is a directed graph, since there is a direction associated with the transitions. In a signal flow graph, the superimposed algebraic coefficients represent transmittance of the path, whereas in state diagram notation, they represent transition rates.

The state diagram portrays in a single diagram the operational and failure states of the system. The state diagram is flexible in that it can serve equally well for a single component or an entire system.

6.7.1 State Definition

Part of the definition of subsystem includes a description of the output states of interest for the assembly. The most common case is that of a two-state subsystem, which has one *good* and one *failed* state. Other subsystems may have three output states: *good*, *degraded*, and *failed*. Still other subsystems may have more levels of degraded states.

To determine the state probabilities, a mathematical model is developed to relate the operating states of the various hardware elements that make up the subsystem to the output states defined for the subsystem family. (A family is a set of functional modules that are interchangeable on a system level.) They may have different reliabilities and different physical parameters. For each subsystem, a different reliability model must be formulated. From a given model, the probabilities of the subsystem existing in one of its defined output states as a function of mission time may be calculated.

Basic State Identification. To identify states, many sources of information are used, including equipment configuration, results of failure mode and effects analysis (FMEA), and optimization program needs. Some states will be *derived*; in other words, they will be obtained by grouping the elementary states. Overall, we establish the equipment configuration's possible states through analysis of the functional block diagram or through a detailed FMEA.

6.7.2 State Diagram Representation

Next, the above inputs are converted to a state diagram for probability evaluation. Using the schematic block diagrams and the operating time profiles, we can develop state diagrams for each subsystem or a major component.

The state diagrams depict all possible internal operating states of a particular subsystem and define the allowable transitions from one state to another. Only a subset of the system states will have an effect on the system operation. These states will be labeled as output states.

State Dependence and Independence.   An independent state is one that does not depend on another system state. The Markov model allows only the representation of independent states.

SYSTEM STATE.   The system state depends on individual component states, such as good, failed, and degraded. Thus, each system state is defined in terms of the individual component states. This does not mean that the system states can be obtained by a simple binomial expansion of the individual component states because in a more detailed analysis we need to compute the sequential probabilities.

For example, assume that the system consists of only two components, A and B. As discussed earlier, we may have to know the probabilities of A failing before B fails and its converse of B failing before A fails, because each of these states may have a different effect on system reliability and fail-safety. Thus, we can distinguish five different system states, whereas the binomial expansion would yield only four states: 1. A good, B good. 2. A good and B fails. 3. B good and A fails. 4. B fails, then A fails. 5. A fails, then B fails. This specific example will be illustrated later in this section.

In the situation where degraded component states are permitted, the number of system states will be even higher.

COMPOUND PROBABILITIES AND SEQUENCE OF FAULTS.   For most systems, the sequence and multiplicity of fault events have an impact on the future system states. The conventional reliability analyses based on reliability block diagrams or fault-trees use Boolean-type representation that cannot properly reflect these conditions. In complex systems, the sequence of faults is important. As discussed previously, if component A fails before component B fails, it may have a completely different effect on the system versus the opposite case. This type of computation cannot be handled by the conventional reliability block diagram, for the RBD can only express the situation that both A and B have failed, but not their failure sequence.

6.7.3 State Transitions

After considering all the states, we then establish the possible transitions from one state to another. Either the functional block diagram or failure mode analysis results can be used to accomplish this task.

State transitions represent the valid transitions between system states. The transitions are characterized by component failure rates. Each state may have zero, one, or more feasible transitions. Zero transitions out of a state normally indicates that it is a system failure state; it is not necessary to consider further transitions. (This is also known as a trapping state.) Multiple transitions out of a state indicate that there is a multiplicity of failure modes corresponding to that state.

First Failures.   We start with the initial state and consider all components and their failure modes in sequence. The transition arrows are then drawn to new system states indicating that the selected component has failed. If there is already an existing arrow between the two states, then the new failure rate can be added to the existing one.

Higher Order Failures.   Second and higher order failures are then considered as the basis for the new arrows to be added to the state diagram developed in the previous step. After the new arrows are drawn, the transition rates are updated.

EXAMPLE

A simple example will illustrate the above process. Assume that we have a simple system consisting of two components A and B, with failure rates λ_A and λ_B, respectively.

We start with the initial (fully operational) system state S_0. Since we have two components, there are two possibilities. Either A may fail first or B may fail first. We will use S_1 to denote the state where A has failed and S_2 to denote the state where component B has failed. In a graphical form, we can represent this as shown in Figure 6.3.

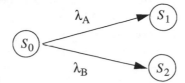

Figure 6.3 First-order Failures.

Figure 6.3 represents the first-order failures. We note that in states S_1 and S_2 we still have one operational component left. Thus, there remains a possibility for the next transition for a system state where no operational components are left. We identify these states as S_3 and S_4. Our state diagram now becomes as shown in Figure 6.4.

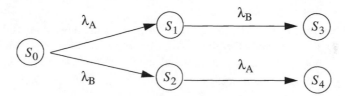

Figure 6.4 Adding Second-order Failures.

Although S_3 and S_4 are system states with no operational components left, they represent two different sequences of failure events. In reaching state S_3 component A failed before B, and in reaching state S_4 component B failed first, followed by A.

Sometimes these probabilities are needed because they may represent different mission outcomes. In other cases, they can be merged into a single state (see Figure 6.5).

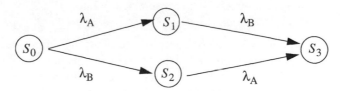

Figure 6.5 Merged States.

To save notation, we will assign S_i to P_i, so that an equivalent representation is as depicted in Figure 6.6.

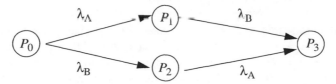

Figure 6.6 Probability Representation.

6.7.4 State Diagram Construction

Although the basic rules guiding the construction of a state diagram are simple, a good understanding of the system being analyzed is necessary. Construction of a state diagram begins with an examination of the system and a determination of the possible states in which it may exist. Specifically, the state diagram is constructed as follows:

1. Begin at the left with a state (circle) identified as S_1 (or as probability P_1). All equipment is initially good in this state.
2. Study the consequences of failing each element (any single-ended part, circuit, or channel defined as a single failure) in each of its failure modes. Group as a common consequence any that result in removing the same or equivalent circuitry from operation.
3. Assign new states (circles) and identify as S_2, S_3, S_4, and so on, for the unique consequences of step (2).
4. Connect arrows from S_1 to each of the new states, and note on each arrow the failure rate or rates of the element or elements whose failure determined transition to the new state.
5. Repeat steps (2), (3), and (4) for each of the new states failing only the elements still operational in that state. Continuously observe for cases where the failures may cause transition to one of the states formerly defined.
6. Continue the process until the initial equipment is totally unserviceable.

For example, in a triple redundant subsystem the possible states are:

1. Fully operational
2. Switched to a two-channel operation
3. System disengaged
4. System operating with an uncorrected failure

The circuit is then further analyzed by failure mode and effects techniques to determine the failure rates for all significant paths between the given states.

To reduce the size of the reliability model, approximations may be needed. These approximations could include truncation at a predetermined number of faults and the merging of states. Some of these approaches will be illustrated later in this chapter.

6.7.5 State Diagram Simplification

To limit the state diagram to a reasonable size, without a major sacrifice in accuracy, longer paths between the initial operational state and the system failure state may be truncated. For example, if one path to a system failure consists of three transitions and another is five transitions, then the longer path may be truncated. The effect of this approximation must be examined in the final model.

6.7.6 Transition Rates

In reliability models, transition rates are obtained from the failure rates. Each component used in a particular subsystem is assigned a failure rate. This rate consists of the base failure rate and the appropriate environment stress factors. Maintenance-related state transitions are computed from repair times.

The state transition rates (failure rates) can be obtained by examining the operational equipment associated with each state and calculating the corresponding failure rate. Where several states can be reached from a single state, an apportionment of the equipment failure rate among the possible transitions must be made, as indicated by the FMEA.

6.7.7 Failure Rate Computation

Failure rate handbooks are available for commercial or military products (Bellcore and MIL-HDBK-217). These procedures are well established, and numerous programs are available because they are easy to develop.

Environment Effects on Failure Rates. It is well known that the environment has a major influence on component failure rates. Environmental factors affecting failure rates include temperature, shock, vibration, and humidity. Many of these factors can be included if failure rates are computed using MIL-HDBK-217 methods.

As a guide, when developing general Markov models, transition rates should be parametrized ($Rate_1 = X$, etc.). In this way, it will be easier to investigate a range of environment conditions on reliability.

6.8 APPROXIMATE SOLUTION OF MARKOV MODEL

For practical work, we are often satisfied with an approximate solution if it is simple in form and easy to evaluate. For example, in trigonometric computations $sin(x)$ can be approximated by x, if x is a small angle.

The simplest way of obtaining an approximate expression is to use power series expansion for the given solution and to use only a few of the initial terms. If we applied this approach directly to the state model, we would have to solve the model and then expand the resulting exponential terms in power series, collect the similar terms, and so on. A simpler approach to this problem is possible as illustrated below.

Consider that a state diagram can be expressed as a sequence of transitions, as shown in Figure 6.7.

Figure 6.7 *N*-state Markov Diagram.

The state probability for the last state (failure state) will be given in Laplace transform form by

$$P_N(s) = \frac{\lambda_1 \lambda_2 \ldots \lambda_N}{(s + \lambda_1)(s + \lambda_2) \ldots (s + \lambda_N)\, s} \qquad (6.24)$$

Expanding the denominator, we obtain:

$$s^{N+1} + s^N(\lambda_1 + \lambda_2 + \ldots + \lambda_N) + s^{N-1}(\ldots) \ldots \qquad (6.25)$$

Substituting this expression in the equation for $P_N(s)$ and then performing the long division, we obtain:

$$P_N(s) = \frac{\lambda_1 \lambda_2 \ldots \lambda_N}{s^{N+1}} - \frac{\lambda_1 \lambda_2 \ldots \lambda_N(\lambda_1 + \lambda_2 + \ldots + \lambda_N)}{s^N} + \ldots - \ldots \qquad (6.26)$$

Equation (6.26) can be easily inverted using inverse Laplace transforms

$$P_N(t) = \frac{\lambda_1 \lambda_2 \ldots \lambda_N t^N}{N!} - \frac{\lambda_1 \lambda_2 \ldots \lambda_N(\lambda_1 + \lambda_2 + \ldots + \lambda_N)t^{N+1}}{(N+1)!} + \ldots - \ldots \qquad (6.27)$$

Using $\Pi\lambda$ to denote the product of all failure rates and $\Sigma\lambda$ to denote the sum of all failure rates, we may rewrite the above formula as follows:

$$P_N(t) = \frac{(\Pi\lambda)\, t^N}{N!} - \frac{(\Pi\lambda)\,(\Sigma\lambda)t^{N+1}}{(N+1)!} + \ldots - \ldots \qquad (6.28)$$

Generally, we use only the first term for the approximation:

$$P_N(t) \approx \frac{(\Pi\lambda)\, t^N}{N!} \qquad (6.29)$$

Since we have an alternating power series, the next term will provide a bound on the absolute error in using this approximation:

$$|\text{Error}| < \frac{(\Pi\lambda)\,(\Sigma\lambda)\, t^{N+1}}{(N+1)!} \qquad (6.30)$$

EXAMPLE

For a given system consisting of two parallel components, each with a failure rate of 10^{-4} failures/hour, and a mission time of one hour (which is much less than the expected average failure time), we have the state diagram shown in Figure 6.8.

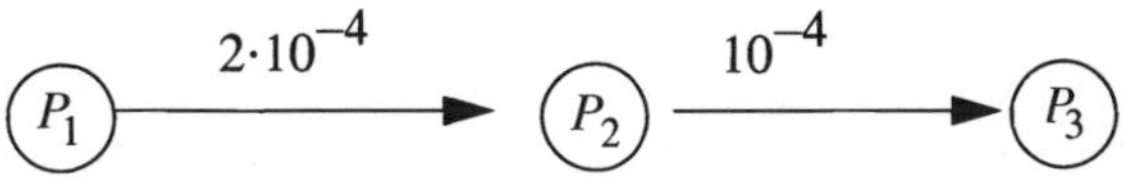

Figure 6.8 Markov Diagram for a Two-Component Parallel System.

In this case, the approximate value for the probability of failure (P_3) will be:

$$P_2(1) \approx \frac{2 \cdot 10^{-4} \cdot 10^{-4} \cdot 1^2}{2!} \approx 10^{-8} \qquad (6.31)$$

The error introduced by the approximation will then be given by

$$|\text{Error}| < \frac{(2 \cdot 10^{-4} \cdot 10^{-4}) \cdot (2 \cdot 10^{-4} + 10^{-4}) \cdot 1^3}{3!} \approx 10^{-12} \tag{6.32}$$

We note that in this case the first-term approximation is well within engineering accuracy.

It is also possible to extend the above concept to approximate evaluation of more complex state diagrams. In these diagrams, the shortest transition path to failure will give the first term in the power series expansion. Unfortunately, the evaluation of error will not be simple.

For more accurate results or for longer mission times, it is best to use a computer program to evaluate the full Markov model state diagram. One such program, CARMS, will be illustrated later in this book.

7

Hardware Reliability Modeling

In this section, we develop Markov reliability models for the basic redundant hardware configurations. The first step in the reliability computation involves the development of detailed state diagrams. Since most of the design alternatives involve different degrees of redundancy, good planning will reduce the amount of work required. This is particularly true when performing component failure rate computations (e.g., to reduce duplication of effort when similar components are used in the system).

An issue to keep in mind when deriving the various state diagrams is to make the state definitions consistent with the classifications established at the system level. Furthermore, since the same state diagrams will be used to compute probabilities for evaluating system safety, states must be selected to enable partitioning of system states into the various failure criticality groups.

7.1 MODELING COMMON CONFIGURATIONS

7.1.1 Single Nonredundant Component

A single component has one good state and one or more failed states. It is represented by the reliability block diagram shown in Figure 7.1.

Figure 7.1 Single-Component Reliability Block Diagram.

67

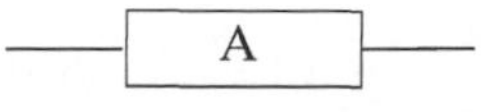

In the simplest case, there will be two states and a single, nonreversible transition between the states. Thus, the states are

State	Description
P_1	Component is operational
P_2	Component has failed

and the Markov diagram for the simplest case can be represented as shown in Figure 7.2.

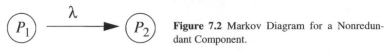

Figure 7.2 Markov Diagram for a Nonredundant Component.

The approximate formula ($\lambda t \ll 1$) for the probability of failure is then given by

$$P_2(t) \approx \lambda t \tag{7.1}$$

The exact solution for the component reliability (the probability of being in state P_1) is given by

$$R(t) = P_1(t) = e^{-\lambda t} \tag{7.2}$$

7.1.2 Single Component with Multiple Failure Modes

This model applies if the given component can fail in several modes and these modes have different effects on the system operation.

The Markov diagram for a component with three failure modes, such as a capacitor that can fail in either open or shorted mode or may experience drift outside the specified range, has the following states:

State	Description
P_1	Component is fully operational
P_2	Component has failed in open mode
P_3	Component has failed in shorted mode
P_4	Component has drifted outside specification values

Note that in this case states P_2 and P_3 will be failed states and P_4 a degraded state.

The Markov diagram for this case is shown in Figure 7.3.

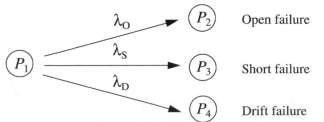

Open failure

Short failure

Drift failure

Figure 7.3 Single Component with Three Failure Modes.

In effect, the total failure rate for the component is given by

$$\lambda_T = \lambda_O + \lambda_S + \lambda_D \qquad (7.3)$$

7.1.3 Single Component with a Degraded State

Sometimes a component may fail in a mode that is degraded but still partially useful for performing some function. In this case, we need to know the following failure rates for the component:

Rate	Description
λ_d	Operational to degraded state
λ_f	Operational to failure state
λ_{df}	Degraded to failure state

The component states in this case are:

State	Description
P_1	Component is fully operational
P_2	Component is in a degraded mode
P_3	Component has failed

The resulting state diagram is shown in Figure 7.4.

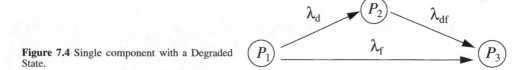

Figure 7.4 Single component with a Degraded State.

7.1.4 Parallel Configurations

Parallel systems are the most frequently analyzed of the redundancy configurations. A parallel configuration assumes that failure of a component will not affect the operation of the remaining components.

The reliability block diagram for a two-component parallel configuration is shown in Figure 7.5.

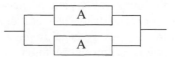

Figure 7.5 Two-Component Parallel Configuration Reliability Block Diagram.

For this two-component parallel configuration, where the components are identical, the states are:

State	Description
P_1	Two components operational
P_2	One component operational
P_3	System failure

The applicable state diagram for a parallel two-component redundant system is shown in Figure 7.6.

$$\boxed{P_1} \xrightarrow{\ 2\lambda\ } \boxed{P_2} \xrightarrow{\ \lambda\ } \boxed{P_3}$$

Figure 7.6 Two-Component Parallel Redundancy.

The approximate formula ($\lambda t \ll 1$) for the probability of failure is given by

$$P_3(t) \approx (\lambda t)^2 \tag{7.4}$$

The exact formula for the reliability of a two-component parallel system is given by

$$R(t) = P_1(t) = 1 - (1 - e^{-\lambda t})^2 \tag{7.5}$$

Similarly, for the three-component parallel system the states are:

State	Description
P_1	Three components operational
P_2	Two components operational
P_3	One component operational
P_4	System failure

and the applicable Markov state diagram is shown in Figure 7.7.

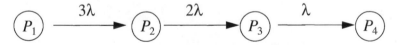

Figure 7.7 Three-Component Parallel Redundancy.

The approximate formula ($\lambda t \ll 1$) for the probability of failure is then given by

$$P_4(t) \approx (\lambda t)^3 \tag{7.6}$$

The exact formula for the reliability of a three-component parallel system is given by

$$R(t) = P_1(t) = 1 - (1 - e^{-\lambda t})^3 \tag{7.7}$$

The cases where the parallel configuration components do not have equal failure rates will be considered later in section 7.2.1.

Unfortunately, true parallelism can be used in only a few situations. Because a failed component cannot always be isolated and a failure of this component can cause a failure of the system. Thus, practical implementations of parallel configurations usually include special fault detection and isolation circuitry. The resulting reliability model is then more complex than that of the simple parallel configuration. The extra states must be included in the final model.

7.1.5 Majority Voting Configuration

Majority voting systems form a subclass of parallel systems. In a majority voting system, all of the components are energized for operation. The system success is determined by the majority rule. The simplest majority voting system consists of three components and a voter. The reliability block diagram for a majority voter configuration is shown in Figure 7.8.

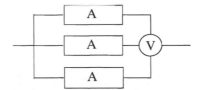

Figure 7.8 Triple Majority Voter Reliability Block Diagram.

This configuration, also known as a triple modular redundancy (TMR) configuration, requires at least two good components for operation. Thus, the system states are (with a perfect monitor):

State	Description
P_1	Three components operational
P_2	Two components operational
P_3	System failure

and the applicable state diagram is shown in Figure 7.9.

Figure 7.9 Three-Component Majority Voting (Triplex-Duplex).

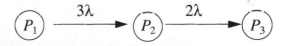

It is obvious that the resulting reliability will be lower than that for a parallel system consisting of three components because the state diagram representing the majority voting system has one less transition to the system failure state. (Note that for short times the reliability is much better than a nonredundant system, but then the reliability degrades at longer running times.)

The approximate formula ($\lambda t \ll 1$) for the probability of failure is given by

$$P_3(t) \approx 3(\lambda t)^2 \tag{7.8}$$

The exact formula for evaluating the reliability of the TMR configuration is:

$$R(t) = P(t) = e^{-3\lambda t} + 3e^{-2\lambda t}(1 - e^{-\lambda t}) \tag{7.9}$$

It is also possible to increase the reliability of the TMR system by making the following modification in the operating sequence; after the first failure has been detected, there are two remaining good components. Since it will not be possible to detect the failed component after the second failure, there is no need to keep both of the remaining components.

Thus, if we keep only one component after the first failure, then we have the following states:

State	Description
P_1	Three components operational
P_2	One component operational (after the first failure)
P_3	System failure

and the resulting state diagram will become as shown in Figure 7.10.

$$P_1 \xrightarrow{3\lambda} P_2 \xrightarrow{\lambda} P_3$$

Figure 7.10 Three-Component Majority Voting (Triplex-Simplex).

The approximate formula ($\lambda t \ll 1$) for the probability of failure is given by

$$P_3(t) \approx \frac{3}{2}(\lambda t)^2 \tag{7.10}$$

However, in systems that have fail-safe requirements, the first configuration is preferred, since after the first failure it is still possible to use the remaining two operational components in a comparison scheme to detect the second failure and then remove both components to protect the system from an undesirable failure mode.

7.1.6 M-of-N Voting Redundancy

This redundancy configuration is known as the NMR (N-Modular Redundancy). The configuration requires that M functional components out of a total of N are needed for the system to remain operational.

In the situation where all the components are identical and a perfect monitor can be assumed, then the resulting reliability is given by

$$R_{NMR}(t) = \sum_{i=m}^{n} \binom{n}{i} \times R(t)^i \times [1 - R(t)]^{n-i} \tag{7.11}$$

The corresponding Markov diagram is of the general form shown in Figure 7.11.

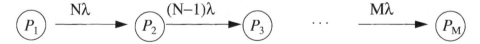

$$P_1 \xrightarrow{N\lambda} P_2 \xrightarrow{(N-1)\lambda} P_3 \quad \cdots \quad \xrightarrow{M\lambda} P_M$$

Figure 7.11 NMR Redundancy Configuration.

Note that the TMR configuration is a 2-of-3 configuration according to the above classification.

7.2 STANDBY CONFIGURATION

Standby redundancy is particularly important in those applications where low power consumption is mandatory, such as in spacecraft systems. Standby systems also yield better reliability than can be achieved using the same quantity of equipment in parallel mode. This happens when the standby condition failure rate is assumed to be zero. If this as-

sumption does not apply, the model needs to be modified to account for the storage failure rate, as will be explained later.

EXAMPLE

Consider a simple system consisting of only two components—a primary and a standby spare—as
shown in Figure 7.12. The spare is passive until switched in.

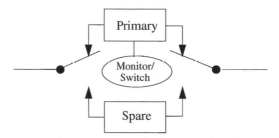

Figure 7.12 Standby Configuration Mechanization.

Both components have the same failure rate, λ, when operating. In the standby mode, the failure rate
is zero (i.e., cold standby). Since only one of these components is energized at a given time, we identify the following states:

State	Description
P_1	Primary component is operational
P_2	Standby component has been switched in and is operational
P_3	System failure

and the following state diagram will apply, shown in Figure 7.13.

Figure 7.13 Single Component with a Standby
Spare.

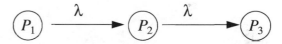

The approximate formula ($\lambda t \ll 1$) for the probability of failure is given by

$$P_3(t) \approx \frac{1}{2}(\lambda t)^2 \tag{7.12}$$

7.2.1 Standby with Nonzero Storage Failure Rate

If the standby component has a nonzero failure rate of λ_s (e.g., because it is energized as a warm or hot component), then we can identify these states:

State	Description
P_1	Both components are good, primary component is operating
P_2	Primary component has failed, secondary has been switched in and is operational
P_3	Standby component has failed, system is still operating with primary component
P_4	Both components have failed, system failure

and use the state diagram shown in Figure 7.14.

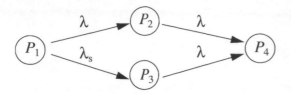

Figure 7.14 Standby with Nonzero Storage Failure Rate.

The previous Markov diagram can be simplified by merging states P_2 and P_3 (see Figure 7.15).

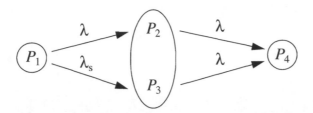

Figure 7.15 Merging of States.

After merging state P_3 into P_2, the new states for the configuration will be:

State	Description
P_1	Both components are good, primary component is operating
P_2	Primary or standby component has failed, only one component is operational
P_4	Both components have failed, system failure

and the new diagram then becomes as shown in Figure 7.16.

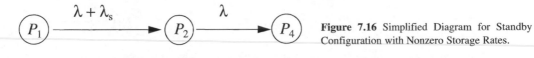

Figure 7.16 Simplified Diagram for Standby Configuration with Nonzero Storage Rates.

The approximate formula ($\lambda t \ll 1$) for the probability of failure is given by

$$P_4(t) \approx \frac{1}{2} (\lambda + \lambda_S) \lambda t^2 \qquad (7.13)$$

The same approach can be extended to standby systems where there are more than one standby components.

As another example, the system states for a redundant configuration with two spares (with nonzero failure rates) will be:

State	Description
P_1	Three good components
P_2	Two good components, one is in failed state
P_3	One good component, two are in failed states

Then, the state diagram for this configuration with nonzero failure rates is shown in Figure 7.17.

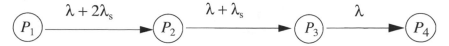

Figure 7.17 Standby Configuration with Two Nonzero Failure Rate Spares.

7.2.2 Single-Component Standby with Monitor

Next, we again examine the standby configuration, but this time we include the effects of failure detector and switch.

The conventional failure detector and switch can fail in one of two modes:

1. In a state where the failure detection ability is disabled.
2. In a state where a false switching to the next standby component has occurred.

If we assign equal failure rates to the primary and secondary components and initially ignore the component storage failure rates, then by assigning λ_{s1} and λ_{s2} to the monitor and switch failure rates for the two modes described above, then the system states will be:

State	Description
P_1	Primary component, fault monitor, and switch are in operating condition
P_2	Primary component is operating, but the switch has failed in a condition, where it will be unable to switch to the secondary
P_3	Secondary component is operating
P_4	System failure

and we will obtain the state diagram shown in Figure 7.18.

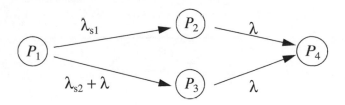

Figure 7.18 Standby Configuration with Fault Monitor and Switch.

Noting that the states P_2 and P_3 are identical in that there is only one operational component left, we can reduce the number of system states:

State	Description
P_1	Primary, fault detector and switch operational
P_2	One operating component
P_3	System failure

and then simplify the state diagram as shown in Figure 7.19.

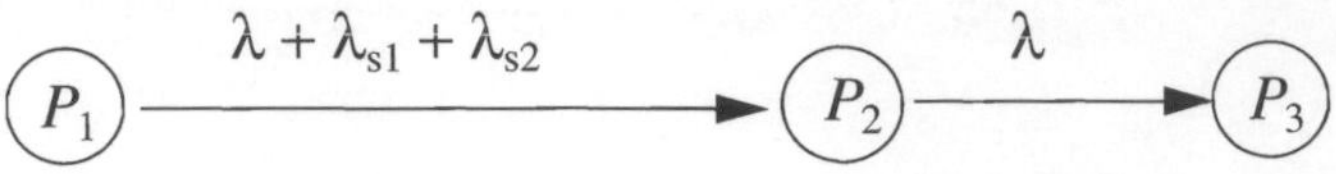

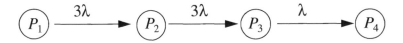

Figure 7.19 Standby Configuration with Monitor and Switch.

The approximate formula ($\lambda t \ll 1$) for the probability of failure is given by

$$P_4(t) \approx \frac{1}{2} \ (\lambda + \lambda_{s1} + \lambda_{s2}) \ \lambda t^2 \qquad (7.14)$$

Interestingly, the fault detector/switch does not act as a serial component. This is in contradiction to the usual assumption that if the detector/switch combination fails, the system fails.

It is possible to extend the same concept to system configurations with more than one standby component. As one gains experience, it will become apparent where simplifications can be made and the number of states in the state diagram reduced. Note that this reduction will be possible only if the component failure rates are the same.

7.2.3 Triple Modular Redundancy with a Spare

It is also possible to include standby redundancy in the TMR system by making the following modification in the operating sequence. After the first failure has been detected, the spare component is switched in and the configuration continues to operate in a majority-voting mode. After the second failure, the system reverts to simplex mode. Here, the system states will be:

State	Description
P_1	Three components operational, spare OK
P_2	Three components operational, spare used
P_3	One component operational (simplex)
P_4	System failure

The resulting state diagram is shown in Figure 7.20.

Figure 7.20 Three-Component Majority Voting with a Spare (Triplex-Triplex-Simplex).

The approximate formula ($\lambda t \ll 1$) for the probability of failure is given by

$$P_3(t) \approx \frac{3}{2} \ (\lambda t)^3 \qquad (7.15)$$

However, in systems that have fail-safe requirements, the first configuration (triplex-duplex) is preferred. The reason is that after the first failure it is still possible to use the remaining two operational components in a comparison scheme to detect the second failure and then remove both components to protect the system from an undesirable failure mode.

7.2.4 Multiple Mode Operation

Many systems are designed for multiple mode operation. Usually, the primary mode is designed to provide high-accuracy, full-performance capability. The secondary mode, sometimes called degraded or backup mode, provides reduced performance or accuracy. With this approach, it is possible to improve the system reliability and fail-safety without the need for full redundancy.

The specific mode capabilities for the multiple mode systems are incorporated in the full system effectiveness model. The mode capability coefficients relate to the degree of full capability needed for mission success.

To illustrate this approach, we will consider a dual sensor system: one sensor is designed for wide-angle operation (lower accuracy and less costly), and the other provides high-accuracy, high-resolution capability. If both sensors are operational, then full system capability can be achieved. If the narrow angle sensor fails, the system is still operational but has lower accuracy. If the wide angle sensor fails, the system is still operational but will require manual support. Here, the states can be designated as follows:

State	Description
P_1	Both sensors are operational
P_2	Only the wide angle sensor is operational
P_3	Only the narrow angle sensor is operational
P_4	Both sensors have failed, system failure

The corresponding Markov diagram is shown in Figure 7.21.

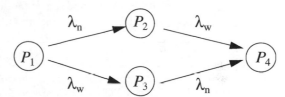

Figure 7.21 Multiple-Mode Configuration.

The design of equipment that is capable of operating in several reduced performance modes is very important in space missions, where weight limitations prohibit incorporation of higher-level redundancy.

Proper multiple-mode design will ensure either full or partial mission accomplishment with a high probability of success.

7.2.5 Load-Sharing Configuration

Load-sharing systems are similar to parallel systems. The major difference is in the load-carrying capabilities. While components in parallel systems are designed to carry full load, in load-sharing systems, each component is designed to carry only part of the load.

If one component fails in a load-sharing system, then the remaining components share the load equally. However, since the components now carry a heavier load, their failure rates will increase due to the additional stress.

As an example, consider a parallel load-sharing system consisting of two components. Under the load-sharing conditions, each component carries only one-half of the load. If under half-load conditions the failure rate for each component is one-fourth of the full load failure rate, then we can identify these states:

State	Description
P_1	Two components operating on a load-sharing basis
P_2	One component has failed, the other carries full load
P_3	Both components have failed, system failure

and then obtain the following state diagram (Figure 7.22).

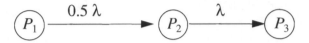

Figure 7.22 Load-sharing System.

Here, the transition rate for the first transition is only one-half that for the standby system. Unfortunately, the load-sharing systems are not easy to design. They are, however, applicable for power supplies or mechanical systems where significant stress differences do occur.

The approximate formula ($\lambda t \ll 1$) for the probability of failure is given by

$$P_3(t) \approx \frac{1}{4}\ (\lambda t)^2 \tag{7.16}$$

7.2.6 Mixed Population

Often, the component population is not uniform and may contain a small number of components that have some defects. The familiar burn-in process is often used to weed out these components. To describe this situation, we postulate the following system states:

State	Description
P_1	Probability that the component is of good quality and is operational
P_2	Probability that the component is of poor quality but is operational
P_3	Probability that the component has failed

This situation can then be modeled by the Markov diagram presented in Figure 7.23.

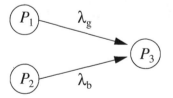

Figure 7.23 Markov Diagram for Mixed-Quality Components.

Initially (at time $t = 0$), the following equations apply:

$$P_1(0) + P_2(0) = 1.0 \tag{7.17}$$

$$P_1(0) \gg P_2(0) \tag{7.18}$$

$$\lambda_B \gg \lambda_G \tag{7.19}$$

Since the failure rate of the poor-quality components will be much higher than that of the good-quality components, the instantaneous failure rate will be decreasing (characteristic of the initial part of the bathtub curve).

7.3 FAULT COVERAGE

Fault coverage is a measure of the system's ability to perform fault detection, fault location, fault containment, or fault recovery. Thus, different measures of fault coverage exist, and they must be specified when requirements are given.

7.3.1 Fault Detection Coverage Definitions

Fault detection coverage is a measure of a system's effectiveness in fault detection. It is often included as a requirement in the specification document.

Mathematical Definition. Fault coverage is mathematically defined as the conditional probability that, given the existence of a fault, the system recovers [Bouricius 71]:

$$C_f = \text{Probability}(\text{Recovery}_{\text{fault}} | \text{Existence}_{\text{fault}}) \qquad (7.20)$$

Fault location coverage is a measure of the system's ability to locate faults whereas fault containment coverage is a measure of the system's ability to contain faults. A unity value here implies that the faults should be localized. Fault recovery is the process of maintaining or regaining operational status after a fault occurs.

7.3.2 Fault Coverage Computation

Fault coverage computation is not a simple process because it is difficult to postulate all potential system faults. The usual approach is to develop a list of faults that can occur in a system. From that list we specify the faults that can be detected (located or contained) and compile a list of faults from which the system can recover.

Consider that a fault occurrence causes a change in a system state. The simplistic approach is to compute the fraction of the faults from which the system can recover divided by the total number of faults [Johnson 89].

A more realistic approach requires detailed failure mode and effects analysis to determine which specific component failure modes will result in system failures that cannot be detected with the available monitors. In addition, failure of the fault monitor must also be included in the reliability model, because after a monitor failure later faults will be undetectable. Note that in this model, fault coverage probability is an output from the model and not an input to it.

7.4 FAULT MONITOR MODELING

During the development of redundancy models, failure-free monitors and switches are usually assumed. In the practical systems, however, the monitor circuit and the switching must be considered.

Detailed development of the more refined models must be based on failure mode and effects analysis. This analysis must consider not only the primary components, but also the monitor and the switch.

7.4.1 Fault Monitoring

Use of redundancy to improve reliability often requires monitoring. Many different mechanization schemes are available for the implementation of monitors. The most common monitor types involve the use of some form of comparison or voting. Comparison monitors compare two signals and disengage when a disagreement is detected. Voting monitors use three or more signals and disengage the faulty signal source at the first failure. After the second failure, the channel is disengaged.

7.4.2 Monitor Interface

The monitor implementation directly affects the reliability improvement that can be attained. Monitor design is further complicated because proper reliability analysis techniques for monitor evaluation are not always used. For example, most redundant system analyses assume that the monitor is a series component in the reliability diagram. As a result, these analyses not only yield incorrect results, but also fail to indicate where improvements could have been obtained. Since the effect of the monitor on system reliability is often misapplied, a simple example will be used to illustrate the basic concepts.

Assume that we have a simple redundant system consisting of one active system and one standby system. The standby system is normally switched in (placed in operation) by the monitor in the case of the primary component failure. This, of course, assumes that the monitor is perfect. A physical monitor, however, will have two major failure modes: false switching and the inability to switch components.

Next, we must consider what will happen as a result of random faults. If the first fault experienced is a false switch of the monitor to the secondary system, then the system will continue to operate, although a loss in redundancy will result. Similarly, if the monitor fails in a mode where it is unable to switch, then the system will also continue to operate. Again, a loss in redundancy will occur. We note that in this situation, the second fault experienced will result in a system failure.

This simple example illustrates why reliability analysis techniques such as reliability block diagrams are not suitable for critical system design. The complexity of the monitor analyses requires a better understanding of the underlying fault process.

As a warning against overdesign, note that as more monitors are added, system reliability may actually decrease. This is intuitive if one considers that the number of possible failure modes increases with the number of components (including monitors).

8

Software Reliability Modeling

The systems of the future will be adding more functional capability in software. Since more than half of all system failures are attributable to faulty software design, it will be necessary to add reliability models capable of representing software faults.

Software reliability is defined as the probability of failure-free operation of a computer program for a specified time in a specified environment. Software reliability has the same effect on the overall system reliability as hardware reliability. However, software reliability differs from hardware reliability in several aspects:

1. Software does not wear out.
2. Software may undergo several updates during the system life cycle.
3. Software fixes may introduce new, unanticipated problems.
4. Software testing will be incomplete due to the complexity of software.
5. Software requires different fault-tolerance techniques than hardware.

Since there are no generally accepted definitions for software error, fault, or failure, we will use the following:

1. A software *error* is due to a mental mistake made by the software developer during the programming process.
2. A software *fault* is a manifestation of a software error.
3. A software *failure* occurs when a fault prevents software from performing its required function within specified limits.

Software errors may be due to a variety of factors, the more important of which are as follows.

1. Incomplete or improper requirement specification.
2. Incomplete or incorrect design document used by the software developer.

3. Errors in program coding.

4. Incomplete testing.

5. Improper bug fixes.

As a result of these factors, most operational software is not failure free. On the average, there are six software faults per 1000 lines of source code instructions, and the average effectiveness of a bug fix is 99.5% [Musa 87].

Numerous computer programs exist for evaluating hardware reliability, but only a few contain provisions for incorporating software reliability. Since no single software reliability model is superior to the others, the analyst should include provisions for a range of individual models.

Software reliability models based on the exponential distribution can be solved using a reliability program based on a Markov process. Use of other distributions will normally require Monte Carlo simulation or special-purpose simulation programs.

8.1 SOFTWARE RELIABILITY MODEL SELECTION

There is a need for a software reliability model that is relatively simple and meaningful. Its parameters should have a physical interpretation. In developing and applying a software reliability model, we have to distinguish two cases:

1. Program development and testing

2. Field operation

In the first case the software is still undergoing changes, and detected faults are eliminated, whereas in the second case the software configuration has been stabilized and the number of inherent faults remains fixed.

Thus, there are two different situations, and each requires a different approach to the software reliability model development.

8.1.1 Reliability Growth Models

The basic software reliability growth models assume that software failures occur as a random nonhomogeneous Poisson process (NHPP). Nonhomogeneous in this context means that the failure process varies in time and is defined by

$$N(0) = 0$$

Independent increments in $[N(t), t \geq 0]$

$$Pr\left([N(t + \Delta t) - N(t)] \geq 2\right) = o(\Delta t)$$

$$Pr\left([N(t + \Delta t) - N(t)] = 1\right) = \lambda(t) + o(\Delta t)$$

$$\lim_{\Delta t \to 0} \frac{o(\Delta t)}{\Delta t} = 0$$

(8.1)

In Eq. (8.1), $N(t)$ represents the number of experienced failures at time t. The above equations state that:

1. At time, $t = 0$, there are no existing failures.
2. Failure times are independent.
3. There are no simultaneous failures.
4. Failure rate is time dependent.

We can obtain the mean value of this failure distribution (the expected number of failures occurring in the execution time interval $[0, t]$) from the equation:

$$E[N(t)] = \mu(t) \equiv \int_0^t \lambda(\tau)d\tau \tag{8.2}$$

The commonly used basic execution time model [Musa 87] is based on the NHPP. In this model, it is assumed that as each failure is corrected, the failure rate will drop by a fixed amount.

To derive this model, we will assume that we can estimate the expected number of total failures, v_0. We will also assume that we can predict (or estimate) the initial failure rate, λ_0.

If n is the mean cumulative number of failures experienced at some point in the testing process, then the basic failure rate is expressed as

$$\lambda(v) = \lambda_0 \left(1 - \frac{v}{v_0}\right) \tag{8.3}$$

where λ_0 = initial failure rate
v = average number of failures experienced at a given point in time
v_0 = total number of failures in the program, detected if given infinite time

In this model, the failure rate $\lambda(v)$ is a linear function of the experienced software failure. The rate of change of $\lambda(v)$ can be determined by taking the derivative:

$$\frac{d}{dv}\lambda(n) = -\frac{\lambda_0}{v_0} \tag{8.4}$$

If we denote the decrement of the software failure rate per failure as

$$\beta \equiv \frac{\lambda_0}{v_0} \tag{8.5}$$

then we can express the failure rate as

$$\lambda(v) = \beta(v_0 - v) \tag{8.6}$$

Since the mean number of software failures experienced is a function of the execution time t, we can write:

$$\lambda(t) = \beta[v_0 - \mu(t)] \tag{8.7}$$

Since $\mu(t)$ is the time integral of $\lambda(t)$ (see defining equation), it follows that $\lambda(t)$ is the derivative of $\mu(t)$. Then we can rewrite the equation as

$$\frac{d}{dt}\mu(t) + \beta\mu(t) = \beta\nu_0 \tag{8.8}$$

Solving the above differential equation for $m(t)$, we obtain:

$$\mu(t) = \nu_0(1 - \exp[-\beta t]) \tag{8.9}$$

The failure rate can be obtained by differentiating Eq. (8.9):

$$\frac{d}{dt}\mu(t) = \lambda(t) = \nu_0\beta \exp[-\beta t] \tag{8.10}$$

From the above we can evaluate the initial failure rate (at $t = 0$) as

$$\lambda_0 = \nu_0\beta \tag{8.11}$$

In addition to the basic execution time model described above, many others have been proposed in the past. Some of the commonly used software reliability models and references to their description are as follows [Brocklehurst 92]:

1. *Jelinski-Moranda (JM)*. This is one of the earliest software reliability models. It assumes that software failures occur at random and that all software faults contribute to unreliability. It also assumes that (a) the failure rate is proportional to the remaining number of software faults, (b) fixes are perfect, (c) no new faults are introduced by the fix, and (d) the failure rate improves by the same amount after each fix.

2. *Generalized Poisson (PM)*. This model is similar to the JM software reliability model but differs in the error count method.

3. *Schneidewind (SM)*. This model is also similar to the JM software reliability model. It assumes that the error detection process changes as testing progresses and that the more recent error counts have more weight.

4. *Bayesian Jelinski-Moranda (BJM)*. This model is also based on JM but uses Bayesian instead of maximum likelihood inference.

5. *Goel-Okumoto (GO)*. This software model is similar to the JM but assumes that the failure rate improves continuously in time.

6. *Musa-Okumoto (MO)*. This model is similar to the GO model, except that it assumes that fixes have a decreasing effect on software reliability than the earlier ones. This assumption leads to a logarithmic Poisson model.

7. *Duane (DU)*. This model is based on the reliability growth model, initially developed for hardware testing. In this model, the software failure rate is assumed to change continuously in time.

8. *Littlewood-Moranda (LM)*. This model is similar to the JM model, except that the faults have different effects on reliability. It assumes that the more frequent faults will be removed earlier; the infrequent ones will be more difficult to detect and thus will be removed later.

9. *Littlewood Nonhomogeneous Poisson Process (LNHPP)*. This model is similar to LM but assumes a continuous change in failure rates when faults are removed from the program.
10. *Littlewood-Verall (LV)*. This model assumes that the software failure rate will vary randomly and that the uncertainty of fix is a function of the fault size and the effectiveness of the fix.
11. *Keiller-Littlewood (KL)*. Similar to the LV model, the KL uses a different expression for reliability growth (shape parameter instead of scale parameter).

Of the above models the last two (Littlewood-Verall and Keiller-Littlewood) are the best in predicting reliability improvements. One recent approach involves combining the reliability models [Lyu 93].

Many of the software reliability models discussed previously can be approximated by a Markov model. We briefly examine the development of such a model.

Let $N(t)$ represent a random variable expressing the number of faults remaining in the program at time t. We further assume that there are n_0 faults at $t = 0$. The Markov process can be stated as follows. In an interval Δt, faults remaining at time $t + \Delta t$ depend only on the state at time t. Thus, the conditional probability is given by

$$\text{Prob}[N(t + \Delta t) = j | N(t) = i] \qquad (8.12)$$

This conditional probability represents the transition between the states representing the number of failures in the program. If we denote the transition function by P_{ij}, then the probability that $N(t + \Delta t)$ is equal to j is given by

$$P[N(t + \Delta t) = j] = \sum_i P_{ij}(t, \Delta t) P[N(t) = i] \qquad (8.13)$$

8.1.2 Operational Software Reliability Models

The previously described models are applicable during the software development and testing phases. However, once the software testing has been completed and the software has been released for field use, there will be no further modifications to it. Thus, we will be able to assume that the failure rate will not change.

8.2 MODELING COMMON SOFTWARE CONFIGURATIONS

In the following, we provide a few examples of software reliability models. By coincidence these examples may duplicate the corresponding hardware model, but the failure rates typically differ

8.2.1 Nonredundant Software Module

A nonredundant software module will have one good state and one or more failed states. It can be represented by the reliability block diagram shown in Figure 8.1.

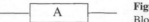

Figure 8.1 Single-Software Module Reliability Block Diagram.

In the simplest case, there will be two states and a single, nonreversible, transition between the states. Thus, the states are:

State	Description
P_1	Software module is operational
P_2	Software module has failed

and the Markov diagram for this case can be represented as shown in Figure 8.2.

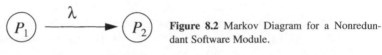

Figure 8.2 Markov Diagram for a Nonredundant Software Module.

The approximate formula ($\lambda t \ll 1$) for the probability of failure is then given by

$$P_2(t) = \lambda t \tag{8.14}$$

The exact solution for the software module reliability (the probability of being in the fully operational state P_1) is given by

$$R(t) = P_1(t) = e^{-\lambda t} \tag{8.15}$$

8.2.2 Multiple Failure Modes in a Software Module

This model applies if the given software module can fail in several modes and these modes have different effects on the system operation. (Some of these may be safe, others unsafe.) For example, if a software module has three modes of failure (A, B, and C) and if these modes are independent, then we can identify the following states:

State	Description
P_1	Module is fully operational
P_2	Mode A failure
P_3	Mode B failure
P_4	Mode C failure

Note that in this case states P_2, P_3, and P_4 are software module failure states and that the summation of these states will yield the total module failure probability. We also assume that after the first failure the system is considered to be in a failed state.

The Markov diagram for this case is shown in Figure 8.3.

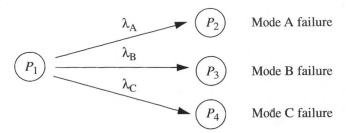

Mode A failure

Mode B failure

Mode C failure

Figure 8.3 Software Module with Three Failure Modes.

The total failure rate for the software module is given by

$$\lambda_m = \lambda_A + \lambda_B + \lambda_C \tag{8.16}$$

8.2.3 Module with a Degraded State

Sometimes a software module may fail in a mode that is degraded but is still partially useful for performing some function. In this case, we need to know the following failure rates for the module:

Rate	Description
λ_d	Operational to degraded state
λ_f	Operational to failure state
λ_{df}	Degraded to failure state

The module states in this case are:

State	Description
P_1	Module is fully operational
P_2	Module is in a degraded mode
P_3	Module has failed

and the resulting state diagram is shown in Figure 8.4.

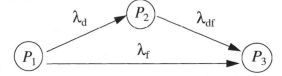

Figure 8.4 Single Software Module with a Degraded State.

8.2.4 Majority Voting in Software

In a majority voting system, all the modules are energized for operation. The system's success is determined by the majority rule. The simplest majority voting system consists of three software modules and a voter. Note that the three modules could be created

by the technique of N-version programming to achieve the required subsystem independence [Knight 86]. The reliability block diagram for a triple modular majority voter configuration is shown in Figure 8.5

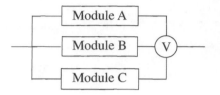

Figure 8.5 Triple Majority Voter Reliability
Block Diagram.

This configuration, also known as the triple modular redundancy (TMR) configuration, requires at least two good modules for operation. Thus, the system states are:

State	Description
P_1	Three modules operational
P_2	Two modules operational
P_3	System failure

and the applicable state diagram is shown in Figure 8.6. Because the modules may not be
completely independent, due to a software common-mode fault, we also supply an imperfect, partial coverage failure rate given by λ_{nc}.

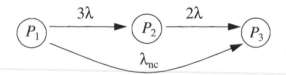

Figure 8.6 Three-Module Majority Voting
(Triplex-Duplex).

It is also possible to increase the reliability of the TMR system by making the following modification in the operating sequence. After the first failure has been detected,
two good modules remain. Since it will not be possible to detect the failed module after
the second failure, we have no need to keep both of the remaining modules. Thus, if we
keep only one module after the first failure, then we have the following states:

State	Description
P_1	Three modules operational
P_2	One module operational (after the first failure)
P_3	System failure

and the resulting state diagram will become as shown in Figure 8.7.

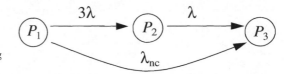

Figure 8.7 Three-Module Majority Voting (Triplex-Simplex).

However, in systems that have fail-safety requirements, the first configuration is preferred, since after the first failure it is still possible to use the remaining two operational modules in a comparison scheme to detect the second failure and then remove both modules to protect the system from an undesirable failure mode.

9

Combined Hardware–Software Reliability Modeling

Almost all of today's complex control systems are computer-based and implement the majority of the control functions in software. Thus, the system operation is dependent on the reliable operation of both hardware and software. In the past, reliability analyses were conducted by performing a separate analysis on the hardware part of the system and then a separate analysis of the software part. This approach is no longer correct because of the close coupling between hardware and software events. Thus, better system reliability models are needed which are capable of handling the combined effects of hardware and software, as well as built-in test capabilities.

9.1 A SIMPLE APPROACH

The simplest approach is to use separate hardware and software reliability models and then use the product rule to combine the resulting reliabilities. In this case, the reliability block diagram is as shown in Figure 9.1.

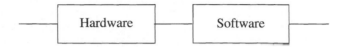

Figure 9.1 Hardware-Software Reliability Block Diagram.

Using the reliability product rule, we have:

$$R_{\text{System}} = R_{\text{Hardware}} \times R_{\text{Software}} \tag{9.1}$$

On the system level, we can recognize the following states:

State	Description
P_1	Hardware and software are operational
P_2	System failure

and the corresponding Markov diagram (see Figure 9.2):

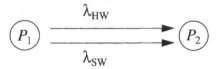

Figure 9.2 Hardware-Software Markov Reliability Model.

with the following failure rates:

Rate	Description
λ_{HW}	Hardware failure rate
λ_{SW}	Software failure rate

Sometimes we may want to distinguish the hardware and software failure states. In this case, we need to split the system failure state in two individual states:

State	Description
P_1	Hardware and software are operational
P_2	Hardware has failed
P_3	Software has failed

We can represent this case in a Markov diagram as shown in Figure 9.3.

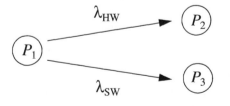

Figure 9.3 Hardware-Software Markov Diagram with Split States.

Note that in this case both P_2 and P_3 are failure states and that the system failure probability will be given by: $P_S = P_2 + P_3$.

   In some situations, only part of the software may fail and the system still may be operational, but degraded. Using the Markov formulation, we can then identify the following system states:

State	Description
P_1	Hardware and software are fully operational
P_2	Hardware has failed
P_3	Partial software failure, but hardware is still operational
P_4	Software and hardware have failed, system failure

The corresponding Markov diagram is presented in Figure 9.4,

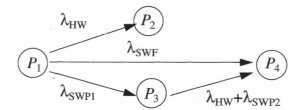

Figure 9.4 Hardware-Software Markov Diagram with a Degraded Software State.

with failure rates:

Rate	Description
λ_{HW}	Hardware failure rate
λ_{SWF}	Software failure rate to failed state
λ_{SWP1}	Software failure rate from operational to degraded state
λ_{SWP2}	Software failure rate from degraded state to full failure state

A more complicated Markov diagram is obtained if the system has repair capability, with the following recovery rates:

Rate	Description
μ_{HW}	Hardware failure recovery rate
μ_{SW}	Software failure recovery rate

The corresponding Markov diagram is as shown in Figure 9.5.

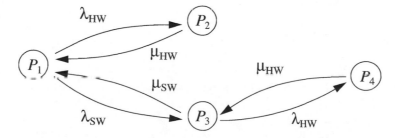

Figure 9.5 Simple Hardware-Software Markov Diagram Showing Recovery.

9.2 MODELING ERRORS AND THEIR SOURCES

The following discussion applies to both hardware and software models as well as the combined hardware/software models. A number of errors must be considered:

1. *Dependency errors.* Dependency errors result if the model does not include dependencies that exist in the system. For example, failure of a simple nonredundant power supply can disable the system. If this effect is not included in the model, then we have a dependency error.

2. *Modeling errors.* Modeling errors are due to the simplifications and assumptions made when developing the model (by definition). Modeling errors are difficult to detect and thus to protect against their occurrence. One approach involves using different modeling techniques, or different modelers, and then comparing the results to detect any discrepancies and to determine their causes.

3. *Model structuring errors.* Model structuring errors include missing states and missing or incorrect state transitions. These errors are also difficult to detect. However, some computer-based checking is feasible to guard against some of these errors.

4. *Parameter errors.* Uncertainty in reliability model parameters, such as failure rates and repair rates, impact the accuracy of reliability computations. One approach involves assuming a range of values for these parameters and then evaluating for worst-case conditions. Use of the worst-case approach, however, could result in a costly solution.

   ACCURACY OF FAILURE RATES.   Failure rates are not highly accurate and are usually limited to two significant figures. Thus, we should not expect the probability of failure computation to be accurate to a dozen or more significant figures. (Note that a calculated probability indicating a reliability of 0.999999 has only one significant figure.)

   ACCURACY OF RECOVERY RATES.   The same accuracy concern also applies to the recovery rates. They are often even less accurate than the failure rates because of the approximations that are made regarding the recovery process.

5. *Solution errors.* Solution errors are introduced by approximate solution techniques, numerical procedures, and simulation. Solution errors can be minimized by use of alternative, higher-accuracy, solution techniques, smaller integration time step, and so on.

10

Modeling of Large and Complex Systems

In the previous sections we examined the basic reliability modeling concepts. In this section we discuss reliability analysis of complex systems.

Proper handling of large models is important in obtaining meaningful answers. For many practical applications, the change from small-model setups to complex models requires more planning, care, and patience in the layout. In this regard, complex RMA design models do not differ from corresponding software designs or other forms of CAD.

10.1 STATE SIMPLIFICATION

The number of states can be reduced in many ways. First, if a particular redundant configuration consists of several identical components, then instead of enumerating every individual state, we can assign states that represent the number of operating components. For example, in a parallel system consisting of, say, four components, we can enumerate the states as four-operational, three-operational, and so on.

The other approach to simplification includes truncating higher order states. By higher order, we mean states that are reached after several transitions. In this case, we are assuming that these transitions will result in a system failure. This approach will produce a more pessimistic estimate; however, the error will be relatively small for high reliability components and short mission times.

10.2 PARTITIONING AND REDUCTION

We need to be able to identify and select a meaningful part of the problem (i.e., the *critical components*) in order to avoid setting up a complex model that will require a long problem solution time. The exponential increase in solution time with number of states makes it difficult to model large systems. Furthermore, because of the large number of states, the program cannot be truly interactive.

One way of handling large systems is to use partitioning and reduction, supported by design approximations and simplifications wherever applicable. In decomposing the system, we cannot ignore potential interactions. At the same time, any insignificant secondary effects should be identified and ignored to reduce the complexity of the reliability model. The specific approach to partitioning will be dependent on the selected design problem.

10.3 SYSTEM STATE MAPPING

State mapping is used to reduce the number of system states. One approach to reducing the complexity of the system state space is to map it to a simpler set. This set is normally selected to provide the needed information without being too detailed. Thus, both the failure and operational states may be mapped to fewer, more general states.

10.3.1 Failure Mapping

Failure state mapping is a two-step process:

1. *Mapping of Failure Modes to Capability States*. The mapping of hardware component failure modes to subsystem performance states relates the causes of failures to the effects on operation. Thus, the failure modes of the components within each subsystem are related to the output states of the subsystem. The data of interest to the program consist of (a) state transition diagrams, which represent the possible states of the equipment within the subsystem, (b) the transition rates between these states, and (c) the logical combination of internal subsystem states that map to output states.

2. *Mapping of Capability States to Mission Outcomes*. The map matrix describes which combinations of the subsystem output states result in performance of the various mission subphases.

10.3.2 Mapping System Failure Severity

When a given system consists of several subsystems, then it is necessary to map the failures in a particular subsystem to the system level. This mapping process for critical failures is illustrated in Figure 10.1. Note that the occurrence of a critical failure in one of the subsystems dominates the outcome at the system level. For example, if there is a critical failure in, say, Subsystem *A*, and there are no failures or a lesser failure in Subsystem *B*, then the resulting failure severity at the system level is *critical*.

Since we are dealing with more than one failure classification, this mapping must cover other failure categories as well, as shown in Figure 10.2. In this case, we follow the same reasoning: the failure criticality at the system level is determined by the most severe failure occurring in one of the subsystems.

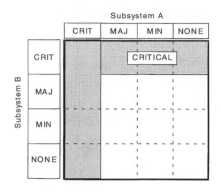

Figure 10.1 Critical Failure State Mapping.

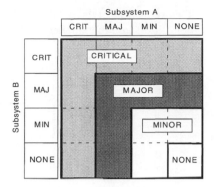

Figure 10.2 Failure Severity Mapping.

In situations where a less detailed failure classification can be applied, use Figure 10.3.

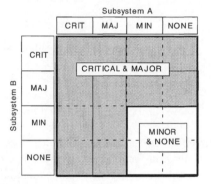

Figure 10.3 Failure Classification Group Reduction.

The above model has only two states at the system level. Thus, this particular mapping is similar to the standard reliability calculations, where only two system states are considered: operational and failed.

10.3.3 Mapping System Capability

To reduce the complexity of the Markov diagram, it is often possible to set up individual Markov diagrams for each of the independent subsystems and then combine them at the system level. To understand this approach to system partitioning, we will examine a system consisting of two data processing clusters, each containing a given number of central processing units (CPUs).

A specific case for two clusters, each with three CPUs, is illustrated in Figure 10.4. Each cluster state is defined by the number of operational CPUs. Thus, there are four distinct states in each cluster consisting of 3, 2, 1, and 0 operational CPUs. If we were to derive a Markov diagram at the system level, then there would be 16 system states.

If we only need to know the number of operational CPUs that are available in the system, then we can reduce these states to seven, each state representing the number of operational CPUs:

6, 5, 4, 3, 2, 1, 0

This reduction in the number of states is particularly effective when the number of CPUs per cluster and the number of clusters increase.

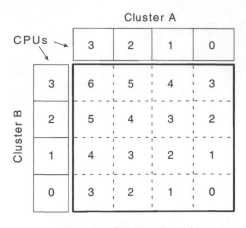

Figure 10.4 Available CPU Mapping.

Figure 10.5 shows how system states are mapped and how the computing capability is obtained at the system level. But we still need to know how to compute the system state probabilities.

This procedure can be best explained if we visualize the situation at the system level. This view can be represented in a three-dimensional diagram, as shown in Figure 10.5. If we consider a more restricted case, where we need two or more operational CPUs in a four-CPU cluster and one or more operational CPUs in a three-CPU cluster, then these configurations are constrained by the shaded area. To compute the probability that this situation will be achieved, we have to add the individual independent probabilities that meet the given conditions. These, of course, can be obtained from the respective Markov diagram for each cluster.

This is a typical application of using mapping to transform a complex problem into a relatively simple one.

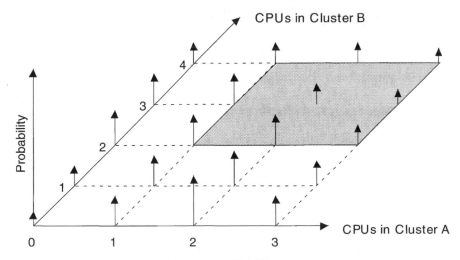

Figure 10.5 Probability Computation Mapping.

10.3.4 Multicluster Systems

If the system contains multiple clusters of CPUs, then the state mapping approach examined in the previous section can be generalized.

As an example, assume that we have five clusters and that each cluster contains three CPUs, for a total of 15 CPUs. The individual clusters are independent, and each cluster contains its own power supplies, memories, and the like. Let us further assume that we have a cluster-level reliability diagram that permits computation of the probabilities of 3, 2, 1, and 0 operational CPUs. We are, however, interested in the state probabilities at the system level, represented by 15, 14, 13, . . . , 0 operational CPUs. Since there are five clusters and each cluster has four states, there are a total of $4^5 = 1024$ states at the system level.

Although the states can be evaluated directly, considerable simplification can be obtained if we represent the computation process in terms of a decision (outcome) tree and then perform the computation one stage at a time. The corresponding outcome tree for our example is shown in Figure 10.6. Numbers on the outcome tree represent the number of operational CPUs at each stage, where a stage represents the addition of a cluster and its associated set of CPUs.

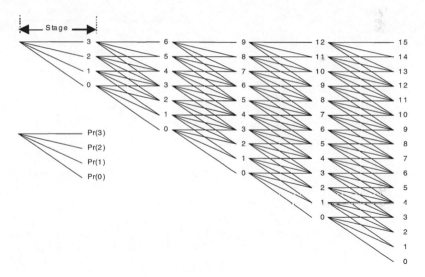

Figure 10.6 Outcome Tree.

The last stage of the outcome tree represents the full set of states (15, 14, 13, . . . 1, 0). To calculate the tree, probabilities are accumulated by convolution as we proceed left to right, with each stage contributing the probabilities of operational CPUs for an additional cluster. As an example, to calculate the probability of eight CPUs operational at stage 3, we use the probabilities of operational CPUs from cluster 3 and those probabilities accumulated from the previous stage as follows:

$$Pr(8)^{\text{Stage 3}} = Pr(2) \times Pr(6)^{\text{Stage 2}} + Pr(3) \times Pr(5)^{\text{Stage 2}} \qquad (10.1)$$

The algorithm for the general case is thus a discrete convolution, where $j = k + l$.

$$Pr(j)^{\text{StageM}} = Pr(k) \otimes Pr(l)^{\text{StageM}-1} \qquad (10.2)$$

However, if we are constrained to a minimum number of CPUs needed for system operation, then the computation process can be further simplified.

Assuming that we have the same configuration as before, but that we need at least eight CPUs for operation, then the outcome tree can be truncated, and all of the system-level states representing less than eight CPUs can be lumped in one failure state. The corresponding outcome tree is shown in Figure 10.7. (The dotted line represents the truncation level.)

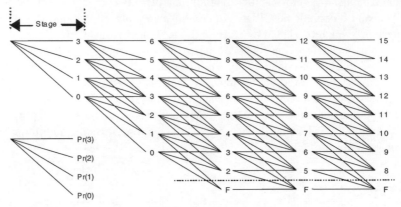

Figure 10.7 Truncated Outcome Tree.

11

Maintainability Modeling

Maintainability analysis typically receives less attention than reliability analysis. It also requires substantial effort to perform a detailed analysis of the repair process. The repair task is particularly difficult during the early design phases, because detailed implementation information is lacking.

Our objective in this chapter is to examine a general maintainability model that is applicable in most practical situations, including the initial design phase. This model considers the multistage nature of the maintenance tasks and illustrates the repair process using Markov stage approximation techniques.

11.1 MAINTAINABILITY DEFINITIONS

Maintainability is defined as the probability that a failed system is restored to operable condition within a specified down time. This definition of maintainability reveals the probabilistic nature of this measure.

11.2 LOGNORMAL DISTRIBUTION

The lognormal distribution is a two-parameter probability, with a probability density function given by

$$f(x) = \frac{1}{\sigma x \sqrt{2\pi}} \exp\left[-\frac{1}{2}\left(\frac{ln\ x - \mu}{\sigma}\right)^2 \right] \qquad \text{(for } x \geq 0\text{)} \qquad (11.1)$$

and

$$f(x) = 0 \qquad \text{(for } x < 0\text{)} \qquad (11.2)$$

Thus, it does not extend below zero, and as such, it is suitable for representing a maintenance task distribution.

11.3 WEIBULL DISTRIBUTION

The Weibull distribution is a two-parameter probability distribution function, with a *failure rate* (sometimes called a *hazard rate*), $r(t)$, given by

$$r(t) = \alpha\lambda t^{\alpha-1}, \qquad (\alpha > 0, \lambda > 0) \tag{11.3}$$

The Weibull *failure density function* is given by

$$f(t) = \alpha\lambda t^{\alpha-1} e^{-\lambda t^{\alpha}} \tag{11.4}$$

It is easy to see that the exponential distribution is a special case of the Weibull distribution, obtained by setting $\alpha = 1$.

Use of the Weibull distribution in availability computations creates a problem because of the difficulty of solving the resulting equations. A similar difficulty is experienced in trying to introduce the Weibull distribution model in the state-space formulation. The approach used in the past has been to assume the exponential distribution. Although this approach simplifies the analysis task, it does introduce inaccuracies because of the rather drastic simplification.

11.4 MAINTAINABILITY PREDICTION

Maintainability prediction is one of the most difficult tasks facing the maintainability engineer. The prediction process is usually based on techniques described in MIL-HDBK 472—*A Handbook of Maintainability Prediction.* This publication describes several different prediction techniques. A technique is usually selected based on the specific system and the available information. Procedures are available for airborne, shipboard, and ground systems. These procedures are applicable throughout the design and development cycle, with various degrees of detail.

It is important that the maintainability predictions be made early in the design phase when the needed changes can be completed without difficult and extensive rework. The maintainability predictions made during this early stage will also pinpoint those areas where critical problems exist. Maintenance characteristics involve the overall system operation and have an effect on personnel, tools, and test equipment.

We should compare the basic objectives of reliability and maintainability at this point. The objective of reliability effort is to reduce the probability of failure. This can be accomplished by reducing the number of failure-causing parts or by introducing redundancy. The first of these approaches will improve maintainability; the second will decrease it because of the added complexity. Since the system objective is to improve availability, a proper tradeoff is needed.

Because of this basic incompatibility, the current practice is to specify reliability and maintainability requirements separately, and require the supplier to conduct separate reliability and maintainability tests.

Although every attempt is made to reduce maintenance time or to eliminate it, scheduled maintenance is still required in some situations. Scheduled maintenance times are not usually included in the model formulation, although they have a major effect on system availability. However, in recent years the use of automatic test equipment (ATE) and built-in test (BIT) has greatly decreased the time needed for failure localization. Use of these techniques has greatly increased system availability.

11.5 MAINTENANCE PHILOSOPHY

Since maintenance operations are expensive, many organizations try to simplify the maintenance procedures and to eliminate intermediate-level shops, while at the same time increasing system availability and reliability.

Two-Level Maintenance. Military services typically use a three-level maintenance system: base, intermediate, and depot. Elimination of the intermediate level would have a major impact on system operation and could result in considerable savings. This decision, however, is highly dependent on both component availability and the capability to detect and repair failures rapidly. Thus, an extensive analysis is required before the decision to eliminate the intermediate repair level is undertaken.

11.6 MAINTAINABILITY MODELS

Conventional reliability block diagrams cannot be used to represent maintenance effects and actions. This is one of the major limitations of the reliability block diagram. However, within the constraints of the Markov model, maintenance operations can be easily implemented. Inclusion of the repair rates and modeling the operation of BIT also permit computation of the dynamic system availability.

Markov models can be used to investigate different maintenance concepts. Maintenance analysis is conducted first to evaluate the effect of maintainability on system performance and then to estimate manpower requirements, maintenance load, required logistics support, and so on.

Effects of Testability and Diagnostics. Testability and diagnostics capabilities have a direct impact on repair time. Thus, the equipment repair rates are derived on the basis of the available testability and diagnostics features built into the equipment or available in external test equipment.

Built-In-Test. As systems become more complex, more emphasis is placed on providing built-in-test (BIT) capabilities to achieve the needed reliability and fail-safety requirements. As mentioned, the reliability effects of the BIT circuitry can be evaluated using Markov model techniques.

Diagnostics. Markov techniques not only model the BIT reliability, but also offer help in determining the optimum way of implementing diagnostic procedures in the system. In this application, the Markov model is used to develop a fault occurrence probability model, and the diagnostic process is developed in such a way that the diagnostic test sequence considers the various fault occurrence probabilities.

11.6.1 Fault Detection, Isolation, and Reconfiguration (FDIR)

Before the system can be maintained or reconfigured, the fault must be detected and isolated. This is where FDIR fits into the redundant system design picture. Fault recovery normally requires automated or manual reconfiguration. Selection of the specific technique depends on system requirements and the operating environment.

Automatic Recovery.   Automatic fault recovery is needed in those situations where only a fast recovery will meet the imposed mission requirements.

Manual Recovery.   Use of manual recovery techniques can reduce system complexity and decrease costs. Manual recovery can range from a simple plug-in replacement to a complete rebuilding of the system.

11.6.2 Repair (Maintenance) Rate

The repair rate expresses the rate at which failed equipment can be returned to operational status.

Exponential Repair Rate.   An exponential repair rate provides a first-cut approximation in modeling. Exponential repair (memoryless), however, is a poor approximation for the repair density function, which usually has a definite peak away from zero repair times.

Lognormal and Weibull Repair Rates.   This is a time-dependent density function, which cannot be easily incorporated in the Markov model but can be approximated with the multiple-stage model. Otherwise, a special program needs to be developed or Monte Carlo simulation used.

11.7 MODELING SYSTEMS WITH REPAIR

The systems considered in previous chapters did not have repair capability. In other words, there were no reverse transitions from a failed state back to an operational state.

The basic repair capability is easily incorporated in the state diagram if we observe certain precautions. First, we have to redefine our states to include the status of the equipment under repair. Next, we have to establish a repair policy that will be a function of the available manpower repair/recovery capabilities. And last, we have to decide which states will be operational and which will be failed states.

Let us consider a few examples. The simplest system that we can model will be one in which we have alternating states of equipment:

$$Up \rightarrow Down \rightarrow Up \rightarrow Down \rightarrow Up \rightarrow \ldots$$

If we have infinite repair capability, then this sequence will never end. In most practical situations, however, we will be working with a limited supply of repair parts and then the sequence will terminate after the part supply has been exhausted. Thus, in the simplest situation, we will have only one spare. In this case, the system states will be:

State	Description
P_1	Initial operating state, system up
P_2	First failure, system down
P_3	First failure repaired, system up
P_4	Second failure, system down

For the Markov model, we will be able to have only one repair action, as shown in Figure 11.1.

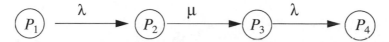

Figure 11.1 System with a Single Repair Action.

We add one more spare, and our diagram becomes as shown in Figure 11.2.

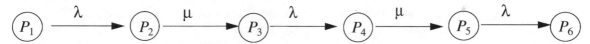

Figure 11.2 System with Two Repair Actions.

In the above examples, we assuméd that our equipment had an exponential failure distribution with a failure rate λ, as well as an exponential repair distribution with repair rate μ.

In the first diagram, Figure 11.1, P_1 and P_3 are equipment up states, and P_2 and P_4 are the down states. The same sequence also applies to the second diagram, Figure 11.2, where the odd-numbered states are the up states and the even-numbered states the down states. The extension to higher order systems is simple; for each additional spare we add two states, one up and one down, and we use transition rates μ and λ for the corresponding transitions.

11.7.1 Unlimited Repair Capability

If we have unlimited repair capability and if we are interested in only the up and down states, then we can obtain a much simpler diagram, as shown in Figure 11.3.

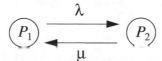

Figure 11.3 Repairable System.

In the analysis of practical systems we will find many modifications of this pattern.

Another simple example will illustrate this point. Assume that our system consists of two parallel components and that we require only one for successful operation. However, if one of the components has failed, then we have repair capability to restore the system to an operating state with a rate of μ. If our parallel components have identical failure rates λ , then our state diagram becomes as shown in Figure 11.4.

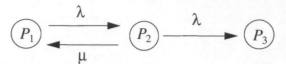

Figure 11.4 Limited Repair.

Note that if we reach state P_3, then the system has failed, and based on our definition of success no further repair is possible. Thus, in our example we are considering the state P_3 to be a catastrophic failure state.

If the system contains some parts that cannot be repaired with the available spares, then the above model has to be modified by introducing an additional transition from state P_1 directly to P_3, as shown in Figure 11.5.

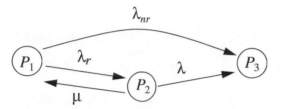

Figure 11.5 Maintenance with Repairable and Nonrepairable Parts.

In Figure 11.5, λ_r is the failure rate for repairable parts, and λ_{nr} is the corresponding failure rate for nonrepairable parts. The total failure rate for this case is given by: $\lambda = \lambda_r + \lambda_{nr}$.

In other applications, however, having two components in failed states may cause only an inconvenience, and we may be permitted to proceed with the repair and then return to an operating state.

In this situation, we have to consider two different cases:

1. When two components are down, we may have two repairmen available who can work independently with an overall repair rate of 2μ, or
2. We can have only one repairman present, which would always result in a repair rate of μ.

These two cases will yield different state diagrams. In the first case, with two repairmen present, the state diagram shown in Figure 11.6 applies.

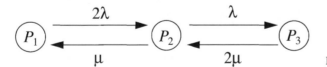

Figure 11.6 Two-Repairman Case.

In the second case, we obtain a similar diagram, except for the repair transition rate, as shown in Figure 11.7.

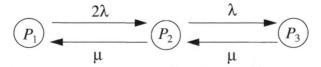

Figure 11.7 One-Repairman Case.

As a review, in repairable systems, we have the situation where after the repair is completed, the system is returned to the operational state. First, there is a definition of states; second, there is an introduction of repair action. Repair is introduced directly in the model. The same model is used, the number of states is not increased, and only an additional transition is incorporated.

The inclusion of repair capability in our state diagram involved consideration of the available manpower. For the above examples, a joint reliability-maintainability-operational policy had to be considered.

If we added a description or evaluation of the expected capability of each state and determined how it would affect the mission outcome, then we would have a system effectiveness model.

11.7.2 Realistic Repair Rates

In the previous discussion, we considered that the repair actions had an exponential distribution, with a constant rate, μ. The concept of constant repair rate is the most often used distribution because of its simplicity. In field experience, however, the actual repair rate may differ considerably from the exponential assumption. Often it is of the characteristic shown in Figure 11.8.

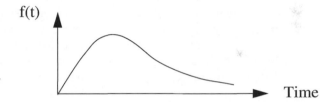

Figure 11.8 Typical Complex Repair Density Function.

Obviously, in this situation the exponential distribution would not give a good fit for the short repair times. The question becomes: what distribution should be used to represent the skewed distribution shown above. A common practice has been to use the lognormal distribution because it has similar shape, although many distributions fall in the same category.

It is difficult to determine why this distribution was selected in the first case; perhaps it was because of the simplicity or the reason that tables were available. It is possible that it was selected without any physical justification. However, once the selection was made, it was assumed as a given and incorporated in maintainability specifications.

In our work, we would like to find some justification for the distributions we select, and we would also like to work with models that are basically linear, although not always of the first order. The lognormal distribution fails in both respects.

Thus, a better approach is needed. We should be able to use a distribution that can be justified on physical principles and at the same time be relatively easy to model and to solve.

11.7.3 Multistage Repair Model

In a more complex model, the specific phases of the maintenance process could be represented, such as fault detection, part replacement, and checkout. An even more complex model could include the constraints introduced by the available resources and test equipment.

The multistage maintainability model is based on the observation that the average repair action consists of a number of stages. In the simplest case, we have a single-stage situation in which only one subtask is involved. As an example, consider the case where a fuse has failed and an indicator signal has been lit. In this case diagnosis is obvious, and the fuse can be replaced immediately. If the indicator light is not available, then we have a two-stage repair process. First, the type of failure must be determined. Second, the failed part has to be replaced. We note that the time duration of these stages cannot be specified exactly because the diagnostic process and the replacement will vary. It is easy to extend this model by adding other stages to account for administrative time, final checkout, and so on.

Although the multistage concept is not new, development of the model in this case is based on parameters that can be easily determined, such as diagnostic time or component replacement time. The distribution of the individual stages can be assumed to obey the exponential approximation. This follows from statistical considerations, since the only information available at this time is the average stage completion time. It is further assumed that the stages have to be completed in sequence. The second assumption follows from practical constraints associated with the repair action. In a real-life situation, the fault must be located before a replacement is undertaken. Thus, the proposed model has a sound physical basis.

Looking at the repair density function, shown in Figure 11.8, we note that the density function starts from zero, rises to a maximum value, and then decays to zero in an asymptotic manner. This type of behavior is characteristic of higher order Markov processes. In a state diagram, this could be expressed as a multistage process, where several tasks need to be performed in a sequence, and the process is completed when all stages are completed.

Returning to our problem formulation, we note that the next simplest process following exponential is a two-stage process, consisting of two tasks in sequence. Thus, we will examine the repair process to see if we can express it as a two-stage process. One way of looking at the repair is to consider that the repair action actually consists of two sequential tasks:

1. Location of the failed component
2. Repair or replacement of the failed component

If the only information available to us consists of the mean times for the completion of each sequential subtask, then we can represent this in the state diagram shown in Figure 11.9.

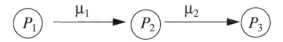

Figure 11.9 Repair with Stages.

Where the system states are:

State	Description
P_1	Equipment is down and fault location is in progress
P_2	Fault has been located and repair/replacement process has started
P_3	Equipment has been returned to operational status

and the repair rates are:

Rate	Description
μ_1	Faulty component location rate
μ_2	Component repair/replacement rate

In our model we now find two repair rates, μ_1 and μ_2, which replace the single repair rate, μ, used in the simple model. These new rates can be obtained by estimating the mean time to locate the failed component and to replace the failed component. If these rates are equal, then we obtain a two-parameter gamma distribution; otherwise we have an Erlang distribution for the resulting repair rate.

The resulting model thus depends on two parameters, μ_1 and μ_2, and as such can assume a number of shapes depending on the value of the two parameters. When this model is applied to actual field repair data, relatively good fit has been obtained. Usually, the fit is at least as good or equal to that given by the fitted lognormal distribution.

The alternative model has a number of distinct advantages over the lognormal model. First, the model is a linear Markov model and as such can be easily introduced in the state diagram representation. Second, since the model is linear, a relatively simple analytical solution can be obtained. Third, the specific rates are meaningful parameters that one should be able to measure or to estimate.

It is also possible to extend the two-stage model to higher order. In this case, we can subdivide the overall repair task into more than two subtasks. As the number of individual subtasks increases, more parameters enter in defining the resulting distribution, with the effect that more control over the resulting distribution shape is obtained. However, there is a tradeoff as to how far one should proceed in this direction and whether the individual parameters can really be easily measured or estimated.

Our original objective was to develop a repair model that would overcome the objections raised against the exponential model. We accomplished this objective by introducing auxiliary states. If we were to calculate the overall repair rate from the failed to the operational state, we would find that this rate would start from zero, increase for a while, and then decrease. Its shape will be similar to but not the same as the lognormal distribution.

Before we complete our discussion of the present topic, we will consider an application of the new model in a practical situation. Returning to an earlier example, repeated in Figure 11.10, we will rework it with the introduction of the new modifications.

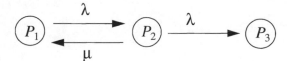

Figure 11.10 Limited Repair Model.

If we add the two-stage representation to the above model, then the resulting state diagram will change, as shown in Figure 11.11.

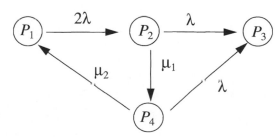

Figure 11.11 Limited Repair with Staged Repair Activity.

In the modified diagram we see a new state, P_4, as well as three new state transition arrows. It is easy to see how μ_1 and μ_2 replaced the original μ. However, we need to explain the introduction of the new transition from state P_4 to P_3. This can be best explained if we briefly review what the actual states represent. P_1 represents the fully operational state where both components are good. P_2 denotes the state where one of the components has failed and we are in the process of locating the failure within that component. P_3 represents the state where both components have failed, and P_4 denotes the state where the failure has been located in the failed component, and we are in the process of repairing or replacing it. It is clear that in states P_2 and P_4 we still have one operational component, and if this component fails then the system will fail. These failures are represented by transitions $P_2 \rightarrow P_3$ and $P_4 \rightarrow P_3$. These transitions are associated with a single-component failure rate, λ.

The multistage maintainability model has been tested against some of the cases reported in the literature with good results. The model appears to follow the empirical distribution quite well. Further work will be needed for a complete validation of the model.

The model can be introduced directly in the state-space system effectiveness model without any further modifications, other than adding extra system states. Its use in future analyses should result in better understanding of the system dynamics and an improved optimization process.

12

Availability Modeling

Availability computations involve both reliability and maintainability. For example, in an airline operational environment, an important aspect is the computation of dynamic availability as a function of flight times and flights flown. In this situation, availability computations serve to determine the necessary fleet size and maintenance.

In a detailed availability analysis, the cyclic behavior of the system operation must be considered. Furthermore, the specific decisions governed by the mission conditions will also affect availability computation. For example, if the decision is made to continue flying a mission while some of the equipment is in a degraded state or some of the redundant equipment has failed, then a higher availability could be obtained. This gain, however, is not free, and it comes at the expense of a reduced mission reliability. This action is normally referred to as a deferred maintenance policy.

Deferred maintenance policy has a complex effect on system effectiveness. To fully evaluate this effect, a simulation is performed. In this case, the Markov model provides the needed framework and simulates the effects of the various maintenance decisions on the system effectiveness. Note that this evaluation cannot be accomplished using the reliability block diagram approach.

12.1 DEFINITION OF AVAILABILITY

Availability is defined as a measure of the degree to which an item is in operable and committable state at the start of the mission, when the mission is called for at unknown (random) time [MIL-STD-721C definition].

A related concept is the operational readiness, which is defined as the ability of a system to respond to an operational plan upon receipt of an operations order. Total calendar time is the usual basis for computing operational readiness.

111

12.2 MEASURES OF AVAILABILITY

Maintainability Acronyms.   Availability computations involve a number of maintenance parameters. These are summarized as follows:

Acronym	Description
MTBM	Mean time between maintenance
MTTR	Mean time to repair
MRT	Mean restore time
MLDT	Mean logistics delay time
MDT	Maintenance down time

12.2.1 Inherent Availability

The most often used and best known availability measure is the inherent availability, A_i, defined by

$$A_i = \frac{MTBM}{MTBM + MTTR} \qquad (12.1)$$

Note that in Eq. (12.1) we use MTBM, mean time between maintenance actions, instead of MTBF, mean time between failures. If we use the latter:

$$A_i = \frac{MTBF}{MTBF + MTTR} \qquad (12.2)$$

For a simple component, with a constant failure rate, λ, and a constant repair rate, μ, the above equation can be expressed as

$$A_i = \frac{MTBF}{MTBF + MTTR} = \frac{\mu}{\lambda + \mu} \qquad (12.3)$$

12.2.2 Instantaneous Availability

The instantaneous availability, $A(t)$, is defined as the probability that the item will be available at time t. For a simple system with a constant failure rate, λ, and a constant repair rate, μ, the instantaneous (transient) availability can be computed from the Markov diagram shown in Figure 12.1.

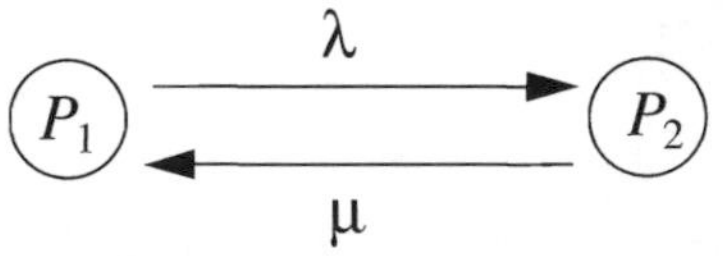

Figure 12.1 Repairable System.

From this diagram we can compute the instantaneous availability, $A(t)$ as:

$$A(t) = P_1(t) = \frac{\mu}{\lambda + \mu} + \frac{\lambda}{\lambda + \mu} \exp\left[-(\lambda + \mu)\, t\right] \qquad (12.4)$$

We note, that at $t = 0$, the instantaneous availability is unity and the steady-state availability is given by the constant term, which is the same as the inherent availability.

12.2.3 Operational Availability

Operational availability, A_o, is given by

$$A_o = \frac{MTBM}{MTBM + MRT}$$

(12.5)

12.3 COMPUTATION OF AVAILABILITY

In computing availability, we have to consider if we need steady-state or dynamic availability.

12.3.1 Steady-state Availability

In general, matrix inversion can be used for computing steady-state availability (assuming there are no trapping or nonrepairable failure states). Applicable equations can be derived from the Markovian formulation by setting derivatives equal to zero.

12.3.2 Dynamic Availability

The steady-state availability of a system can be computed from the known values of MTTF and MTTR (if given) or by matrix inversion. However, many complex systems never reach a steady-state availability, and as such the steady-state value is no longer a valid tradeoff factor. The dynamic Markov model provides a convenient approach to computing the dynamic system availability as the specified operational profile evolves.

For the remaining systems, by letting the dynamic model run to equilibrium (corresponding to a suitable simulation time), we can arrive at a steady-state value.

13

Safety Modeling

Safety engineering is another branch of the basic system disciplines. In an aircraft environment, safety engineering is concerned with the crew, operating personnel, and passenger safety. Its basic purpose is to reduce the probability of catastrophic failure. In medical applications, the primary emphasis of safety engineering is on preventing occurrence of life-threatening incidents.

The safety engineering objectives in many cases will conflict with other system objectives. Maximum safety will introduce additional complexity, result in more aborted missions, and in general decrease system performance. Thus, in many of the current systems, safety devices will result in an overall decrease in system reliability and increased maintenance load.

13.1 SAFETY DEFINITIONS

Safety is defined as freedom from those conditions that can cause death, injury, occupational illness, or damage to or loss of equipment or property [definition from MIL-STD-882]. In a safety analysis, system failures are classified according to their effect on the system and the operator(s). See Table 13.1.

TABLE 13.1   MIL-STD-882 Failure Criticality Categories

Category	Type	Description
I	Catastrophic	Catastrophic failure states are those that may cause death or loss of the system.
II	Critical	Critical failures will not result in injury, occupational illness, or system damage but will have a major impact on system capabilities.
III	Marginal	Marginal failures may cause minor injury, minor occupational illness, or minor system damage.
IV	Negligible	These failures will not result in injury, occupational illness, or system damage.

13.2 DESIGN FOR SAFETY

A new system design must include provisions for safety. This is particularly important in those systems where a failure may result in catastrophic conditions. Thus, the computation of system safety must be evaluated in addition to reliability, maintainability, and system availability.

Since the system fail-safety requirements are introduced as constraints during the system design process, it is important to specify these requirements as *quantitative* goals. If the system fail-safety requirements are specified qualitatively, as for example: *no single failure shall cause a catastrophic failure*, then it is still possible that the probability of a catastrophic failure may be unacceptably high due to the occurrence of a second failure.

The probability of critical failures can be reduced by several different techniques. These techniques are similar to those used for reliability improvement: reduction of failure rates and use of redundancy. For example, we often find redundancy is used to improve safety. A dual flight control system that disconnects the failed element is a system of this type. In this case, the resulting total equipment reliability is less than that of a single system, but the probability of critical failure is less.

13.3 SAFETY ANALYSES

The reliability goal is to reduce the probability of operational failures, whereas safety is concerned with reducing the probability of critical failures.

The analytical techniques used for safety analyses are still relatively primitive and deal mostly with static-type analyses.

Using an extended Markov model, we can conduct safety analysis concurrently with reliability analysis. When developing the extended model, it will be important to mark the states according to both reliability (operational or failed) and safety (safe or unsafe) classifications (Table 13.2).

TABLE 13.2   MIL-STD-882 System State Classification

State Type	Description
1	Fully operational
2	Fail-operational
3	Fail-degraded
4	Fail-safe
5	Fail-unsafe

Fail-safe and Fail-operate States.   In mission-critical systems, the initial faults should not result in a critical system failure (fail-safe). Furthermore, in some systems the first fault should not cause performance degradation (fail-operate).

Since the system states are mutually exclusive, it is only necessary to identify the unsafe states and sum the probabilities associated with these states to compute the probability of unsafe operation. In most systems, the safety and reliability analyses must be conducted concurrently because of the interaction of system elements and dynamic

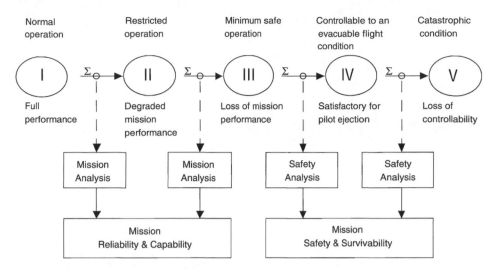

Figure 13.1 Outline of Combined Reliability-Safety Analysis.

reconfiguration capability and the need to achieve the required balance between reliability and safety.

A complete system analysis should include the secondary equipment that is used only after the primary system fails. For example, this equipment may include launch escape equipment, ejection seats, and parachutes. Consideration of these devices does not greatly complicate the analysis because they can be considered to operate only after a failure has occurred in the primary system.

An overview of the analysis approach is presented in Figure 13.1. Summation operators, Σ, indicate that the corresponding state failure probabilities are summed. These are then displayed and used in further analyses.

14

Markov Model Evaluation

Evaluating a Markov model (MM) can be time consuming or, at worst, feasible only for the simplest systems—unless one uses proper techniques. In general, most practical applications of the Markov model require computer support for deriving and solving state equations based on the user-specified state diagram.

14.1 MANUAL EVALUATION

Obtaining a solution to a Markov model involves three separate steps: setting up the model, deriving equations, and solving state equations.

14.1.1 Setting up the Model

Developing a Markov state diagram for manual evaluation consists of determining the system states, the transitions between these states, and the transition rates. It also includes labeling the states as operational, degraded, or failed.

14.1.2 Deriving Equations

The Markov state diagram developed in the preceding step must be converted to a set of linear differential equations. The manual derivation of the Markov model equations from the state diagram is time consuming and error prone for Markov models with four or more states.

14.1.3 Solving State Equations

Solving the state differential equations manually is normally limited to a few states. A number of solution techniques exist, such as Laplace transforms, that can simplify this task. Except in those cases where the equations can be easily derived, the complexity of the analytical solution makes them prohibitive.

Analytical Solution.   An analytical solution of the state equations is feasible only for simple problems or for those that are highly regular. Even if an analytical solution can be found, they cannot be easily evaluated, and the effect of parameter variation on the system cannot be determined unless one uses a symbolic equation evaluation program, such as Mathcad.

Computational effort increases as the number of states in the system increases. The rise in computations is partly counteracted in that the number of valid state transitions does not increase as fast as the state population for most practical problems.

Laplace Transform Solution.   The use of Laplace transforms in engineering is well known. Important applications are in control system stability evaluation, circuit analysis, and so on. Laplace transforms provide a convenient way of solving simpler models. Since the Laplace transform method is widely used in scholastic publications, a short discussion is in order.

Solution of the Markov state equations using this approach involves two steps:

1. State equations are transformed to their Laplace counterparts. This step is relatively simple because the state equations are linear and of first order.
2. The resulting Laplace transform domain equations are inverted to obtain their time-domain solutions. This step can be performed either analytically or by using approximate numerical inversion techniques. Some highly stable Laplace transform inversion methods are available. These methods, however, are not well known and thus not widely used.

Numerical Integration.   Manual numerical integration of these equations must be ruled out because it is a time-consuming process. If the mission times are short and if the failure rates are small, then approximations can be used that may satisfy the accuracy requirements.

14.2 COMPUTER-ASSISTED EVALUATION

Computer support is needed for the solution of most practical reliability problems. Since many of the reliability, availability, and maintainability parameters need to be predicted early in the design stage, the basic requirements of a reliability analysis tool are the following:

1. Provide a framework and language in which to state reliability problems.
2. Allow the comparison of alternative designs in a fast, interactive fashion.

3. Allow an approach flexible enough to model various situations encountered in practice.

4. Provide insight into assumptions concerning system life characteristics (such as which components are critical).

Computer-assisted evaluation of Markov models requires the same three steps of setup, derivation, and solution, but provides an alternative approach.

14.2.1 Setting up the Model

Interactive development of the Markov model is much simpler than that in the manual mode, because several modes of model specification are available. For example, the setup of a Markov model in a symbolic or graphical form is much easier than manually developing the set of Markov state equations. The symbolic representation provides the necessary specification for detailed equation derivation.

As data are entered in the program, they can be checked to determine whether they conform to the required format. Although this checking will not ensure that the correct values have been entered, it will guarantee that the simulation program will run, and possibly aid in the debugging effort. For example, consistency checking can ensure that the graphical state diagram representation matches the database parameter specification and provide diagnostics to the user.

14.2.2 Deriving Equations

The Markov model entered in the preceding step must be converted to a set of linear differential equations. This task can be easily performed by the computer because the state diagram provides all of the required information.

Since the system state probability equations are derived from the system state transition diagram in a formal manner, errors due to manual derivation of equations will be reduced.

14.2.3 Solving State Equations

Solving the state differential equations by computer is a straightforward process. However, if the equations are stiff (with greatly differing characteristic roots), the solution time will increase.

Computation of State Probabilities. Markov models yield linear differential equations for the state probabilities. These equations must be solved to obtain the final state probabilities. Solution of these equations involves several factors:

1. *Numerical integration methods.* Differential equations representing a Markov model are integrated to obtain the state probabilities. Since the solution accuracy is dependent on equation characteristics, a suitable numerical integration method will have to be selected.

2. *Integration step.* Numerical integration proceeds stepwise, with the integration step corresponding to the time advance. The selected step size will affect solution

time and solution accuracy. A smaller time step will normally yield higher accuracy, but will result in longer computation time. Many of the numerical integration methods support automatic and adaptive integration step selection.

3. *Stability of solution method.* A stable solution may not always be obtainable. Instability may be due to a large step size, the particular solution method, and the type of problem.

4. *Solution accuracy.* Solution accuracy will depend on the integration step size and the precision of computation. More accurate results will require the use of double-precision computation.

   Mathematical analyses seldom use approximations, whereas in engineering analyses, we always have to deal with approximate data. Since the accuracy of the solution is limited by the input data accuracy for engineering problems, the design problem solution should reflect this limited knowledge. Usually, the number of significant digits in the input data will be determined by the type of data associated with the particular component.

   Once a detailed solution of the problem has been obtained, we must review all approximations and, perhaps, conduct a detailed component tolerance and error analyses.

5. *Potential speed improvements.* Floating point processors or hardware accelerators should always be considered for numerical applications.

14.2.4 Related Issues

To achieve the fastest turnaround, the complete model evaluation process must be considered. Automation plays three roles: data entry time is minimized, data error frequency is minimized, and problem solution time is made sufficiently short to support an interactive design environment. Of course, this means that efficient numerical solution techniques should be selected, and due to the characteristics of the models, several solution algorithms are usually included in the Markov model solution package.

Other advantages of using a computer-assisted approach include:

1. *Reduced skill level.* To apply Markov modeling to system analysis, it is important to reduce the skill level needed for model development and yet retain model flexibility and applicability. This objective can be accomplished by identifying and automating those tasks that are time consuming and of a routine nature.

   The approach used is similar to those used in other engineering disciplines, ranging from electronic circuit analysis to finite element modeling of mechanical systems. In these areas, most of the routine tasks have already been automated, resulting in a cost-effective solution of design problems.

2. *Decreased training time.* The simplicity of the computer-assisted and directed modeling process will reduce the time needed for user training. The availability of a graphical data entry mode is appealing to the initial user because the model that the user will enter will be represented in a visual form.

3. *Decreased modeling time.* Model development time is reduced because the model can be described in a graphical form ready for translation. This model will

usually consist of a state diagram representing system states and the available transitions. Once again, development of the state diagram is easier than development and solution of the state equations.

4. *Improved reliability of computation.* Improved reliability will be due mainly to the use of automatic state equation derivation and on-line checking support.

5. *Interactive modeling environment.* A Markov model can be developed directly in an interactive environment without first sketching it on paper. This approach has the advantage that all of the data are captured in form, suitable for later archiving and modifications. With a labeling capability, the Markov model can be made self-documenting.

6. *Model library support.* An existing Markov model can also be recalled and suitably modified. If these models are similar to the ones proposed, then considerable saving in data entry is possible.

14.3 APPROXIMATE SOLUTIONS AND THEIR LIMITATIONS

Approximations allow a convenient way for fast evaluation of different redundancy configurations. Often the redundancy schemes can be ranked by a simple comparison of their approximate solutions. Approximate solutions of the Markov models were discussed earlier in Chapter 6.

14.4 MARKOV MODEL EVALUATION TOOLS

Very few tools for the reliability analysis of fault-tolerant systems have made an impact on the commercial CAD market. This lack of tools remains surprising despite the frequent use of terms such as *mission-critical* and *fail-safe* in describing various applications. Unless these are hollow words, some sort of analysis must cover the design, yet which tools?

When addressing this issue, first note that the distinction between tools for *fault-tolerant system* analysis and *conventional reliability* analysis is important, for the tool user can already choose among several commercially available MIL-STD-217 software packages. However, for those working at the conceptual and design phase of a fault-tolerant architecture, where different redundant configurations are traded off, the available tools remain limited. A potentially useful tool would use a method such as Markov modeling via state diagrams.

For instances of where computer-aided methods would prove useful, one only has to search through the recent reliability literature. As a prototypical example, *IEEE Transactions on Reliability* regularly publishes a reliability analysis study on some specific fault-tolerant system (labeled X). The author of a typical study will sketch the Markov model state diagram for the system and solve the differential equations analytically. This task will be repeated by the next author, presenting an analysis of system Y, which differs from system X in minor ways. Clearly, automating the modeling tasks will reduce the designer's effort in the long run. This leads to the following thought to keep in mind: Although redundancy in the design of fault-tolerant systems is desirable, redundancy in the manual derivation of state equations is wasted effort.

User-oriented, interactive Markov model packages that support the various system analyses outlined earlier do not currently exist. The key deficiencies of the presently available programs are as follows.

1. *Long Setup Time.* These programs require considerable setup effort because of their batch orientation. This is because the models have been developed for use on mainframes or upper-end minicomputers.

2. *Unique Modeling Language.* To use these programs, the user must learn a unique modeling language and follow rigid data formatting rules. Often special coding forms must be used and code conventions memorized. An on-line data integrity check is seldom provided, and the model debugging time may be appreciable.

3. *Rigid Models.* These programs are not flexible and extensible. Rigid models complicate derived probability computations. Only those problems that fit the established models can be evaluated. Since approximations must be made to fit the models, overall solution accuracy suffers.

   Many of the RMS problems require considerable flexibility in modeling. For example, improvements in modeling efficiency can be achieved by proper partitioning of the system. However, as the system is partitioned and individual models are evaluated, it becomes necessary to combine the individual solutions to obtain system-level results. This recombination process involves a substantial amount of computations that should be performed within the modeling environment to achieve efficiency and reduce potential errors.

4. *Limited Interactive Capabilities.* As already mentioned, most existing programs are batch oriented and use remote terminal access modes. Although these programs could be converted to run in a PC environment, this approach would not be desirable because of the lack of interactive capability and limited graphics display capability.

   Lack of a graphics interface means that the data may have to be translated to the specific format required by the plotting program and that the plot parameters also have to be specified.

5. *Complex Plotting Interface.* Plotting capability is usually supplied in a stand-alone format and is not interactive. To obtain a plot of the results, a complex setup procedure must be followed.

The goal then is to provide tools that allow the designer to parametrically input data or automatically generate reliability models for fault-tolerant systems. The tools, and not the user, will be responsible for deriving and solving the equations, storing diagrams, and creating the documentation. To illustrate this concept, we use the Computer-Aided Rate Modeling and Simulation program (CARMS) as a design tool. CARMS uses Markov modeling as a fault-tolerant design methodology and also adds automation and intelligent features to the design and documentation process. Besides reducing the designer's effort, this program will also provide faster design turnaround time. (The user, however, will still be responsible for validating the outputs from these tools.)

14.5 CARMS

CARMS is an integrated Markov modeling and simulation tool. Its features include a state diagram-based CAD environment for model setup, a spreadsheet-like interface for data entry, an expert system link for automatic model construction, and an interactive graphics interface for displaying simulation results. Primary applications are in engineering design, reliability, operations research, scientific, and statistical modeling.

We find that by using CARMS, complex design cycles can be shortened, simplified, and better understood and documented. A brief overview is provided in this section; the CARMS User's Manual and Reference Manual can be found in Chapters 19–21.

CARMS Introduction. CARMS excels as a general-purpose tool suitable for reliability, maintainability, and availability evaluation. It is designed to solve a broad spectrum of reliability and other mathematically related problems.[1]

A combination of text- and graphics-based data input makes the program ideal for solving problems when a product, operations, system, or engineering design is at the conceptual phase. In this phase, flexibility, ease of use, and speed are prime requirements in determining the ideal course of action and probing the "what if?" scenarios.

Unlike the traditional methods of computer-based evaluation, CARMS features an interactive environment that allows the user to quickly change data values and graphical representations of a given system. Menu-driven commands and help screens are supported.

Key CARMS Features. Listed below are the key features of the CARMS program:

- Spreadsheet-like data input screen.
- Vector-based graphics for constructing transition diagrams.
- Expert-system front end that automates model construction.
- Symbolic algebra for simplifying reliability, maintainability, and availability problems.
- Graphical display of results as a function of time.
- Generation of reports to printer, plotter, or file.
- Choice of numerical routines for solving a range of problems.

Other CARMS Features. CARMS is extensible in that the data input is human readable and an application programming interface is provided. The Windows features include universal printer support, export of graphics to the clipboard, and the familiar help system (see Tables 14.1 through 14.4 for support features).

---

[1]Reliability is usually defined as "the probability that a system will perform its intended function for a given period of time under stated environmental conditions." This definition can be extended to describe the system performance or life characteristics as a continuous function of time. Availability refers to the probability or percentage of up time during the mission time or system life cycle. It can also refer to the availability of the system at the start of the mission. Availability is in part determined by the maintenance policy.

TABLE 14.1   Model Development Support

Feature	Description
Alegebraic support	Create formulas for failure rates or for calculating probability. Adding failure rates, multiplying by common factors, and so on, are possible.
Unit conversion	Use engineering mode on data. For example, type 10K instead of 10000 and CARMS converts to the correct units.
Base rate capability	Model the system by using named base rates. For example, a commonly used failure rate can be named *lambda* and given a value.
Clipboard with cut and paste	Use clipboard to include diagrams in word processor documents, and transfer formulas and data using Windows cut and paste.
Configurable model size	Model data sizes can be configured. For larger problems, which require more memory, the maximum limits can be adjusted upward.
Expert system front end	Expert system front end allows parametric input models. This is valuable for creating large models automatically.
Font support	Choose from Windows fonts to display state diagram. All available Windows fonts and sizes are supported. Greek symbols are supported for display formulas using the equivalent English, Latin character and the symbol font. For example, choosing the symbol font and typing l will create a λ.
Context-sensitive help	Use standard Windows help system. The drawing window has context sensitivity to the help.
Spreadsheet interface	Use the unique spreadsheet interface to model data. This gives an alternate view of the data and provides faster data entry.

TABLE 14.2   CARMS Database and Libraries

Feature	Description
Human readable database	Input data are human-readable and modifiable, permitting translation to other database formats.
Built-in configurable editor	Input files can be edited with a user-definable editor. Data files are text-based and so can be edited easily.
Model conversion	Choose from other model views and automatically convert to Markov models (from fault trees, Stochastic Petri nets, etc.).
Input library selection	Models can be selected from a large example library, or a parametric model may be used.

TABLE 14.3   CARMS Outputs

Feature	Description
Vector-based diagram	State diagram uses vector graphics for drawing and display. All diagram objects can be moved and resized.
Time domain output	Probability can be displayed as a function of simulation time. Simulation time can be restarted or continued.
Selectable state view	The user should pick only the states desired to be viewed during simulation. This allows one to interactively compare various states of interest.
Color output	Graph output can be modified to desired colors.
Multiple views or programs	One can view among several representations of data or run multiple instances of CARMS.

TABLE 14.4   CARMS External Interfaces

Feature	Description
Windows interface	Conventional Windows interface eases learning. Most of the interface commands follow the common user interface guidelines.
Macro Windows support	Windows macros can be used to program tasks.
DLL/DDE interface	CARMS is object callable via dynamic link library (DLL) or dynamic data exchange (DDE) conventions. Thus, one can use conventional programming languages (Ada, C) to communicate with CARMS.

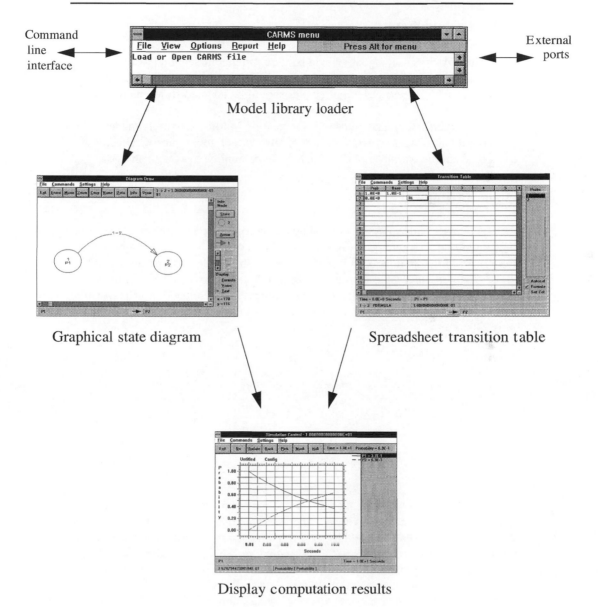

Figure 14.1 CARMS Interactive Environment.

14.5.1 CARMS Views

The structure of CARMS follows a strategy of providing several views of the working model (see Figure 14.1). Each one of the views, **Diagram Draw, Transition Table,** and **Simulation Control,** can be accessed from the main menu. The views are contained within separate windows and with their own local menus. The drawing view provides methods to create state diagrams. The table view allows spreadsheet access to the data displayed in the diagram. The simulation view controls the calculation of state probabilities.

14.5.2 Methodology

The CARMS user's goals should be to set up the model at a level where parametric inputs and formula abstraction make the overall task easier and the final configuration potentially reusable. These general principles should be adhered to when creating any reliability model.

The specific rules and guidelines for creating Markov reliability models rely on logical and probabilistic arguments. As a brief introduction to a typical CARMS use, we will give one example on how a Markov model can be applied to system analysis.

14.5.3 Example

A 1-of-N parallel system is a simple candidate for Markov modeling. Successful fault-tolerant operation is achieved if at least one out of N initial parallel processors remains operational at mission completion (the reliability block diagram or RBD in Figure 14.2). In a particular case, the requirements might call for a specified reliability after X hours. The individual processors have independent failure rates of λ. The question raised may be: How many processors are required to complete the mission with a given probability of success?

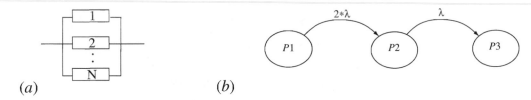

(a) (b)

Figure 14.2 (a) RBD for 1-of-N System. (b) CARMS Markov Model for 1-of-2 System.

The Markov model state diagram of this system for $N = 2$ is shown in part (b) of the figure. Shown are the states (Circles) and associated state probabilities (P-labels). There are three state probabilities for the 1-of-2 system: corresponding to both processors working (P_1); one processor working (P_2); and neither working (P_3 = failed state). The state diagram models the probability flow from the initial state to the final state, with the transitions governed by the component failure rates (λ).

Initially, all components are working. The system is in the first state with a probability of $P_1(t = 0) = 1.0$. The probability of the system failing is $P_3(t)$. The reliability of the system after time t is $R(t) = 1 - P_3(t)$. Each of these state probabilities must be solved either analytically (through differential equations) or numerically by a Markov model simulator.

We can solve this problem interactively via CARMS (Chapters 19–21). First, the system can be modeled through the built-in graphical diagramming tool using standard mouse or pointing device commands, or through the automatic model-building input. The analyst then runs the simulation to obtain results (e.g., finding the reliability for a fixed-hour mission).

14.5.4 System Requirements and Compatibility

CARMS runs on PC-compatible computers under the Windows user environment. The suggested minimum requirements include:

- Windows 3.1 with 2 MB of memory.
- VGA, super VGA, or video graphics adaptor compatible with Windows.
- Pointing device such as a mouse or trackball (optional).
- Math coprocessor (optional).

14.5.5 Application Summary

CARMS provides a high-level approach to simulation analysis in which much of the lower-level detail stays hidden. In a way, CARMS is similar to graphical schematic input for circuit modeling tools or to high-level software languages. In all cases, the lower level details (such as probability equations) are hidden from the user. If possible, most designers prefer to work in methods that abstract away as much of the complexity as possible but do not lose their representational power. As a system becomes more complex, higher levels of model representation will be required (see Table 14.5). Some of these higher levels of representation include Stochastic Petri nets.

TABLE 14.5 Description Levels

Top-Level	Intermediate-Level	Low-Level
Graphical state diagram/rules	Markov model	State equations

In summary, the CARMS tool provides the following features:

1. Graphical user interface (GUI) input for constructing state diagrams and tables.
2. Time-resolved simulation for solving Markov models.
3. External ports for tool integration.
4. Expert system for automatic model building, sensitivity control, and model translation.

Including reliability analysis, several of the application areas that CARMS can be applied to are listed in Table 14.6.

TABLE 14.6 CARMS Application

Area	Typical Applications
Reliability engineering	Reliability evaluation, fault-tolerant system reliability analysis
Operations research	Maintainability and availability evaluation, waiting line and servicing (queueing) modeling, inventory system analysis, traffic flow modeling, computer and system engineering
Fault-tolerant system design	Computer system performance evaluation, state diagram analysis
Software-engineering	Petri net simulations, Markov chain fault modeling
Statistics	Probability evaluation, Markov analysis, renewal and queueing

The CARMS User's Manual (Chapter 19) gives complete details on how to use the program.

15

Effectiveness Modeling

15.1 SYSTEM EFFECTIVENESS

System effectiveness is a dynamic measure indicating the expected level of system performance. It is a compound measure that combines the system physical performance parameters with probabilistic measures. In other words, system effectiveness attempts to express the degree of accomplishing a specified mission.

A system effectiveness computation involves capability, availability, and dependability factors. *Capability* is determined by a detailed analysis of the system performance capability. *Availability* is obtained from the system availability modeling and depends on system reliability and maintenance policies. *Dependability* is a dynamic reliability measure.

15.2 DESIRABLE CHARACTERISTICS OF A SYSTEM EFFECTIVENESS MODEL

1. The system effectiveness model should be simple and have intuitive appeal. Its role in the system design process should be clearly indicated. If possible, the model should be in a form familiar to the system designer.
2. The system effectiveness model should have a wide range of applicability. It should be capable of modeling all of the known redundancy configurations and of handling maintenance and multimode system operation.
3. It should be capable of accepting the basic system parameters—failure rates, repair rates, attrition rates, multiphase operation, and so on.
4. The system effectiveness model should be descriptive. It should have a topological representation so that the model can be easily visualized. An example of this type of representation is the logic diagram or circuit schematic. To achieve the acceptance of system effectiveness techniques, a visual representation is a must.

5. The system effectiveness model should be suitable for computer evaluation. Since most of the analysis work is done using interactive computers, setup and simulation times should be fast. A direct computer simulation will greatly enhance analysis efficiency and decrease the analysis cost. A majority of the present models require a multitude of different computations before the model can be exercised.

6. The system effectiveness model should include the capabilities of evaluating all of the significant "-ilities": reliability, maintainability, availability, fail-safety, penetrability, survivability, vulnerability, and capability. The model should also be able to incorporate any new "-ilities" as they become defined.

7. A desirable feature would be to have all of the necessary coefficients appear in algebraic form. This would greatly simplify data-handling and input-output operations in the computer.

After examining these characteristics, it is apparent that this list is long and demanding. At first sight, it may appear that the chance of arriving at a satisfactory model meeting the above requirements would be low or nonexistent based on previous experience. Fortunately, an approach exists which can satisfy a majority of the system effectiveness requirements. This model is based on the system state representation with a structure familiar to the majority of system engineers. Our objective will then be to adopt this model to system effectiveness and to illustrate typical applications.

Background. The basic system effectiveness model received wide publicity in the 1960s. A detailed description of this model appeared in the final Weapon System Effectiveness Industry Advisory Committee (WSEIAC) report published in 1965. Although a detailed description of the model is given, the rationale used to select this model is not mentioned [Barber 65].

The WSEIAC model is given as (see Figure 15.1):

$$E = A \times D \times C \tag{15.1}$$

Effectiveness = Availability x Dependability x Capability

$$\bar{E} = \bar{A}^{\mathsf{T}} * [D] * [C]$$

$$
\left[\frac{E_1}{E_2}\right] =
\left[A_1 \;\middle|\; A_2 \;\middle|\; A_3 \;\middle|\; A_4\right]
\times
\begin{bmatrix}
D_{11} & D_{12} & D_{13} & D_{14} \\
D_{21} & D_{22} & D_{23} & D_{24} \\
D_{31} & D_{32} & D_{33} & D_{34} \\
D_{41} & D_{42} & D_{43} & D_{44}
\end{bmatrix}
\times
\begin{bmatrix}
C_{11} & C_{12} \\
C_{21} & C_{22} \\
C_{31} & C_{32} \\
C_{41} & C_{42}
\end{bmatrix}
$$

$$E_k = \sum_{j=1}^{n} \sum_{i=1}^{n} A_i \, D_{ij} \, C_{jk}$$

Figure 15.1 System Effectiveness Definition.

where E = *System effectiveness,* a measure of the extent to which a system may be expected to achieve a set of specific mission requirements and is a function of availability, dependability, and capability.

A = *Availability,* a measure of the system condition at the start of the mission and a function of the relationships among hardware, personnel, and procedures.

D = *Dependability,* a quantitative measure of the system condition at one or more points during the mission, given the system's conditions at the start of the mission. It may be stated as the probability (or probabilities, or other suitable mission-oriented measure) that the system will enter or occupy any of the significant states during a specified mission.

C = *Capability,* a measure of the system's ability to achieve the mission objective, given the system's condition(s) during the mission, and specifically accounts for the system's performance spectrum.

A number of variations of the basic formula are described in the WSEIAC final report. In all of these variations, availability, dependability, and capability are the common elements.

The most significant features of this model are that the representation is static and that it involves discrete time points and probabilities associated with these time points. Unfortunately, neither the transient solution nor the steady-state value can be expressed as a simple product of readiness and reliability.

Similar limitations apply to capability quantifications. The WSEIAC model does not account for transitions that occur during system states during the mission interval. In other words, it is not possible to evaluate system effectiveness in those cases where part of the mission is completed under fully operational conditions and the remainder in a degraded mode of operation.

Thus, the WSEIAC model has the same limitations as the conventional reliability block diagram and the various reliability models based on Boolean logic. Some of these limitations were also recognized by the original WSEIAC team.

15.3 STATE-SPACE SYSTEM EFFECTIVENESS MODEL

The state-space system effectiveness model was developed to alleviate the difficulties inherent in the WSEIAC model. In concept it is similar to the WSEIAC model, but it differs in the way the mathematical model is formulated.

The basic form of the new system effectiveness model is similar to the state model used in system analysis and discussed in Chapter 6. The usual notation for the general state model is

$$x' = Ax + Bu$$
$$v = Cx + Du \tag{15.2}$$

where x = system state vector
v = output vector
A = state coefficient matrix
$B, C,$ and D = matrices that relate input, output, and state vectors
x' = time derivative of the state vector

In the system effectiveness formulation, the basic elements assume the following meaning:

x = system state probabilities

v = system effectiveness

C = capability vector

A = transition rate matrix

B, D = not defined at this time and assumed to be null

Thus, our new system effectiveness model becomes:

$$P' = AP$$

$$E = CP \tag{15.3}$$

after a change in notation by letting P represent state probabilities and E system effectiveness. Note that in this formulation, availability does not appear as a factor but is introduced as initial state probabilities at the beginning of the mission. Furthermore, the A coefficient matrix contains only system failure and repair rates.

Although the above representation is deceptively simple, computational difficulties are encountered if a manual solution is attempted. To reduce the computational burden, interactive modeling programs are available to compute the needed quantities. The resulting model is a dynamic one and easily permits incorporation of mission baseline configurations. Model modification allows the analyst to investigate a number of different equipment configurations.

Figure 15.2 depicts the structure and development of the state diagram. The figure shows four different transition rate groupings, representing the major events that will result in a system state change. The *State Probabilities* block contains the basic state probabilities for the system.

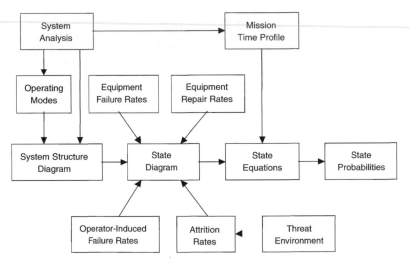

Figure 15.2 Markov State Diagram Development.

The system effectiveness model evaluation process can be represented graphically as shown in Figure 15.3.

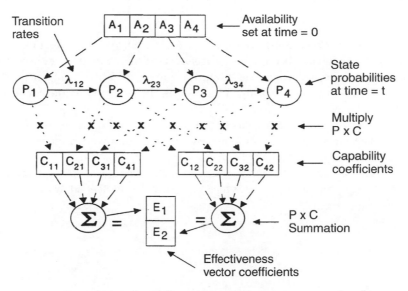

Figure 15.3 Performability and System Effectiveness Computation.

15.4 COST-EFFECTIVENESS

Cost-effectiveness is an interdisciplinary approach based on theories from engineering, economics, and mathematics [English 68]. It is an analytical technique for evaluating the broad management and economic implications of alternative choices of action, with the objective of assisting in the identification of the preferred choice.

The simplest criterion for cost-effectiveness is selecting the lowest cost alternative. Another selection criterion is to achieve best performance for the money available. In the most general case, cost-effectiveness compares several designs, each of which has somewhat different primary and secondary performance characteristics.

15.4.1 Logistics

Most logistics operations are expensive and directly affect system operation and effectiveness. Thus, it is important to optimize all of the logistics operations. This involves detailed logistics analyses, including reliability, maintainability, and specific logistics policies. Most of these analyses require the use of extended Markov model techniques. In the past, there have been a few Markov model applications in the logistics area, for applications such as inventory control or the study of maintenance facility operations.

Repair Policies. Typical repair policies include throwaway versus repair decisions, determining where the repair should be conducted and determining the needed number of personnel, among others. Most of these decisions will require the support of Markov model analyses.

Maintenance Shop Operations. Maintenance shop operation decisions involve determining the number of repair personnel needed, the quantity of specialized test equipment, the expected arrival rate of failed components, types of repair actions to be undertaken, and so on. Again, many of these decisions will require Markov model support.

Sparing. A major concern in spares provisioning is to sustain system effectiveness. The expected number of system component failures for a specific mission can be obtained from a detailed reliability analysis. If this model is further extended to include maintainability aspects, a more detailed and accurate Markov model can be derived to represent the sparing process and to determine the sparing level needed to satisfy system effectiveness requirements.

16

Support Analyses

To conduct a full reliability analysis of the system, more than just reliability data are needed. In this section we consider a number of analyses that must be completed before a reliability analysis is initiated. These analyses include mission definition and FMEA.

Later in this chapter, we will consider the role of Markov modeling in system trade-off studies.

16.1 MISSION DEFINITION

Mission objectives are usually presented in the system specification document. (The basic objectives are customer defined and as such must be considered as part of the system requirements.) During the analysis process, the mission definition is converted to a flow diagram format that shows how the mission scenario is partitioned into phases, and further indicates the functional requirements for each phase. Obviously, the sequence of specific mission tasks or operations and their role towards the mission accomplishment must be understood before design begins.

Multiphase Operation.   Systems that are designed to support multiphase operation often use system reconfiguration to eliminate excess equipment (due to weight restrictions, storage space, etc.). Then during operation, different equipment configurations are created dynamically for the various operational phases. Ideally, for a good design, some of the equipment will be used throughout the complete cycle.

The conventional reliability block diagram approach requires a separate block diagram for each phase. However, these diagrams are not independent because the final probability conditions of one state carry over to the next state. For reliability block diagrams (RBDs) there is no easy way of expressing the inherent dependency and adjusting state probabilities. As a result, use of reliability block diagrams in multiphase operations requires approximations. The Markov model, however, can handle these situations with relative ease.

Multiphase Breakdown.   A detailed description should be developed for the mission profile, including time information. This information is presented in the form of a *phase-time-equipment* diagram. The information gathered in the previous steps should be sufficient to develop a resource utilization diagram.

Multimission Systems.   Many existing systems are designed to support different applications. Both the embedded computer and reconfigurable hardware make interoperability feasible, with new applications continually appearing. The reliability evaluation of these system configurations is difficult to handle using conventional analyses. A multimission specification requires detailed descriptions for each of the required missions.

Again, in this case, a Markov model approach permits a detailed reliability analysis, including system effectiveness evaluation over the proposed operating modes. Optimization of multimission scenarios requires the assignment of expected use factors to each allowable mission.

16.1.1 Mission Outcome Tree

As missions grow more complex, it will become more difficult to develop detailed reliability and optimization models. A useful approach for describing mission outcomes is to construct a mission outcome tree from the nominal mission profile. A tree's first-level function may form multiple branches representing whether that function is performed in a good, degraded, or failed manner. Horizontal lines represent good states. Branches with negative slopes represent either degraded or failed states.

Functions.   Using the first-level elements of the functional flow diagrams to describe mission outcomes provides a valuable method of associating system operating states with mission values. The functions themselves may be either in-line or support. The mission tree is constructed from in-line functions. Support functions do not appear directly on the tree but are accounted for when evaluating the probabilities of the various operating states for each in-line function.

For example, for a given in-line function to be in a good state, all hardware and software elements associated with that function and all support functions required for that in-line function must be in specified operating states.

Mission Values.   Values are assigned to mission outcomes, which are described by first-level functions. Hardware failure modes (or operating states) are defined, and their effect on functions can be described. Thus, probabilities can be established for the operating states of all single-thread and potentially redundant hardware elements throughout the mission. Then the probabilities of the various valuable mission outcomes may be determined.

16.1.2 Reconfigurable Systems

The availability of distributed networks and data processing allows the development of reconfigurable systems. Reconfiguration may involve reassignment of computing resources, as well as data processing tasks. The evaluation of reconfigurable systems is complicated by having to consider the many possibilities for creating operational configurations.

16.2 FAILURE MODE, EFFECT, AND CRITICALITY ANALYSIS (FMECA)

The purpose of FMECA is to evaluate the functional impact of each potential functional or hardware failure on mission success, personnel and system safety, system performance, maintainability, and maintenance requirements. Each of these failures is ranked according to the severity of its effect. In evaluating severity, the worst possible consequences of a failure must be considered, and degree of injury, property damage, or system damage must be assigned.

FMECA provides the information needed for deriving the applicable models and state transitions. FMECA also helps to uncover potential weaknesses and to prevent fault propagation.

To control the complexity of FMECA, the system is partitioned into independent components. Potential faults in each of these components are considered in sequence, and their effect on the mission outcome is determined.

Furthermore, the effects of a component failure must be considered at several levels within the system hierarchy, with the final effect considered at the system level. The failure effect analysis is closely related to the state diagram development. Much effort can be saved if the lower level state diagrams are prepared at the same time that the failure effects analysis is conducted.

Analysis Process.   The hardware failure modes and mission effect analysis thus become a two-part process. First, the failure modes of hardware elements that comprise each independent assembly are correlated to the performance states defined for that family of independent assembly performance states. Such a model needs to be constructed for each independent assembly.

The second part of the process relates the performance states of each independent assembly family to the mission outcome tree via a map matrix. This matrix indicates which of the independent family performance states are necessary to achieve each mission subphase. Since the probabilities of the performance states of any set of independent assemblies can be determined from their models, the map matrix provides the logic to compute the probability of any subphase of the mission outcome tree. Thus, the correlation of hardware failure modes to the mission outcome is complete.

In addition to the failure modes, it is also important to obtain failure frequencies because different component failure modes will normally have a different effect at the system level. A fault in the system implies the transition to one of the failure states. The failure effects analysis maps these states to the mission outcome.

FMECA involves the following steps:

1. Identifying interface functions, expected performance, and defining failures for the system definition.
2. Constructing functional and reliability block diagrams.
3. Identifying failure modes for components and their interfaces.
4. Evaluating worst possible consequences of the failure
5. Identifying failure detection methods and compensating provisions.
6. Identifying corrective actions to eliminate the failure or to reduce the risk.

Important failure conditions include:

1. Premature operation.
2. Failure to operate at a prescribed time.
3. Intermittent operation.
4. Failure to cease operation at a prescribed time.
5. Loss of output or failure during operation.
6. Degraded output or operational capability.
7. Other unique failure conditions.

During FMECA, we must also investigate failures that occur on the indicators. Failure mechanisms that must be indicated to the operator include:

1. *Normal.* An indication to the operator when the system is operating normally.
2. *Abnormal.* An indication that is evident to an operator when the system has malfunctioned or failed.
3. *Incorrect.* An erroneous indication to the operator due to the malfunction or failure of an indicator.

FMECA must be performed before detailed Markov reliability models of the system can be derived. It is important to know not only the various faults that can be encountered, but also their effect on the system and, in particular, how they affect the system state transitions.

Since determining the potential failure modes requires considerable experience, this task is normally performed by an experienced design engineer, who is familiar with the basic components and their failure modes. To reduce the number of system states corresponding to various levels of degradation, failure category states should be used, such as critical and fail-operational.

16.2.1 Failure Criticality Analysis

A formal procedure for performing failure criticality analysis is outlined in MIL-STD-1629, *Procedures for Performing a Failure Mode, Effects and Criticality Analysis.*

Individual failures vary in the severity of their effects on system performance and mission outcome. The first steps in improving system reliability should focus on reducing the probability of critical failures.

Each identified failure must be evaluated according to its criticality for the system performance and mission outcome. Based on the results of this analysis, the parts whose failure will result in critical conditions can be determined. Classification of part failures in terms of their criticality is needed for the development of detailed state diagrams and for further optimization.

Failure Severity Categories. Severity classification provides a *qualitative* measure of the worst potential consequences resulting from design error or item failure. FMECA uses the failure criticality categories of MIL-STD-882, *System Safety Program Requirements.* This standard presents another classification of system failures according to their effect on the system (see Table 16.1).

TABLE 16.1 Failure Criticality Categories

Category	Type	Description
I	Catastrophic	Catastrophic failure states are those that may cause death or loss of the system.
II	Critical	Critical failures will not result in injury, occupational illness, or system damage, but will have a major impact on system capabilities, including mission loss.
III	Marginal	Marginal failures may cause minor injury, minor occupational illness, or minor system damage.
IV	Negligible	These failures will not cause injury, occupational illness, or system damage, but will result in unscheduled maintenance or repair.

Failure mode criticality number, C_m, is calculated from

$$C_m = \beta \alpha \lambda_p t \tag{16.1}$$

where the parameters are defined as

Parameter	Description
C_m	Criticality number for failure mode
β	Conditional probability of mission loss
α	Failure mode ratio
λ_p	Part failure rate
t	Duration of applicable mission phase (time)

Failure probability of occurrence levels are shown in Table 16.2.

TABLE 16.2 Probability of Fault Occurrence

Level	Range	Name
A	$0.2 < p \leq 1.0$	Frequent
B	$0.1 < p \leq 0.2$	Reasonably probable
C	$0.01 < p \leq 0.1$	Occasional
D	$0.001 < p \leq 0.01$	Remote
E	$0 \leq p \leq 0.001$	Extremely unlikely

Failure effect probability, β, classifications are given in Table 16.3.

TABLE 16.3 Failure Effect Probability Levels

β Value	Failure Effect
1.0	Actual loss
$0.1 < \beta < 1.0$	Probable loss
$0 < \beta \leq 0.1$	Possible loss
0	No effect

Item Criticality. Criticality is the relative measure of the consequences of a failure mode and its frequency of occurrence. It is the number of failures of a specific type expected due to the item's failure modes. The specific type of system failure is expressed by the severity classification for the item's failure modes. For a particular severity classification and mission phase, the criticality number of an item, C_r, is given by

$$C_r = \sum_{n=1}^{j} (\beta\alpha\lambda_p t)_n \qquad n = 1, 2, \ldots, j \tag{16.2}$$

where

Parameter	Description
C_r	Criticality number for the item
n	Failure modes for the item in category r
j	Number of failure modes in category r

Note: Other parameters as in the previous parameter

Failure Rate Determination. The failure rates used in FMECA are the same as those used in conventional reliability analyses. For military projects, MIL-HDBK-217 is the primary source. Commercial sources such as the Bellcore reliability data are also available.

Numerous commercial programs are available that support failure rate determination under different temperature and stress environments.

Limitations of FMECA. Although failure analyses often assume independence among different faults to simplify analysis, this assumption is not always valid. Examples of common dependent components include power supplies, system buses, and similar devices serving several components, where a failure of one redundant component may disable a common component.

16.2.2 Fault Propagation

To improve reliability, faults should not propagate to other system components. For example, a power supply failure resulting from a fault in one module should not affect operation of other system components that are driven by other power supplies.

16.3 MARKOV MODEL IN SUPPORT OF TRADEOFF ANALYSES

The Markov model is becoming the most important method in system tradeoff studies for reliability, maintainability, and availability analyses. To be useful, the following characteristics will have to be considered.

Fast Model Evaluation. Rapid response is necessary in an interactive environment to permit evaluation of different models. Otherwise, the longer computation time will require waiting for the computer, reducing the number of configurations that can be investigated, and increasing tradeoff analysis manpower cost.

Flexibility.   The Markov model will be used by different design team members during the design process. The development of models will require that some standard conventions be established to permit Markov model interchange between groups. These conventions will include state labeling and use of compatible time units. The modular structure of the Markov model makes them attractive for use in a design team environment. The overall process will be iterative and will continue until all of the system constraints have been met.

Users.   The key design team users of the Markov model will be the following:

- *Reliability analyst.* The reliability analyst will provide the initial model description and supply the failure rates. The analyst will be responsible for producing the initial definition of system states and for defining the potential transitions to fault states.
- *Maintainability analyst.* The maintainability analyst will build on the model previously developed by the reliability analyst. The analyst will conduct additional analysis, supply the applicable repair rates, identify the potential transitions, and formulate the planned maintenance policies.
- *Systems analyst.* The system analyst will use an extended Markov model that already contains the applicable reliability and maintainability inputs in a tradeoff study. Modeling the dynamic RMA performance of the system will allow optimization of the system to achieve the desired effectiveness level.
- *Logistics analyst.* The logistics analyst will base his evaluation on the model that already contains all of the key RMA parameters and the selected system configuration. The analyst may add further refinements to the model or modify it as needed for more detailed and specialized analyses.

Interface with Other Programs.   The results of the design support analyses are normally incorporated in other reports; therefore, it is important to provide a means of automatically transferring this information to other programs without the need for continuous transcription. Avoiding specialized translation programs, the approach is to provide a simple, yet flexible, interface. Furthermore, many of the common programs, such as word processing, incorporate flexible data reformatting and editing capabilities. Thus, it is more important to transfer the raw data reliably and universally than to provide a unique transfer protocol.

16.4 FUTURE TRENDS IN SYSTEM ENGINEERING

System engineering is an integrated task involving a collection of tools, procedures, concepts, hardware, and an attitude capable of blending the techniques. The same attitude is also needed in the management of the system engineering effort. The system engineer's most difficult obstacle at the present time is not the technical problem but a management team that is not sympathetic or lacks understanding of the basic system approach.

As indicated earlier, the trend in system engineering is changing, and in the near future we should expect more emphasis to be placed on scientific management techniques.

The application of fast computers will accelerate this trend, and the old, firmly established myth that computers can provide only solutions but not make decisions will be dispelled. For confirmation, one only needs to examine the current generation of computers and the functions they perform.

We can expect that the trend toward more powerful systems with better and more cost-effective performance will continue. These systems will be subject to severe constraints on both design and operation. The real-time, mission-critical applications will require automated recovery and dynamic reconfiguration capabilities.

16.4.1 Computation

Computations performed by these systems will be complex and highly varied. Computational complexity will continue to increase, yet at the same time a higher degree of reliability will be required of all computations. There will also be a larger variety of computational tasks as new computer applications are introduced. Because of this variety, it will be more difficult to assess the system operational status.

Computations will have a range of priorities. Many future systems will have to operate in real time and be able to respond to emergencies. Multiple priority levels to provide proper resource scheduling will help to meet these requirements.

16.4.2 Performance

Performance requirements emphasize speed and accuracy. In addition, good failure recovery capability will be required. New performance criteria, such as performability, will be introduced, mainly to aid system optimization. Employing system effectiveness criteria, users can introduce the reliability and availability parameters in the evaluation process.

In the future, we can envision more complex performance evaluations that will also consider the effects of operator and external environment-induced failures. These effects are not normally independent. For example, a pilot error may result in disconnecting some operational equipment and thus reducing the system redundancy level. Similarly, damage may have the same effect as equipment failure caused by internal effects. Thus, both of these failure causes will have a major effect on equipment configuration and the resulting reliability.

As these additional elements are introduced, the model will grow in complexity, and the presently used reliability analysis techniques will have to be extended.

16.4.3 Reliability

Many of the future systems will have to support a variety of modes of operation, while retaining the basic reconfiguration capabilities. To meet the operational needs, emphasis will have to be placed not only on the design of reconfigurable systems, but also on the reliability of switching systems and the major interconnection links. Use of redundancy will further increase the complexity of the systems; therefore, the design process will have to consider reliability, maintainability, and testing needs. Quantitative redundancy evaluation determines whether measures of dependable operation satisfy the system requirements.

16.4.4 Limited Human Intervention

The complexity of the computational tasks and the needed response speed usually will rule out human intervention. Thus, in these systems, most of the operator input will be in a supervisory capacity, acting to handle unexpected situations. The limitations of human intervention will require built-in capability for supporting executive functions. This serves to retain an acceptable level of operation when reconfiguring hardware and software programs, thus guaranteeing operation in the case of system faults.

To meet these requirements, automatic detection of errors, automatic recovery capabilities, and backup hardware can be used. A multiple-priority concept will permit the system to continue to operate in the case of hardware or software faults. This will be accomplished by deferring the processing of the lower priority tasks.

16.4.5 Impact on Modeling

In the future, modeling methodology for system design will become more important because of the increasing system complexity and emphasis on system fail-safety.

Complexity.   Future systems will be more complex. They will contain more electronics, use more redundancy, require higher system safety, and so on. All of these requirements will place further demands on system analysis capabilities, including the use of more complex Markov models.

Fail-safety.   There will be more emphasis on system fail-safety. Even the less complex future systems will need to be more reliable and as such will require fault-tolerance and fail-safety. We can expect that the majority of critical systems will use fail-safety analysis as an integral design tool. The integration of the various analyses will not only result in a more representative model but will also provide more meaningful performance indices.

17

Application Examples

17.1 AVIONICS SYSTEM EFFECTIVENESS EVALUATION

The starting point for avionics system design is a clear understanding of the requirements imposed by the planned missions. The next step involves selecting potential configurations and evaluating their effectiveness.

In this chapter, we illustrate the avionics system effectiveness evaluation procedures using a system effectiveness model based on a Markov process. The basic problem discussed here was adapted from AFSC-TR-65-2, Volume III, Example A [Barber 65]. This is an old application but serves its purpose in providing a fundamental mission-critical, yet nonproprietary, example.

17.1.1 Problem

Determine the system effectiveness of an avionics system developed for a tactical fighter-bomber aircraft. Effectiveness indicates how well the mission achieves its objectives.

17.1.2 Mission Definition

At any time, when an executive order is received, the aircraft shall take off immediately, receive a target assignment, proceed to the target area, deliver the weapon within 500 feet of the target, and then return to the operating base.

To simplify our sample problem, we will assume that the avionics system consists of only three major subsystems, which contain one or mode equipment sets. These available components are listed in Table 17.1.

TABLE 17.1   Available Equipment

Subsystem	Equipment
Fire control	Radar (search)
	Radar (terrain-avoidance)
	Toss-bomb computer
	Sight system
Doppler navigator	Doppler navigator
Communications	UHF direction finder
Identification	TACAN
Navigation	Instrument landing system
	UHF transceiver
	Identification equipment

The identified equipments are independent of each other; that is, the condition of any of the equipment does not influence the operation of any other.

17.1.3 Equipment Functions

The fire control subsystem is employed in actual weapon delivery. It provides a radar display of the target and computation of the weapon release point in the toss-bombing mode. It also provides, through the sight subsystem, the aiming point for "lay-down" delivery. The terrain avoidance equipment provides automatic control of aircraft altitude.

The Doppler navigator provides the prime navigation function by computing and displaying information on both present position and distance/heading to target. Alternative navigation capabilities are provided by TACAN (tactical air navigation) and UHF (ultra high frequency) direction finder.

The instrument landing system (ILS) provides the ability to land the aircraft under ceiling and visibility conditions that would otherwise prevent landing.

The UHF transmitter-receiver is the only communications device and is employed for all in-flight radio communication. Audio amplifier equipment is employed with the UHF transmitter-receiver and may be considered part of that equipment.

The identification equipment (IFF—identification friend or foe) provides coded identification signal in response to an interrogation by friendly forces. Failure to provide the proper response could result in friendly fire.

17.1.4 Functional Breakdown

The essential functions performed by the avionics system are listed in Table 17.2.

TABLE 17.2   Avionics Functions

	Function
1	Communication
2	Identification
3	Navigation
4	Penetration
5	Weapon Delivery
6	Landing

17.1.5 System Block Diagram

The applicable block diagram is shown in Figure 17.1.

Functions

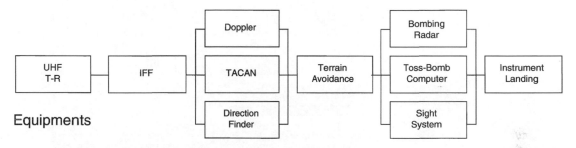

Equipments

Figure 17.1 Avionics System Block Diagram.

17.1.6 Mission Profile

Three different modes of delivery are available, as shown in Table 17.3.

TABLE 17.3 Weapon Delivery Modes

Mode	Description
VL	Visual lay-down
VT	Visual toss
BT	Blind toss

Basic mission breakdown is shown in Table 17.4.

TABLE 17.4 Mission Time Specification

Phase	Time (hours)		Mission Phase Description
	Start	End	
1	0.00	0.50	En route to target
2	0.50	0.60	Target identification
3	0.60	0.65	Weapon delivery
4	0.65	1.15	Return to assigned base
5	1.15	1.20	Land aircraft

A timeline representation of the mission is presented in Figure 17.2.

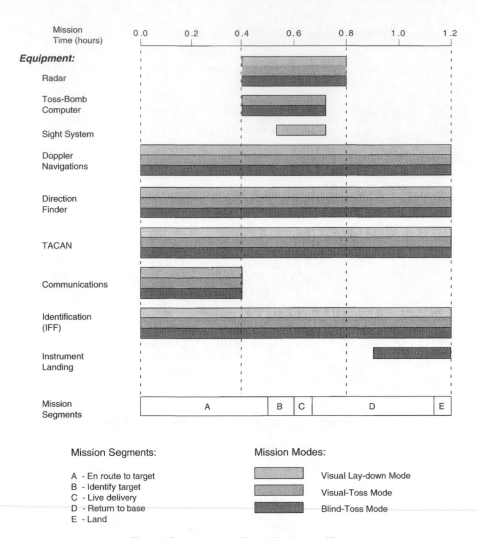

Figure 17.2 Mission Profile and Equipment Usage.

At the mission level, the mission is either fully accomplished or failed. At a lower level, however, we can provide a more detailed breakdown related to the causes of failure to accomplish the full mission, or partial accomplishment of mission goals. These mission outcomes may be represented in a tree form, as shown in Figure 17.3.

For the specific mission requirement, the key figure of merit (FOM) is the probability that the full mission was accomplished. Accomplishment of the full mission, however, depends on the successful performance of several individual functions (see Table 17.5).

System effectiveness is influenced by a great variety of factors. In our example, the key factors to consider are shown in Table 17.6.

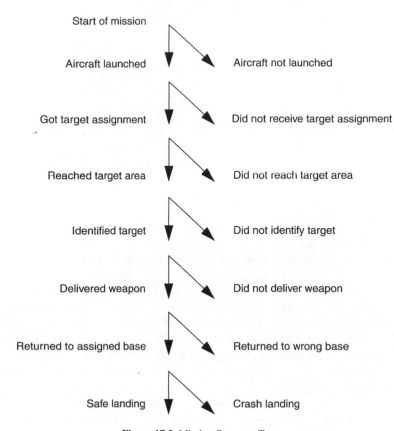

Figure 17.3 Mission Outcome Tree.

TABLE 17.5 Mission Functions

	Function	Key Equipment
1	Takeoff	
2	Receipt and acknowledgment of target assignment	Communications
3	Navigation to a point not more than five miles from the target	Navigation
4	Proper identification when interrogated	Identification — IFF
5	Penetration of enemy defenses	Terrain-avoidance radar
6	Identification of target and weapon delivery within 500 feet of target	Search radar
7	Navigation to within 10 miles of assigned opening base	Navigation, direction finding
8	Landing	Instrument landing system

TABLE 17.6 Factors Influencing System Effectiveness

Area	Factors
Operational conditions	Physical environment (climate)
	Day versus night conditions
	Good (VFR) versus bad (IFR) weather
	Modes of weapon delivery
	Enemy counteractions
	Actions by friendly forces
Support situation	Ground operating environment
	Ground support equipment
	Maintenance personnel availability
	Repair philosophy
	Spare part availability

Some of the key factors are as follows.

The operating environment will be semitropical, with the ground temperatures ranging from 70° to 105° F, and 60 to100% humidity. Atmospheric conditions that result in improper radar functions are anticipated 1% of the time. The operating environment (temperature and humidity) will have a direct effect on the failure rates. Atmospheric conditions will have to be considered when evaluating radar system capability.

Daylight conditions exist for 14 hours of the day (58% of the time). Bad weather (IFR) conditions exist, on the average, 20% of the time, day or night.

Visibility conditions are such that the instrument landing system is essential to safe landing 5% of the time.

Visibility and tactical requirements affect the weapon delivery mode. Visual delivery mode can be used only during daylight VFR conditions. The tactical requirements are such that the lay-down mode will be preferred 80% of the time. If toss-bombing is preferred, the visual method will be selected whenever possible, that is, weather and daylight permitting.

Enemy defensive action, that is, the enemy's ability to destroy the intruding aircraft, is such that:

1. A 30% loss of aircraft is anticipated for aircraft approaching at altitudes in excess of 1000 feet at normal attack speed.

2. A 5% loss of aircraft is anticipated for aircraft approaching at altitudes less than 1000 feet at normal attack speed.

Friendly defenses require that 90% of the aircraft entering the defense area be challenged. If the friendly aircraft does not properly respond to the challenge, a 10% destruction of the aircraft by friendly defense exists. (This includes secondary methods of identification, such as visual.)

It is expected that a TACAN ground station will be available, operating, and within range 50% of the time. A UHF ground station will be available, operating, and within range 40% of the time. Sufficient ground support equipment (GSE) will be provided so that no delays in repair due to this factor will occur. The quantity, availability and skill levels of the maintenance personnel will be reflected in the stated MTTR figures. All repairs to the avionics system will be made through replacement of flight-line replaceable units (LRU). Sufficient spare units will be available.

17.1.7 System Effectiveness Model

The system effectiveness model must express the probability of successfully completing the stated mission as a function of

1. The effectiveness of the system in each of the three delivery modes.
2. The probability of employing each delivery mode.

This model can be represented by the equation:

$$E = \sum_{i=1}^{3} E_i \times p_i \qquad (17.1)$$

where E = System effectiveness
E_i = System effectiveness in mode i
p_i = Probability of using mode i

In the given problem, we will be considering three different delivery modes. The value of p_i will be determined from tactical as well as operational considerations. The values of E_i will be derived by combining the effectiveness figures for each of the applicable mission modes.

Depending on the design phase when the system effectiveness is evaluated, sources of the available data will vary. During the design definition phase, system effectiveness prediction will be based on failure and maintenance rates derived from previous projects. Later, when more information is available from development prototype testing or filed experience, the needed failure and maintenance rates will be updated.

Since the primary purpose of this chapter is to illustrate system effectiveness evaluation procedures, detailed derivation of the failure and repair rates will not be given. The values used in the numerical example are given in Table 17.7; they were extracted from the same reference:

TABLE 17.7 Avionics System Failure and Repair Rates

Equipment	MTBF (hours)	Failure Rate/hr	MTTR (hours)	Repair Rate/hr
Bombing radar	32	0.0312	6	0.167
Terrain avoidance radar	40	0.0250	8	0.125
Toss-bomb computer	20	0.0500	4	0.250
Sight system	200	0.0050	2	0.500
Doppler navigator	20	0.0500	15	0.067
Direction finder	100	0.0100	2	0.500
TACAN	50	0.0200	4	0.250
Instrument landing	150	0.0067	3	0.333
Communications	70	0.0143	2	0.500
Identification (IFF)	100	0.0100	3	0.333

Equipment availability using the Markov-type system effectiveness model is relatively simple, because we can use the basic model. If we can assume that the steady-state conditions apply, then we can use:

$$\text{Availability} = \frac{MTBF}{MTBF + MTTR} \qquad (17.2)$$

where MTBF = mean time between failures
MTTR = mean time to repair

In certain instances, however, we cannot use the steady-state model, because the steady-state conditions cannot be achieved and the actual equipment availability may be lower than that indicated by Eq. (17.2).

17.1.8 Markov Model Development

Using the Markov-type system effectiveness formulation, we have a number of alternatives available for computing *equipment availability.* We can set up a dynamic model for determining availability and then select representative mission and allowable maintenance activity times. We can also simulate a number of sequential missions with the given constraints and thus obtain more accurate results. Similarly, *mission success probability* can be evaluated by eliminating repair rates during the mission (because equipment cannot be repaired during flight).

To illustrate the availability computation, we will select a subsystem. To begin with, we choose the communications subsystem, which consists of the UHF transmitter-receiver. The appropriate failure rate is 0.0143 failures/hour, and the corresponding repair rate is 0.500 repairs/hour. The applicable state diagram is shown in Figure 17.4.

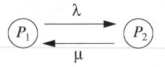

Figure 17.4 Markov Diagram for a Single Component with Repair.

After substitution, we obtain Figure 17.5.

Figure 17.5 Markov Diagram for Communications Subsystem.

In this state diagram, state P_1 represents an operational communications subsystem and state P_2 the failed state. The initial conditions for states P_1 and P_2 are determined as follows:

1. If at the start of the state probability computation all of the communications equipment is operational and fully checked out, then at $t = 0$ we set $P_1(0) = 1.0$ and $P_2(0) = 0.0$.
2. If we are starting at some other point, say after the return from a typical mission, then the corresponding probabilities are determined by the state probabilities at the end of that mission.

If we are interested only in the steady-state availability figures, then we can use the steady-state computation.

The next subsystem in the equipment list is IFF. For this subsystem, again, we can develop the appropriate state diagram, as shown in Figure 17.6, where P_3 is the operational state, and P_4 is the failed state. Initial conditions for this subsystem can be derived in the same manner as discussed earlier.

Figure 17.6 Markov Diagram for Identification Subsystem.

Our next subsystem—navigation—consists of three navigational components, which are essentially working in parallel (in a reliability modeling sense). For this subsystem, we have to consider three equipment states as given in Table 17.8.

TABLE 17.8 Navigation Equipment Status

State	Doppler	TACAN	Direction Finder
P_5	Operating	Operating	Operating
P_6	Operating	Operating	Down
P_7	Operating	Down	Operating
P_8	Down	Operating	Operating
P_9	Operating	Down	Down
P_{10}	Down	Operating	Down
P_{11}	Down	Down	Operating
P_{12}	Down	Down	Down

The resulting state diagram for the navigation subsystem is presented in Figure 17.7.

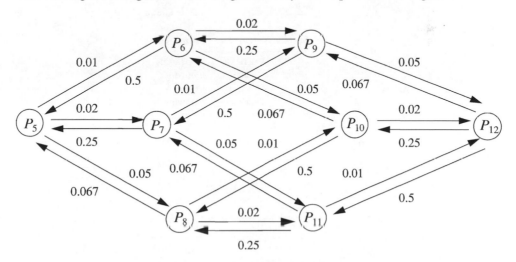

Figure 17.7 Markov Diagram for Navigation Subsystem.

An alternative formulation would be to consider the three types of equipment making up the navigation subsystem to be independent; then calculate their availabilities separately, as we did earlier for the communications and IFF subsystems; and finally, obtain the availability values by using probability product rule. In using this approach we would require a separate state diagram for each navigation subsystem component.

The bombing subsystem also consists of three parallel equipment combinations, but the evaluation conditions are different. In the blind-toss bombing mode, we require only the bombing radar and the toss-bomb computer. In the visual-toss mode, we require only the toss-bomb computer, and for lay-down delivery only the sight system.

In this situation, again, we have to make a choice in selecting the representation. Under the definitions stated above, the sight system will be used separately and thus should be set up as an independent model. That leaves the combination of the bombing radar and the toss-bomb computer. Again, we can handle these either individually or as a combination. We will select the latter approach for this example.

The state diagram for the sight subsystem is shown in Figure 17.8. The visual toss-bomb computer can be modeled in a similar way (see Figure 17.9).

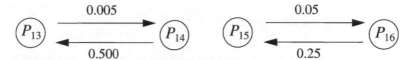

Figure 17.8 Markov Diagram for Sight Subsystem.

Figure 17.9 Markov Diagram for Toss-bomb Computer.

In these figures, P_{13} and P_{15} represent the operating states and P_{14} and P_{16} the failed states.

For the blind-toss mode, our state diagram will have four distinct states as designated in Table 17.9.

TABLE 17.9 Blind-toss Mode States

State	Radar	Toss-bomb Computer
P_{17}	Operating	Operating
P_{18}	Operating	Down
P_{19}	Down	Operating
P_{20}	Down	Down

The corresponding state diagram takes the form shown in Figure 17.10.

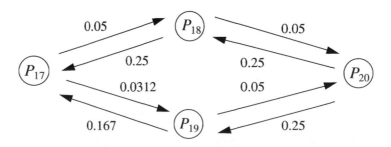

Figure 17.10 Markov Diagram for Blind-toss Subsystem.

The instrument landing system (ILS) and the terrain avoidance radar subsystems are single independent subsystems. Their state diagrams are presented in Figures 17.11 and 17.12.

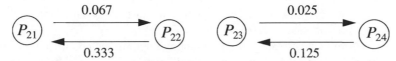

Figure 17.11 Markov Diagram for Instrument Landing Subsystem.

Figure 17.12 Markov Diagram for Terrain-Avoidance Radar.

17.1.9 Probability of Launch

Under field operating conditions, launch is not always ruled out just because some equipment is not operational. Since in some cases, bombing capability exists with even some inoperative equipment, the probability of launch in a degraded mode should be considered. Estimates of the probabilities of launch for the various equipment states are given in Table 17.10.

TABLE 17.10   Probabilities of Launch

State	Equipment	Probability of Launch
1	Communications	1.0
2		0.0
3	Identification (IFF)	1.0
4		0.2
5	Navigation	1.0
6		1.0
7		1.0
8		0.1
9		0.8
10		0.0
11		0.0
12		0.0
13	Lay-down sight system	1.0
14		0.8
15	Visual toss with computer	1.0
16		0.7
17	Blind-toss radar and computer	1.0
18		0.5
19		0.0
20		0.0
21	Instrument landing	1.0
22		0.95
23	Terrain-avoidance radar	1.0
24		0.0

17.1.10 Determination of Capability

Next, we have to determine capability parameters for each functional set of equipment. In our problem, the communications functions are required only for target assignment changes, after the aircraft has taken off. It will be estimated that in 90% of the cases specific target assignments will be made before the aircraft is out of range. In the remaining 10% of cases, an unsuccessful mission will result.

We will further estimate that environmental conditions and difficulties with ground equipment will prevent the required communication in 5% of the cases while the aircraft is within the operating range of the base station.

The capability of the communications subsystem is expressed as the probability that the target designation or change is received and acknowledged by the aircraft. Thus, in the operational state, the capability C_1 will be given by

$$C_1 = (0.90)(0.95) = 0.855$$

In the nonoperational state, communications capability is zero.

During the attack phase, the aircraft is in danger of being attacked (it is not able to identify itself properly) and destroyed by friendly forces. The identification equipment in the operational state will have a capability of unity. However, destruction of the aircraft is not certain if the IFF equipment is not operational. In this state the aircraft will survive if

1. It is not challenged
2. It is challenged but is not destroyed

If we assume that the probability of challenge is 0.90 and the probability of destruction is 0.10, then

$$C_4 = (1.0) - (0.9)(0.1) = 0.91$$

The aircraft must be able to navigate to within 5 miles of the target area by the use of navigation equipment. From this point, further target identification will be accomplished by other means. On the return flight, the aircraft must be able to navigate within 10 miles of its assigned base.

While the navigation information is supplied by three different sets of equipment, the capability of each is different, (see Table 17.11).

TABLE 17.11   Navigation Equipment Capability

Equipment	Capability
Doppler	0.95
TACAN	0.9
Direction finder	0.8

Since the TACAN and direction finding equipment requires availability of external signals from an associated ground station, the probabilities that these signals may not be available must be considered.

While the Doppler can be used at any time it is operating properly, the TACAN ground station will be available only 50% of the time, and the direction finder (DF) ground station only 40% of the time. Thus, the actual capabilities for the equipment will be:

$$C_{\text{Doppler}} = 0.95$$

$$C_{\text{TACAN}} = (0.9)(0.5) = 0.45$$

$$C_{\text{DF}} = (0.8)(0.4) = 0.32$$

Next, we will consider the capabilities for the eight distinct states of the navigation subsystem. The capability of each state will be the capability of the operating equipment whose individual capability is the highest, if all equipment is equally available.

In the situation where both TACAN and DF equipment is available, but the Doppler has failed (state P_8), the probabilities that the ground station for TACAN and DF will be available must also be considered. Assuming independence between the TACAN and DF ground stations, we find that the capability in this state is:

$$C_8 = \text{(Probability that TACAN can be used)(TACAN capability)}$$

$$+ \text{(Probability that only DF can be used)(DF capability)}$$

$$= (0.5)(0.9) + (1.0 - 0.5)(0.4)(0.8) = 0.61$$

The target can be identified either visually or by means of radar equipment. The ability to deliver a weapon within 500 feet of an identified target is dependent on the mode of the delivery. For our example, these probabilities could be either based on previous experience or estimated. Weapon delivery modes and capabilities are listed in Table 17.12.

TABLE 17.12 Weapon Delivery Capabilities by Mode and State

Deliver Mode	Mode State	Radar State	Toss-bomb Computer State	Sight System State	Capability
Lay-down	L_1	—	—	Operational	0.90
	L_0	—	—	Down	0.70
Visual toss	V_1	—	Operational	—	0.80
	V_0	—	Down	—	0.60
Blind toss	B_1	Operational	Operational	—	0.75
	B_2	Operational	Down	—	0.40
	B_3	Down	Operational	—	0.00
	B_4	Down	Down	—	0.00

The instrument landing system, when properly functioning, has a capability of 0.99; that is, a landing without damage to the aircraft or injury to the pilot can be made 99 out of 100 times. In weather during which this equipment is not needed, the probability of successful landing is 1.0.

If we assume that visual landing procedures are possible 95% of the time, then the probability of successful landing is:

C_{21} = (Probability of visual landing)(Probability of successful landing under visual conditions) + (Probability of ILS landing)(Probability of successful landing under ILS conditions)

$$= (0.95)(1.0) + (0.05)(0.99) = 0.995$$

If the ILS system is not operable, then no capability to land under ILS conditions will exist and the overall landing capability is 0.95.

The terrain-avoidance function of the radar is the only avionics equipment that contributes to the aircraft's penetration ability. This equipment permits flying the aircraft at normal attack speeds at low altitudes. Without this equipment, such low-level approaches are not possible.

If we assume that the anticipated losses due to enemy action are 5% for low altitude approaches and 30% for high-altitude approaches, and that the atmospheric conditions that result in improper radar return are anticipated 1% of the time, the penetration capabilities (the probability of penetrating enemy defenses), when the enemy action effectiveness is considered, are:

$$C_{23} = \text{(Probability that radar permits low-level approach)}$$
$$\text{(Probability of survival, given low approach)} +$$
$$\text{(Probability radar does not permit low approach)}$$
$$\text{(Probability of survival, given high approach)}$$

$$= (0.99)(0.05) + (0.01)(0.70) = 0.9474$$

$$C_{24} = \text{(Probability of survival, given high approach)}$$

$$= 0.70$$

The state capabilities are summarized in Table 17.13.

TABLE 17.13   State Capabilities

State	Equipment	Capability
1	Communications	0.855
2		0.000
3	Identification (IFF)	1.000
4		0.910
5	Navigation	0.950
6		0.950
7		0.950
8		0.610
9		0.950
10		0450
11		0.320
12		0.000
13	Lay-down	0.900
14	Sight system	0.700
15	Visual toss with computer	0.800
16		0.600
17	Blind-toss	0.750
18	Radar and computer	0.400
19		0.000
20		0.000
21	Instrument landing	0.9995
22		0.950
23	Terrain-avoidance radar	0.9475
24		0.700

In the previous sections, we derived all of the pertinent state diagrams for the individual subsystems. Our next task will be to compute the subsystem availability parameters. As discussed earlier, we have the choice of using either the steady-state availabilities, shown in Table 17.13, or the dynamic probabilities for the initial conditions.

Initially, we may want to start with a reliability-type computation and assume that all of the equipment is operational at $t = 0$. In this case, we introduce initial conditions of unity in states 1, 3, 5, 13, 15, 17, 21, and 23. The initial conditions of other states are set to zero.

Next, we select the first time phase. In our example, 1000 hours of operation will be sufficient to establish the steady-state conditions. At the end of 1000 hours, the probabilities associated with each state will be the desired availability figures. If we multiply these probabilities by the probability of launch (given in Table 17.10), then the necessary initial conditions for availability can be established.

In the next step, we remove all transitions associated with repair activities. (This implies that we do not have in-flight repair capability.) We also have to set transition rates equal to zero for equipment that will be deenergized during the first mission phase.

Examining the mission profile and equipment usage diagram (Figure 17.2), we can identify the mission phases. In our example, these will be 0.4, 0.7, and 0.9 hours.

At time $t = 0$, we deenergize terrain-avoidance and bombing radar and toss-bomb computer. At 0.4 hours, we energize the terrain-avoidance and bombing radar and the toss-bomb computer and deenergize the communications subsystem. At 0.7 hours, we deenergize the toss-bomb computer, at 0.8 hours we deenergize the terrain-avoidance and bombing radar. At 0.9 hours the ILS system is energized, and at 1.2 hours we stop the simulation.

At this point, we have computed all of the required probabilities for each identified state and are ready to apply the capability coefficients (Table 17.13). Summing these values for each subsystem, we can determine the subsystem effectiveness values.

The individual functional effectiveness parameters may now be combined to evaluate the effectiveness of each mission type. Using the conventional approach (assuming that subsystems are independent and that their effectiveness can be combined using the product rule), we form a product containing all of the subsystem effectiveness values that are necessary for a specific mission.

In our example, communications, identification, navigation, landing, and penetration subsystems are common to all mission types. They differ only in the equipment needs for a specific mission. Thus, we can combine states 1–12 and 21–24 in the common group, and work with states 13–14 for lay-down delivery, 15–16 for visual-toss mode, and 17–20 for blind-toss mode.

A single, overall system effectiveness figure may be obtained from

$$E = E_{LD} \times P_{LD} + E_{VT} \times P_{VT} + E_{BT} \times P_{BT} \tag{17.3}$$

where the subscripts denote the type of the mission

E = mission effectiveness
P = probability that a particular mission will be flown

P_{LD} (Probability of lay-down delivery)
   = (Probability of daytime mission)(Probability of good weather conditions)(Probability that lay-down delivery is preferred)
   = (0.58)(0.8)(0.8) = 0.3712

P_{VT} (probability of visual-toss delivery)

= (Probability of daytime mission)(Probability of good weather conditions)
  (Probability that toss bombing is preferred)

= (0.58)(0.8)(0.2) = 0.0928

P_{BT} (Probability of blind-toss delivery)

= (Probability of night mission) + (Probability of bad weather conditions)
  −(Probability of night mission and bad weather conditions)

= (0.42)(0.2) − (0.42)(0.02) = 0.536

17.1.11 Application of Model Results

Since this example considers evaluation performed during the program definition phase, we are interested in using the obtained system effectiveness parameters to establish the plan needed to accomplish a specific mission.

If one system has a probability, p, of accomplishing the mission, then the probability, S, that at least one of N systems will accomplish the mission is

$$S = 1 - (1 - p)^N \qquad (17.4)$$

To determine the number of systems required to attain a required value of S, Eq. (17.4) must be solved for N. This solution yields:

$$N = \frac{ln(1 - S)}{ln(1 - p)} \qquad (17.5)$$

Consider the relationship for S values of 0.95 and 0.90. That is, any point on the 95% curve shows the number of systems of effectiveness required to provide 0.95 assurance of successful mission completion. Thus, for the upper curve, note that for the system effectiveness of 0.24 computed in the previous section, 11 systems will be required.

While the many inputs to the model represent the effects of a wide range of influencing factors, the system designer has control over only some of the factors. These include the capability, reliability, and maintainability of the equipment.

If each of these factors is varied over some predetermined range and the resulting effectiveness values are compared, an indication of the areas of potential payoff will be available.

17.1.12 CARMS Implementation of Model

Shown in Figure 17.13 is the complete parametric Markov model, implemented as a CARMS state diagram. The named transition rates can be adjusted, depending on the particular mission, and then evaluated for a specific mission time. The CARMS file is called `syseff.mm`. Details on how to load and modify the file are presented in the next chapter.

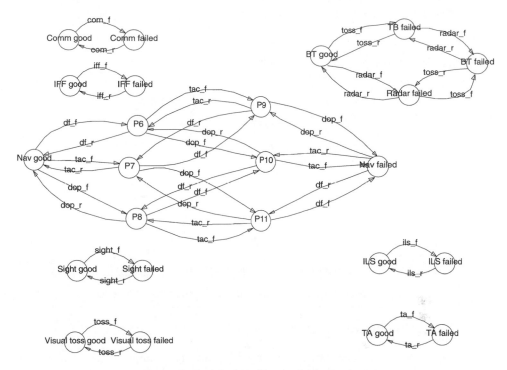

Figure 17.13 CARMS Markov Model for Example.

17.2 OTHER APPLICATIONS

Although many applications discussed earlier were typical of mission-critical systems, Markov modeling has several other applications.

17.2.1 Business Applications

The most common application of the Markov model in business applications is in analyzing service (i.e., queueing) operations. Since almost every service operation has customers, servers, and waiting lines of customers to be served, there are many applications of this type. The specific analyses conducted consider the effects of different service structure on the expected performance and thus on the profitability of the operation.

EXAMPLE

As an illustration, we will consider the use of a Markov model in analyzing a service operation, such as are encountered in banks and supermarkets. The generic system can be represented as shown in Figure 17.14.

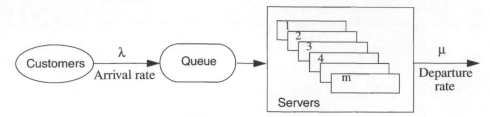

Figure 17.14 Generic Service System.

The generic state transition diagram for Figure 17.15 is as depicted in Figure 17.15.

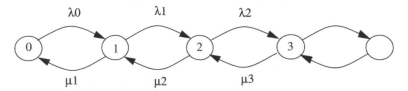

Figure 17.15 State-transition Diagram for a Service System.

The numbers in the circles indicate the number of customers in the queue.

17.2.2 Inventory Control

Markov models can also be applied to inventory control. As an illustration, we will examine a highly approximated case.

EXAMPLE

We will assume that the initial supply (inventory) of a certain component consists of n units. We will further assume that the demand for these components is low and is exponentially distributed with a rate λ. Since the price of an individual component is assumed to be relatively high, a single-item re-order for the component will be placed only after the component has been requested. The delivery time of the component will be assumed to be exponentially distributed with a mean value of ρ.

This example will result in the state transition diagram shown in Figure 17.16.

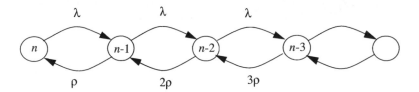

Figure 17.16 State-transition Diagram for Inventory Control.

The numbers in the circles represent the various inventory levels.

17.2.3 Chemistry

Many chemical processes are formulated using rate equations. Although these processes are not probabilistic in the sense of a Markov model, they have a similar mathematical formulation. Thus, the same simulation techniques developed for the Markov model evaluation could be used to investigate chemical processes.

EXAMPLE

Consider the case where a chemical reaction occurs which changes A to B. This reaction can be represented graphically (see Figure 17.17).

Figure 17.17 Nonreversible Chemical Reaction $A \xrightarrow{\ \kappa\ } B$

The corresponding nonreversible mass action equations are:

$$\frac{dA}{dt} = -\kappa A$$

$$\frac{dB}{dt} = -\kappa B$$

(17.6)

Note the similarity of the above equations to those for a single-component reliability. Whereas in the chemical reaction A changes to B, in the reliability model the component goes from operational to failure state. The key differences are that the chemical reaction model is deterministic and the reliability model is stochastic.

17.2.4 Ecology

Ecology is another area where the Markov modeling process can be applied with success. Since many ecological processes are characterized by rate equations and follow the Markov model assumptions, the Markov model is widely used in this area. The primary objective of Markov model analysis will be to investigate the dynamic behavior of ecological systems.

Ecological model development is similar to the chemistry example presented earlier.

17.2.5 Nonlinear Models

Although not covered in this text, nonlinear modeling has applications for system evaluation. Transition rates in these models may depend on several states. Usually, they are expressed in the form:

$$R = k \times P_n \times P_m \times \ldots$$

(17.7)

In general, these models are more difficult to solve than Markov models and are often difficult to justify due to the number of empirical parameters involved (and potential combinations).

Predator-Prey Model.   This model is widely used in biology and ecology. In the simplest case, we have two species x (prey) and y (predator) and a simple coupling depending on xy. The equations describing this model are given by

$$\frac{dx}{dt} = Ax - Byx \qquad A,B,C,D \geq 0$$

$$\frac{dy}{dt} = -Cy + Dyx \qquad x,y \geq 0$$

(17.8)

As an illustration, we will assume that x represents the number of rabbits (prey) and y the number of foxes (predators) in a given region of the country. Without the presence of foxes, the rabbit population would grow with an exponential growth rate A. The actual rate, however, will be reduced due to the interaction between the two species. This rate, B, represents the rabbit attrition rate due to the fox population.

The foxes without the rabbit population will have a death rate represented by C. This rate, however, will be modified by the current rabbit population and will be proportional to the product of number of rabbits and number of foxes. The coefficient D represents the effect of the prey on the growth rate of the predators.

Lanchester Engagement Model. One of the earliest nonlinear models, the Lanchester model (named after F. W. Lanchester), was developed to simulate military engagements. In the simplest case (general defense situation), the following assumptions are made:

1. Two opposing forces are engaged in a fight. The units are similar but have different attrition rates.
2. Each unit on either side is within the weapon range of all units of the other side.
3. Attrition rate coefficients for both sides are constant and are known.
4. Each unit knows the general area in which the opposing units are located but is not informed about the consequences of its own fire.
5. Fire from the surviving units is distributed uniformly over the area in which opposing units are located.

A variation of the above is the two-sided attack case, where the last two assumptions are changed to:

4. Each unit is informed about the location of the remaining opposing units so that when a target is destroyed, fire may be immediately shifted to a new target.
5. Fire is uniformly distributed over remaining units.

The first formulation is known as the *linear law,* and the second is known as the *square law.* These names describe the characteristics of dynamic changes in the troop concentrations.

Based on these two assumptions, the linear law can be represented as the following differential equations:

$$\frac{dn}{dt} = -K_m mn$$

$$\frac{dm}{dt} = -K_n mn$$

(17.9)

and the square law as

$$\frac{dn}{dt} = -K_m m$$

$$\frac{dm}{dt} = -K_n n$$

(17.10)

where m and n are the opposing force strengths and K_m and K_n are the attrition coefficients. The initial conditions at time t are the initial troop strengths:

$$n(0) = n_0 \qquad m(0) = m_0 \tag{17.11}$$

Equations (17.9–17.11) are symmetrical; that is, they represent the cases in which both sides are under cover or are engaged in open combat. They can be easily changed to an asymmetrical form to represent the situation where one side is attacking and the other is defending.

18

Practical Design of Fault-Tolerant Systems

18.1 FAULT-RECOVERY PROCESS

One of the key problems encountered in the design of fault-tolerant systems involves the design and modeling of the fault-recovery process. To achieve the desired reliability improvement, the interaction between the components must be controlled to avoid fault propagation to adjacent components or to other subsystems.

Since the fault-tolerant system is vulnerable during the recovery process, a dependable recovery scheme must be implemented. Unfortunately, the fault-recovery process is difficult to analyze and to model. As a result, many assumptions are made, some of which may not always be justifiable, and the implemented system reliability may not reach the expected goals.

To improve recovery, the emphasis should be on protecting the recovery process because of its criticality. One way to accomplish this is to adapt some of the critical region protection schemes used in concurrent systems to the fault-recovery process (i.e., fault containment regions [Lala 91]).

During the recovery process, we need to know where some of the potential problem areas lie and what valid assumptions we can make. This task may require dynamic simulation capability to examine the recovery process and to identify potential system failure modes.

18.2 RELIABILITY PROBLEM SOLUTION

Before a solution method is selected, a detailed analysis of the problem must be performed, assisted by the available engineering analysis tools. In selecting a method, emphasis should be on simplicity, for a practical design is based on justifiable approximations and intelligent decisions.

169

"The purpose of computing is insight, not numbers," states R.W. Hamming [Hamming 73]. Thus, analysis during the early design phase should be the identification of the critical factors affecting the various design decisions. To accomplish this task, the designer should be able to identify not only those components that have major impact on reliability, but also those factors that will limit the achievement of the stated reliability goals. We need not only to evaluate a specific design but also to determine how to improve it if it does not meet the specified design goals. In the end, the fault-tolerant design must also be balanced to retain cost-effectiveness.

18.3 HANDLING LARGE AND COMPLEX SYSTEMS

One way of handling large systems is to use partitioning and reduction, supported by design approximations and simplifications wherever applicable. In partitioning the system, we cannot ignore potential interactions. At the same time, any insignificant secondary effects should be identified and ignored to reduce the complexity of the reliability model.

We need the ability to identify and to select a meaningful part of the problem (i.e., the *critical components*) in order to avoid setting up a complex model that will require a long problem solution time. The exponential increase in solution time makes it difficult to model large systems. Furthermore, a large number of states prevents the program from being truly interactive.

18.3.1 Accuracy of Computation

Once a detailed solution of the problem has been obtained, we must review all approximations and, perhaps, conduct a detailed component tolerance and error analyses.

MATHEMATICAL VERSUS ENGINEERING ANALYSES.   Mathematical analyses seldom use approximations, whereas in engineering analyses, we always have to deal with approximate data. Since the accuracy of the solution is limited by the input data accuracy for engineering problems, the design problem solution should reflect this limited knowledge. Usually, the number of significant digits in the input data will be determined by the type of data associated with the particular component.

ACCURACY OF FAILURE RATES.   Failure rates are not highly accurate and are usually limited to two significant figures. Thus, we should not expect that the probability of failure computation will be accurate to a dozen or more significant figures. (Note that a calculated probability indicating a reliability of 0.999999 has only one significant figure.)

ACCURACY OF RECOVERY RATES.   The same accuracy concern also applies to the recovery rates. They are often even less accurate than the failure rates because of the approximations that are made regarding the recovery process.

18.4 DESIGN ILLUSTRATION

To illustrate the application of a simple initial design approach, we will examine a previously analyzed problem [White 91]. We selected this example because it involves a relatively simple system and the authors already have completed an accurate reliability computation for this configuration. A top-level system block diagram of this system is presented in Figure 18.1.

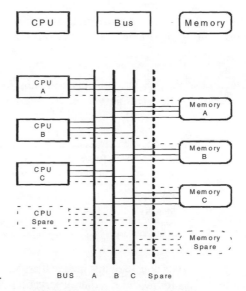

Figure 18.1 System Configuration.

Each of the individual subsystems—CPU, memory, and bus—consist of three operational blocks and a standby spare component for each subsystem. After the switched spare component has failed, the subsystem reverts to a simplex operation. The failure and recovery rates for the individual components are shown in Table 18.1. From this table, we can see that the recovery rates are orders of magnitude higher than the corresponding failure rates. This condition results in increased computation time when the resulting Markov model is solved (i.e., a *stiff* problem). We also note that the memory subsystem has the highest failure rate, making it the critical subsystem.

TABLE 18.1 Failure and Recovery Rates

Component	Failure Rate	Recovery Rate
Processor	10^{-4}/hour	10^4/hour
Memory module	5×10^{-4}/hour	10^3/hour
Bus	10^{-5}/hour	10^3/hour

Next, we will develop reliability models for the individual subsystems. Since all of the subsystems use the same redundancy scheme, only one model will be needed. The corresponding ideal Markov state diagram for each is presented in Figure 18.2.

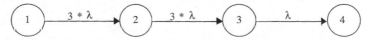

Figure 18.2 Markov Diagram for a Triple Majority Voter with a Spare.

In the Figure 18.2, the fault-recovery process failures are ignored. Thus, this diagram represents the highest reliability that could be obtained under *ideal* conditions (perfect switching and recovery).

The next step is to perform initial approximate computations for each subsystem, based on perfect recovery and no interaction between the individual subsystems. Since at this point we are interested only in approximate values, we can resort to using the approximate formula for the Markov diagram represented in Figure 18.2. This approximate value (representing the first term in power series expansion) is given by

$$3 \times \lambda^3/2 \qquad (18.1)$$

We can use Eq. (18.1) to calculate the approximate probabilities of failure for the given subsystems. The resulting values, for one-hour mission time, are given in the following table.

Subsystem	Failure Rate (per hour)	Failure Probability
Processor	10^{-4}	1.5×10^{-12}
Memory	5×10^{-4}	1.875×10^{-10}
Bus	10^{-5}	1.5×10^{-15}

From this table, we can conclude that the most critical case in this problem will be the memory subsystem. This follows our earlier observation that the nonredundant memory subsystem had the highest failure rate. Since we are adding the same type of redundancy to all subsystems, their relative reliability ranking will remain the same. The other two subsystems, processor and bus, will have relatively minor effects on the system failure probability.

The next step will be to examine the effects of the recovery process to determine how it will affect system reliability. The Markov diagram developed earlier and shown in Figure 18.2 did not include the recovery process. With the recovery process included, the Markov diagram becomes more complex, as shown in Figure 18.3. In this figure, ρ denotes the recovery rate (recoveries/hour). Note that this diagram applies only to a single subsystem.

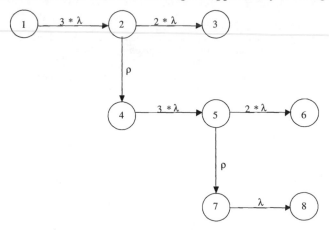

Figure 18.3 Markov Diagram with Recovery.

In Figure 18.3, states 2 and 5 are the recovery-mode states. If there is another failure while the subsystem is in the recovery state, then the system is assumed to fail (the conservative approach). These transitions will be to states 3 and 6. Note again that we are still considering only a single subsystem.

Since the diagram in Figure 18.3 includes fast recovery processes, denoted by ρ, that do not lend themselves to easy approximate computations, it must be converted to a simpler one. Simplifying the first branch is shown in the following steps.

First, isolate the essential transitions:

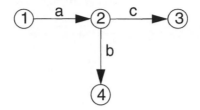

This can be decomposed to:

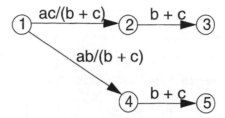

And finally, this simplifies to

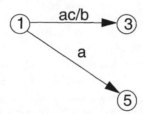

The approach is to convert it to a semi-Markov diagram as shown in Figure 18.4.

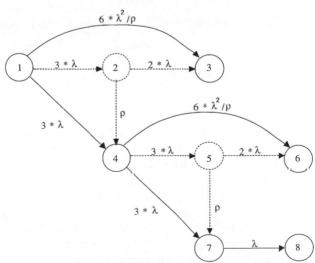

Figure 18.4 Approximate Semi-Markov Diagram.

The dashed (- - -) lines indicate those transitions that have been eliminated by the approximation process. In this diagram we can still distinguish the main path, represented by transitions $1 \rightarrow 4 \rightarrow 7 \rightarrow 8$, which was represented in Figure 18.3. On closer examination of Figure 18.4, we note that the transitions to the failure states due to the imperfect recovery process are of lower power order, first and second, than the main path represented by the third order. Table 18.2 shows the approximate values when introducing the first-order recovery failure rate approximation for a one-hour mission.

TABLE 18.2   Approximate Redundant Component Failure Probabilities (Imperfect Recovery)

Subsystem	Failure Rate/Hour	Recovery Rate/Hour	Failure Probability $= 1.5\,(\lambda t)^3 + 6\,\frac{\lambda^2}{\rho}\,t$
Processor	10^{-4}	10^4	7.5×10^{-12}
Memory	5×10^{-4}	10^3	1.69×10^{-9}
Bus	10^{-5}	10^3	6×10^{-13}

18.4.1 Errors Due to Approximations

In the previous section, we used some rather drastic approximations to obtain a quick estimate for the probability of system failure. At this point, however, we have to question the accuracy of this simple solution to a rather complex problem. For comparison we need the failure probability for the full system model. Fortunately, the results for the full model were reported in a form suitable for comparison [White 91].

According to [White 91], the complete model for the example problem consisted of 227 states and required 2.1 hours (7878 seconds) to compute on a DEC VAX 11/750 computer. Their simplified model consisted of 83 states and took only 4.3 minutes (258 seconds) to compute on the same computer and yielded essentially the same value for the probability of failure. A comparison of the reported system probability of failures and our approximation is given in Table 18.3.

TABLE 18.3   Comparison of Failure Probabilities

Method	Prob(Failure)	Difference (%)
Full model	1.808×10^{-9}	0
Memory subsystem approximation	1.69×10^{-9}	-6.5%

From Table 18.3, we can conclude that the approximation used is within the usual "engineering accuracy" range. The approximate value is lower than the one given for the full model, because the effects of other subsystems on the system probability of failure were ignored.

Next, we will examine the effect on solution accuracy using only the first term in the power series expansion. In this case, we look only at the subsystem Markov diagram solutions with recovery. This comparison is shown in Table 18.4.

From Table 18.4 we can conclude that the first-term approximation is within our acceptable accuracy range. In this case, the approximation provides us with a quick method

TABLE 18.4   Comparison of Submodel Accuracy

Method	Prob(Failure)	Difference (%)
Full submodel	1.6847×10^{-9}	0
Semi-Markov simplification	1.6873×10^{-9}	+0.15%
First-term approximation	1.69×10^{-9}	+0.3%

to estimate probability of failure during the early design phases. After the initial architecture has been defined in more detail, full reliability analysis should be performed using the available tools.

18.4.2 Summary of Design Example

The above conclusions apply only to the specific example examined. However, in the actual design of fault-tolerant systems, similar useful and safe approximations can be made during the early design phases and with acceptable results. The primary purpose of making approximations is to control the complexity of the design representation and at the same time identify the critical components early. The simple example illustrated the fault-tolerant design process, from which we can summarize the key findings:

1. *What can we learn from the example?* The most important lesson learned was that it was possible to start with relatively simple Markov models for the early design decisions. Not only does such a model simplify the initial design evaluation, but it also helps to identify the critical system components.

2. *What are the limits on reliability improvement?* From the analysis, the limiting subsystem in this particular system is the memory subsystem. We also note that the recovery process has a primary impact on resulting system reliability. For example, adding more spares to the memory subsystem will not affect resulting reliability, unless the recovery process is improved. As the reliability of the memory subsystem improves, the reliability of the other subsystems may dominate. This requires the development of additional reliability models.

   Note that the use of higher reliability components will have more impact on the resulting reliability than adding complexity to the model. For example, a 10% improvement in part reliability will reduce the probability of failure by almost 20%. Again, this conclusion applies only to the specific problem being considered. The actual improvements, in general, will be system and configuration dependent.

3. *What else is needed for further improvements?* In addition to modifications discussed above, alternative redundancy configurations could be considered. These, however, will require new models and another design iteration. It is also important to realize that as the reliability of the critical subsystem improves, it may no longer be the critical subsystem on a system level. Thus, during the design process, the individual subsystem models, as well as models on the system level, should be continuously reevaluated.

   The design of the monitor and recovery scheme used is crucial, since according to the assumptions, a failure during recovery results in system failure. Better recovery approaches and a well-designed monitor (which may be nonredundant and therefore the weak link) can avoid this problem. Section 18.5.3 considers the monitor design in detail.

Lastly, if the designer in the example case had depended entirely on a detailed Markov model with thousands of system states, then it is doubtful that he or she would have been able to reach the same understanding of the system. The alternative is to use verifiable formal specification for the system and automate the model generation and calculation as much as possible. This necessitates fast algorithms and powerful computing systems such as those in the REST (Reliability Estimation System Testbed) approach [Nicol 92, 93].

18.5 ADVANCED SOFTWARE FAULT-TOLERANT TECHNOLOGY

New approaches to fault-tolerant software design will be needed to meet the increasing reliability, survivability, and maintainability goals in software-dependent systems. The need for improved software fault-tolerance in complex systems is supported by field failure data indicating that, on average, software failures account for 25 to 50% of all system failures, while the computer hardware failures account for less than 10% [Hecht 86a, b; Levendel 89; NRC 86; Tang 93].

The majority of software failures are due to design errors. Some of the design problems are introduced at the system design level because hardware and software development efforts follow two separate development paths, as prescribed by the conventional design process. In this approach, hardware designers are not concerned with software failures, and software designers assume that hardware will never fail and that unexpected errors will never occur. As a result, when the development effort reaches the hardware and software integration phase and the lack of an integrated system-level fault tolerance concept is discovered, it's usually too late for another design iteration.

The longer term technical challenge will be to develop new design techniques to improve software fault-tolerance to the level currently achievable in hardware design. To achieve this objective will require the use of formal software description languages, guidelines for instrumenting software programs for fault detection, development of new support tools, and improved test techniques.

18.5.1 Software Fault Statistics

Software fault-tolerance implementation problems can be understood by examining actual statistics related to software development as well as actual field experience. Two such case studies are reviewed next.

One study cites an Air Force project experience and presents software defects corrected during the software development cycle [Sheldon 92]. The data are summarized by problem type and by development phase. In the first category, the percentage of defects are due to *Requirements Translation* (36%) and *Logic Design* (28%). In the second category, the largest percentages of defects are discovered during *System Integration* (48%), *Software Integration* (15%), and *Flight Test* (13%) program phases. Since the largest group of software defects are due to requirements translation, it explains why the majority of defects are discovered late, and at considerable expense, in the program cycle. This may also imply that some of the system performance requirements are discovered only during the system and field testing phases and were not included in the original requirements specification.

The second study reports a summary of 27,788 software failures, collected over an eight-month period, of seven DEC VAXclusters used at NASA Ames Research Center [Tang 93]. Major failure classifications included were *Machine* (CPU and memory), *I/O* (Disk, Tape, and Network), *Software*, and *Unknown* failures. In this time interval, *Machine* failures accounted for 2% of the total with a 99.7% recovery probability; *I/O* for 42.9% with 99.6% recovery; *Software* for 25.3% with 10.1% recovery; and *Unknown* with 29.8% and 61.8% recovery. Shared resources were a major source of reliability problems.

The above data again indicate the key role of the software failures in system field performance. Noteworthy is the large percentage of unknown failures, which makes it difficult to institute corrective actions. Also note that these data apply to DEC VAX system software that has undergone considerable testing and years of field experience and improvements.

18.5.2 State-of-the-Practice in Software Fault-Tolerance

Implementing software fault-tolerance is not always cost-effective. Not only have some of the programming-based approaches failed to yield the desired reliability improvement goals, but there is also a scarcity of reliable software fault detection techniques, causing the software debugging and testing to account for a major share of the system development costs. Approaches to developing fault-tolerant software include the following.

Programming Techniques. Current software fault-tolerance techniques [Simcox 88] include such approaches as the use of self-testing, redundant computations, multiple-version programming [Anderson 85a,b; Eckhardt 85; Knight 86a, b; Littlewood 87; Shimeall 91], recovery blocks, hybrid forward and backward recovery [Vick 90], and data diversity. None of these techniques is completely satisfactory because they may violate the basic fault-tolerant system design requirement of fault independence (i.e., software *A* and *B* both critically fail due to the same fault). Furthermore, software designers seldom consider potential hardware failures, thus increasing the number of faults that cannot be detected by the operational program (or common-mode faults).

Testing Techniques. Although major advances have been made in software testing, recent experience shows that extensive testing of widely available operating systems, even with tens of thousands of beta sites, still fail to uncover all of the software defects. [Butler 93] provides a detailed discussion of the impossibility of quantifying the reliability of ultra-reliable, life-critical systems.

A recent review of the commercial fault-tolerant software design processes is available [Goel 91]. However, it does not cover the fail-safe, fault-tolerant systems developed for military avionics applications.

18.5.3 Basics of Fault-Tolerant Software Design

Improved computer hardware designs come from better understanding of fault-tolerant hardware system architectures, by developing improved techniques for fault detection, improved design support tools, and improved hardware testing techniques. In addition, formal techniques have been developed for describing hardware architectures, and simulation tools are now available which accept this formal description language. Unfortunately, similar improvements have not been routinely achieved in fault-tolerant software design [Weinstock 93].

An important factor in fault-tolerant system design is knowledge of the system operational status. In the hardware systems, this is achieved by instrumentation. For example, in a car we find instrumentation that indicates the status of the critical systems, such as electrical, braking, cooling, and engine systems, implemented as instruments or as warning lights. These displays not only serve as diagnostic aids but also help to avoid potential accidents and expensive major system failures.

Software systems seldom indicate operational status. Thus the first indication of a nonworking system is when it fails to respond to user commands or is outputting random characters. As a result, the internal operation of software is usually invisible to either the user or tester of the program, and often the only recovery capability is by system reboot, hoping that the problem has disappeared. This approach is not acceptable for mission-critical real-time systems, where continuous operation is desired and data loss cannot be tolerated. Here, status may be used by Byzantine agreement and system diagnosis redundancy schemes to improve fault tolerance [Barborak 93].

The key factor in fault-tolerant system design is the ability to detect a fault that may lead to system failure. This implies that the design must include features or extra circuitry for the specific purpose of fault detection. It is also important to have an independent fault detection capability, because a fault in the system may otherwise disable the fault detection capability and thus prevent recovery. Frequent violations of this simple principle can be found in many software programs, where the operating program is assumed to be capable of locating its own faults.

Fault information can be obtained by instrumenting the program—that is, by strategically inserting *software probes* into the program to extract data for use as status indication, fault detection, fault isolation, and fail-safe recovery. These software probes consist of added software instructions or modules that may be permanent or temporary parts of the program. They extract program status information that is processed by an independent monitor, thus satisfying the key fault-tolerance requirement of independence.

Once a fault has been identified and located, it must be isolated (contained) to prevent it from creating a chain reaction and corrupting other parts of the system. As an example, the rationale for the Ada exception statement is to contain a fault and keep it from propagating within a program.

It is also important to provide for the detection and recovery from unexpected faults caused by software, hardware transients, or external events [Jalotte 86]. This type of recovery usually requires an independent external monitor that can monitor system operation and sense that major deviations from the expected behavior have occurred and then control the recovery process. Fault recovery based on error detecting codes and self-testing has been considered [Cha 87] and found to be effective in data transfer and storage applications.

Several arguments form the basis for software monitoring. First, software monitoring is needed to provide a consistent fault-monitoring capability throughout the system. Second, software monitoring can help to detect hardware faults. Third, reliable software status information will be needed for the system resource manager to identify the location of a failed component and to enable proper reconfiguration of the remaining components. Fourth, comprehensive software monitoring reduces the uncertainty associated with the unresolved software fault causes, thus enabling better maintenance and corrective actions.

The software monitoring concept can be adapted to the different requirements as development continues. During the early development phases, the full capabilities of software probes will be needed. Later, as the system attains maturity, monitoring levels can be reduced or readily changed.

18.5.4 Software Probes

Software probes have been used for system performance monitoring and debugging support [Pitarys 88; Probert 82], with extended monitoring provided by hybrid hardware/software monitors [Van Karsen 86]. In a previous investigation, we established that the use of software probes can provide the needed status for monitoring and can improve both software and hardware fault detection and isolation [Pukite 89c]. Implementing software probes results in a slight increase in program overhead and execution time, but this increase can be minimized with proper design.

The ease of software probe implementation will depend on several factors, including complexity of the program, degree of fault location resolution desired, and number of probes to be implemented.

The location of the software monitoring points depends on the type of software probes used in the monitoring process. Similarly, the software probe itself will be determined by the information transmitted by the probes. This information will range from a simple event indication to a complex acquisition of critical parameter values. We can identify three types of probes (event, entry, and exit) [Pukite 89c], with each having different levels of monitoring capabilities.

1. *Event probes.* Event probes are single probes that mark events within or around software modules. This type of probe is most useful in programs that have a linear structure. Timing checks to verify correct operation involve only the time between adjacent probes.

2. *Entry/Exit Probes.* Entry/exit probes are used in pairs to identify the beginning and end of software modules. These probes aid in identifying faulty modules by using two timing checks. The result is a more complex algorithm, but with better fault detection/fault isolation (FD/FI) capabilities.

3. *Hybrid Probes.* By converting some of the entry/exit probes into event probes, we can combine the best features of each probe. This probe reduction eliminates the risk of process saturation, which occurs when too many probes are present. Timing checks are still performed, but we now use both event and entry/exit, which creates an even larger and more complex monitoring algorithm.

Selection of the probe locations requires an understanding of program functions and construction. Since most of this detailed knowledge is created during the design phase, an early introduction of software probes will also ease program debugging and testing. Use of software probes is not limited to new designs. They may be implemented in existing software, provided that a detailed structure of the program is known. The available aids to an optimal probe placement include program *control flow* and *data flow* diagrams. The control flow represents the sequence of program steps and the allowable branch points. The data flow diagram represents the flow of data within the program.

After the probe locations have been selected, program testing should also require *probe testing*. Testing can be performed by using either software simulation or the actual system.

Introduction of software probes in the system will affect program execution speed and memory requirements. Both of these factors will be minimal in a well-designed system. The processing overhead will include data conversion and parameter computation. The time required for transmitting the probe information is small: for example, if a direct write to an output port is used, then transmission of probe information will require only one to two instruction cycles per probe. Transmission of additional information, such as tag or parameter values, will result in longer transmission times. We should expect a 2 to 5% decrease in execution speed and a 2 to 5% increase in memory requirements due to the addition of software probes [Pukite 89c].

Estimation of fault-detection coverage achieved through software probes will require further research because this topic has not received sufficient attention in the past. Fault simulation appears to be the least expensive approach for determining fault coverage.

The reliability of software probe fault detection will depend on a number of complex factors and requires detailed analysis and modeling [Scott 87]. A new reliability model, capable of representing the probes and dynamic changes of the system, will need to be developed.

The design of the software fault monitor differs from its hardware counterpart in one major respect. Whereas the fault types in hardware are relatively well known and their effects can be analyzed using failure mode and effects analysis (FMEA), software FMEA becomes complex because software faults are often unpredictable and unexpected [Reifer 79]. Therefore, the hardware fault monitor must be designed to detect a known class of hardware failures, and the software fault monitor must be designed to detect software faults whose locations are not always known.

The monitoring information required to isolate faults and to support recovery capability includes software structure, the allowable range of key parameter values, the allowable transitions within the program, and the program event timing information. Examples include: (1) valid transition event messages, (2) time interval between probe messages, (3) allowable parameter range for inputs and outputs, and (4) stack information.

The information supplied by the probes *alone* will not indicate a potential fault. This information must be further processed until decisions are made. The monitoring functions consist of observation of control and data flow in the software, verification that the required functions are completed within acceptable time limits, and integrity cross-checks.

The actual processing can range from a simple GO/NOGO indication to a more enhanced processing involving possible determination of fault location and cause. The latter computation would involve a quantitative assessment of the fault conditions. In some situations, local processing may also be used to limit the amount of data transmitted via the software probes. However, local processing *itself* may be disabled during a system fault, as well as fault-related information.

Different monitor configurations can be used during the various system development phases, with implementations ranging from a dual or TMR fault monitors[1] to a simple fault-recording device. In the latter case, off-line monitoring would be used for fault and performance data processing.

----

[1]As an example of what might happen in a real situation, should a monitor processor fail, its function could be reassigned to a different mission processor by a system executive or diagnosis program.

The probe database contains both the dynamic probe data and the target system description data. If the target software is embedded with many probes, the task of setting up the probe database can be extensive, so automated methods for placing probes and retaining locations may be wise. Techniques include the use of semantic analyzers that detect program transitions, calculate the corresponding transition times, and combine this information into a database lookup table.

Additional hardware, such as a separate clock, timer, or counter, or even a modified architecture, may be needed by the monitor processor to perform more accurate tests on the target processor [Johnson 82; Tsai 90]. When using a hardware timer, the monitor simply does the timer load, save, start, and stop, thus reducing its software overhead. As configured, the timer would have the responsibility of notifying the monitor when too much time has elapsed and the monitor would then determine if an actual fault had occurred. Several timers may be needed to obtain the desired accuracy and monitor the start and stop probe times.

In addition, the normal program execution in the target processor can be interrupted and delayed by external interrupt and direct memory access (DMA) processing. Since bus lines control these activities, bus signals can identify when an interrupt occurs or when a DMA processor is granted the bus. The interrupt service routine can also be embedded with software probes to improve monitoring capability. These events, if not processed by the monitor, will also have an impact on the software itself and may trigger a false alarm if not handled properly. When a disruptive process occurs at the target, the monitor must be able to recognize this and respond accordingly, so that the system operation is not corrupted.

To interface the software monitor to the target system probes, a communications channel must be available. This communications channel may be a system bus, RS-232 serial port, Ethernet link, and so on. Additional interfaces may be provided from the monitor to the system health monitor, fault data recording unit, or a maintenance interface to provide off-line testing capability. If I/O channels are used for transmitting probe information, then channel assignments can be used to determine fault data origin without additional decoding. For example, if different I/O channels were assigned to the key parameters, these values could be automatically recorded by channel-sensitive recording devices.

Other important system functions can be included in the monitor. For example, the monitor can supply the information needed to evaluate the processor operational performance. In this case, a software monitor provides information about potential processing overload in the system.

The monitoring concept can also be used to test the integrity of the software during the acceptance phase. To support this application, interactive monitoring can be added.

A conceptual example of an extended expert system/decision module is presented in Figure 18.5 [based on Pukite 89c]. In this implementation, system data, containing potential fault information, are collected from a variety of independent sources. The extracted information is then used to display status information, to determine if any faults have occurred, and to direct redundancy and reconfiguration management.

18.5.5 Design and Development Tools

The design of fault-tolerant software along with software instrumentation, software probe documentation, and program maintenance will require a formal software description language to attain the same capabilities that are currently available for hardware design. One approach is to follow a path taken by VHDL (VHSIC Hardware Description Language) in defining structure, functions, and behavior of the hardware part of the system. Thus, a high-level software description language (HLSDL) could be developed and used to describe program data structure, data flow, control flow, program structure, specific probe locations, and probe types. The use of HLSDL could also ease software maintenance document preparation. Since such a description language is not yet available, VHDL can be adapted to this task.

To support the fault-tolerant software development process, new computer tools will have to be developed, including simulators to verify program functionality and tools for software instrumentation and probe location. The use of these tools will lead to more reliable software and will reduce the time needed for debugging.

New software reliability prediction tools will also be needed. As studies have shown, present software reliability prediction techniques are not well suited for analyzing fault-tolerant programs [Hecht 84, 86b; Kumar 86; Pukite 89b; Reifer 79; Sumita 86].

18.5.6 Future Needs

Use of the software fault-monitoring concept is one potential approach to achieving higher system reliability and survivability. Although the feasibility of the basic concept has been demonstrated [Pukite 89c], open research problems remain. In particular, better understanding of implementing software probes and their interface to the fault monitor is needed. A detailed comparison of the software monitoring concept versus the state-of-the-practice fault-tolerance methods and cost-effectiveness evaluation also needs to be performed.

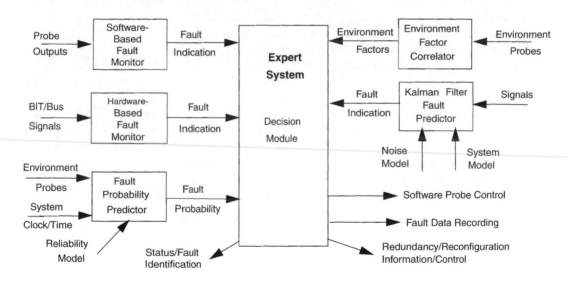

Figure 18.5 Expert System/Decision Module.

18.6 FAULT-TOLERANT SYSTEM DESIGN GUIDELINES

To summarize, when designing fault-tolerant systems, the system analyst and the designer must understand the details of the process: what options are available to meet the objectives, which parameters are approximate, and which parameters are secondary (can be neglected). Software-based system designers, in particular, will need methods to handle the overwhelming state-space complexity. In the future, much of the reliability improvement will come from intelligent testing and monitoring.

Knowledge of the design process determines the need for specific design tools. Tools (or a toolkit) supported by an interactive and integrated environment should be capable of providing reasonably fast answers to design problems. In the development of this environment, emphasis should be placed on information integration, because information is accessed and modified by the various tools.

Support tool designers must realize that the information and data available during the early-design phase will be approximate. Thus, even in the best case, the computed answers to the design problems will also be only approximate and will not require the computing process to achieve ultra-high accuracy.

Since there are no fault-tolerant design reference texts that stress the practical aspects of the design process, it will be important to develop suitable guidelines. Specifically, a practical fault-tolerant system design procedure manual is needed to support future system design efforts.

19

CARMS User's Guide

19.1 INTRODUCTION

CARMS (Computer-Aided Rate Modeling and Simulation) is an integrated, general-purpose tool suitable for reliability, maintainability, and availability (RMA) evaluation. It is designed to solve a broad spectrum of RMA and other mathematically related problems, and, in particular, is well-suited for fault-tolerant system design. CARMS is based on the discrete space, continuous-time Markov model. A combination of text- and graphics-based data input makes the program ideal for problems in which an engineering design is at the conceptual phase. In this phase, flexibility, ease of use, and speed are prime requirements in determining the ideal course of action and probing tradeoff scenarios. Unlike the traditional methods of computer-based RMA evaluation, CARMS features an interactive environment that allows the user to quickly change data values and graphical views of a given system (see Fig. 19.1). Menu-driven commands and help screens are also available.

The features of CARMS include:

- Spreadsheet-like data input screen.
- Vector-based graphics for constructing transition diagrams.
- Expert-system front end that automates model construction.
- Symbolic algebra for simplifying reliability, maintainability, and availability problems.
- Graphical display of results as a function of time.
- Generation of reports to printer, plotter, or file.
- Choice of numerical routines for solving a range of problems.

185

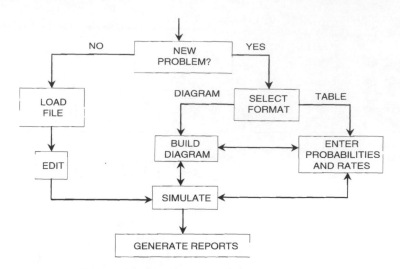

Figure 19.1 CARMS Road Map.

19.2 REQUIREMENTS

The CARMS program requires a PC-compatible computer running the Microsoft DOS/Windows 3.1 operating system and environment. An Intel x87 math coprocessor chip is not required, although it will speed up the simulation if installed. A mouse configured for Windows is useful but is not required to run the program.

19.3 APPLICATION

CARMS computes the likelihood of events based on a probabilistic model that the analyst using the tool defines. A typical model will describe probability flow from one state to another as a function of time. The interactive portion of CARMS enables the user to create and experiment with the model without deriving the probability equations. This is the basic CARMS approach for modeling fault-tolerant design configurations.

19.3.1 The Method

A convenient starting point for fault-tolerant reliability analysis is a listing of equipment that must be working satisfactorily. The state of the system can then be described in terms of the operation or failure of the equipment.

First, note that a system has a finite probability of being in one of two distinct states; one that is operational and one that is failed. The way that these states are interconnected is dependent on the failure modes and transition rates.

As an example, consider a system consisting of a primary and secondary communications channel. The system states under these conditions will be:

1. Primary channel operating (system operational) with failure rate λ_1.
2. Secondary channel operating (system operational) with failure rate λ_2.
3. No operating channels (both channels have failed—system failure).

The block diagram of the system is shown in Figure 19.2.

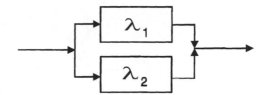

Figure 19.2 Dual-element Parallel System.

Starting with the feasible system states, CARMS uses a graphical method to develop the system reliability model. Called the state transition diagram, this representation allows the user to specify the transitions from one operating state to another operating (or failed) state. The state diagram corresponding to the block diagram is shown in Figure 19.3.

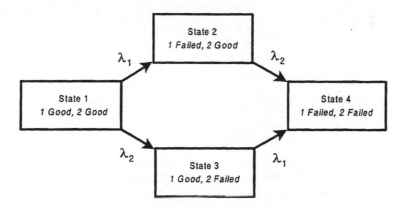

Figure 19.3 State Diagram for Parallel System.

From this state diagram, Markov equations can be formulated for each state. These equations express state probabilities for each state, $P_n(t)$, as functions of time. We can write these for illustration purposes as

$$\frac{d}{dt}P_1(t) = -(\lambda_1 + \lambda_2) \times P_1(t) \qquad P_1(0) = 1.0$$

$$\frac{d}{dt}P_2(t) = \lambda_1 \times P_1(t) - \lambda_2 \times P_2(t) \qquad P_2(0) = 0$$

$$\frac{d}{dt}P_3(t) = \lambda_2 \times P_1(t) - \lambda_1 \times P_3(t) \qquad P_3(0) = 0 \tag{19.1}$$

$$\frac{d}{dt}P_4(t) = \lambda_2 \times P_2(t) + \lambda_1 \times P_3(t) \qquad P_4(0) = 0$$

These differential equations can then be transformed into a matrix for solution:

$$
\begin{bmatrix}
\dfrac{d}{dt}P_1(t) \\[2mm]
\dfrac{d}{dt}P_2(t) \\[2mm]
\dfrac{d}{dt}P_3(t) \\[2mm]
\dfrac{d}{dt}P_4(t)
\end{bmatrix}
=
\begin{bmatrix}
-(\lambda_1 + \lambda_2) & 0 & 0 & 0 \\
\lambda_1 & -\lambda_2 & 0 & 0 \\
\lambda_2 & 0 & -\lambda_1 & 0 \\
0 & \lambda_2 & \lambda_1 & 0
\end{bmatrix}
\times
\begin{bmatrix}
P_1(t) \\
P_2(t) \\
P_3(t) \\
P_4(t)
\end{bmatrix}
\tag{19.2}
$$

Given the implicit structure of these equations, it makes sense to view the model from a different perspective. Typically, this is done by associating the probabilities, initial conditions, and transition rates in tabular form or *transition matrix* form (Figure 19.4).

Initial Conditions		Transition Matrix			
Prob		From P_1	From P_2	From P_3	From P_4
$P_1(0)$	To P_1				
$P_2(0)$	To P_2	λ_1			
$P_3(0)$	To P_3	λ_2			
$P_4(0)$	To P_4		λ_2	λ_1	

Figure 19.4 Transition Table.

From here it is possible to convert the transition matrix into a spreadsheet-like interface that most computer users are familiar with. Shown in Figure 19.5 are the data arranged using references to other spreadsheet cells. This is referred to as the CARMS **Transition Table** view, or simply **Table** view.

	Prob	Base	1	2	3	4
1	$P_1(0)$	λ_1				
2	$P_2(0)$	λ_2	B1			
3	$P_3(0)$		B2			
4	$P_4(0)$			B2	B1	

Figure 19.5 Transition Table in CARMS Spreadsheet Format.

By working backwards from the **Transition Table** view, it becomes obvious that the original matrix has a direct representation in spreadsheet format. Thus, the necessary differential equations can be derived in a form suitable for solution directly from the **Transition Table**. This step is performed automatically within the CARMS program. The flexibility of CARMS allows either a table or diagram to be used for problem formulation. Shown in Figure 19.6 is the state diagram for the model, where B1 = λ_1, B2 = λ_2 are the cell references to the failure rates.[1]

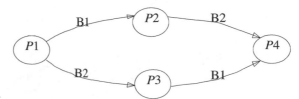

Figure 19.6 CARMS State Diagram.

Therefore, the standard method of setting up the matrix and differential equations can be replaced with the CARMS method of graphically inputting the state diagram with a mouse or keyboard (Figure 19.7).

Conventional Markov Model Method

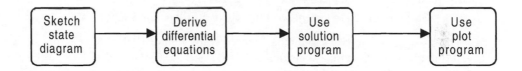

CARMS Approach

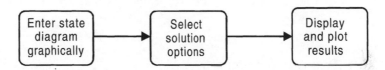

Figure 19.7 Approaches to Creating Markov Models.

To gain some familiarity with the approach, consider a few more state diagram examples:

1. Single-element
2. Two-element parallel
3. Two-element standby
4. Single element with multiple failure modes

19.3.2 Single-Element State Diagram

Let the states be defined as follows:

State 1—element is working satisfactorily

State 2—element is not working (failed state)

---

[1]Instead of B1 and B2, we can also use named variables such as lambda1 and lambda2, or λ1and λ2. To do this, input a ***Name*** into the corresponding "Base" cell.

The state diagram in this case is represented by the displayed figure (Figure 19.8). Note from the direction of the arrow that a transition is only possible from state 1 (circle labeled 1) to state 2 (circle labeled 2). The transition (failure) rate is indicated above the arrow and in this case is expressed by B1. Transition rate units can be expected failures/hour, and so on. These must be constant with respect to time.

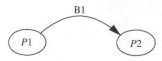

Figure 19.8 Single-Element State Diagram.

19.3.3 Two-Element Parallel

Assuming two identical elements operating in parallel, we can designate the states as follows:

State 1—both elements working satisfactorily

State 2—one element working satisfactorily

State 3—neither element working satisfactorily (failed state)

The corresponding state diagram is represented by Figure 19.9. If the circuits are working simultaneously, the initial transition rate is B1 + B1 = 2*B1, since either of the elements can fail. After the initial failure, only the remaining element can fail; hence, the transition rate is given by B1.

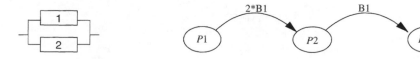

Figure 19.9 Two-Element Parallel System.

19.3.4 Two-Element Standby

This diagram contrasts to the two-element parallel state diagram. Here, if the two elements are not working concurrently but one is in standby mode, the states need to be redesignated:

State 1—primary element working satisfactorily

State 2—secondary (standby or backup) working satisfactorily

State 3—secondary element not working (failed state)

The slightly modified state diagram is represented by Figure 19.10. If the primary and secondary circuits are identical, such as is the case for the preceding two-element example, then B1 = B2. However, situations may arise where the standby is less reliable than the primary, so that B2 would be larger than B1.

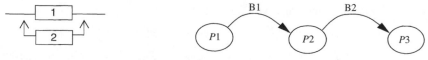

Figure 19.10 Two-Element Standby.

19.3.5 Single Element with Multiple Failure Modes

To accurately model more complicated systems, all possible failure modes may need to be included. For example, where a single element may fail in one of two ways:

State 1—element working satisfactorily
State 2—element failed with failure mode 1
State 3—element failed with failure mode 1
State 4—element failed with failure mode 1 or 2

The corresponding transition diagram is shown in Figure 19.11. Here, B1 and B2 differ in value, and state 4 is indicated as the sum of P_2 and P_3. The transition arrows leading to state 4 are derived in that no transition rates are associated with it.

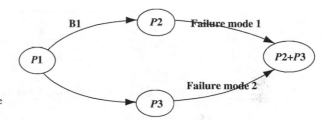

Figure 19.11 Single Element with Multiple Failure Modes.

19.4 INSTALLATION

19.4.1 CARMS Package

The CARMS package consists of a user's guide, a distribution disk, and the function key template. The distribution disk contains the program needed to run the simulator as well as several example files and help file. Late changes can be found in the README file supplied. To protect the disk, it may be wise to make a backup.

19.4.2 Distribution Disk

The CARMS program is available from the Internet, and a copy of the program can be downloaded to a disk at the Website location http://umn.edu/~puk/carms.html.

To install the CARMS program, run the automatic installation program SETUP.EXE. Otherwise, copy the entire contents of the demo disk(s) to your hard disk (preferably in a directory called \CARMS directly under the root directory) or run the disk from a floppy drive. Files included on the disk are as follows:

1. CARMS.EXE   The CARMS program.
2. CARMS.HLP   Help file for the program.
3. README   Last minute changes not in CARMS documentation.
4. DAINA.INI   Windows initialization file.
5. *.MM, *.PRO   Additional CARMS model files.
6. WAES.EXE   Expert system front-end program
7. ESMETHOD.EXE   Method selection program

19.4.3 Running the CARMS Program

Within the Windows environment, click on the CARMS icon in the CARMS program group. Otherwise, load CARMS.EXE as a program item and then launch on that item. To automatically load a CARMS data file, supply the file name on the command line. If preferred, the working directory can be set to the commonly used database files.

The CARMS operational views are shown in Figure 19.12 as a state transition diagram. We can freely move between these views via the menu commands or hot keys. Each of the different environments (1 through 5) will be discussed in the following pages.

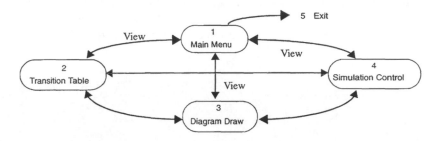

Figure 19.12 Main Menu Launches to CARMS Views.

1. Main Menu.   The main menu display (see Figure 19.13) allows the user to load a file from the database or to choose how to interactively build or solve a model through the *View* menu selection. As the program commands are executed, a history of messages will appear within the window. The main menu is the first view to appear on the screen after starting CARMS.

Figure 19.13 CARMS Main Menu.

2. Transition Table (spreadsheet).   The *Transition Table* (see Figure 19.14) is a spreadsheet-like environment. Data can be modified in a manner similar to con-

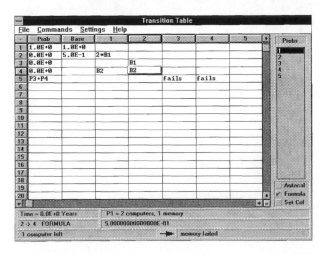

Figure 19.14 CARMS Transition Table View.

ventional spreadsheets. Nongraphical models can be built quickly through the table commands. Alternatively, the diagram values can be modified within this view.

3. Diagram Draw (state diagram).   The easiest way to grasp the method of model building and data entry is to start from the graphical entry view called **Diagram Draw** (see Figure 19.15). To start constructing a state diagram, it is only necessary to click and drag with the mouse (see the **State** and **Arrow** commands in the commands reference).

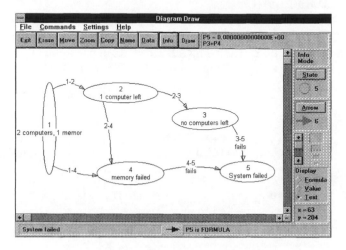

Figure 19.15 CARMS Diagram Draw View.

By using the mouse and keystrokes, or the Windows macro capability, one can rapidly construct a transition diagram. The auxiliary commands in the menu and the dialog buttons allow the states and arrows of the diagram to be named, manipulated, probed, and assigned values.

4. Simulation Control (graphical results display).   To predict reliability, maintainability, or availability as a function of time, it is often convenient to plot the results. CARMS provides a graphical **Simulation Control** interface (see Figure 19.16) that not only will control the simulation time and model updating, but will

Figure 19.16 CARMS Simulation Control View.

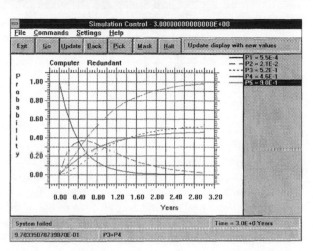

also show the intermediate results. The user can further specify which curves to display, print, or plot. Several sample models can be found in the example files. *Note:* Before running the simulator, it is necessary to enter at least two states and at least one transition rate to the transition table or diagram.

5. Exit to Windows.   To quit the program and exit to Windows, the user must be in the **Main Menu** view.

19.4.4 Data Entry

Data entry to the CARMS model can be accomplished through the **Diagram Draw** or **Transition Table**. The **Diagram Draw** requires only that the user click on states or arrow midpoints with the **Data** mode on (see Figure 19.17).

Click on midpoint to change transition data

1→2
1.0E−1

Click on circle to change
state data

1
1.0E+0

2
0.0E+0

Figure 19.17 Drawing States and Transitions.

After the state diagram has been set up through **Diagram Draw**, the values given to the states and transitions can be globally viewed through the **Transition Table**. The first column of the **Transition Table** (labeled "Prob") is dedicated to the values of state probabilities, the second (labeled "Base") is dedicated to frequently used transition rates, and the rest of the spreadsheet to the transition matrix. The tail locations, or "From" states, are listed as the column headers, while the "To" states are listed as the row labels (see Figure 19.18).

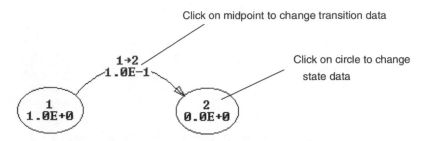

"Prob" column   "Base" column   "From" state

Transition Table

File	Commands	Settings	Help				
-	Prob	Base	1	2	3	4	5
1	1.0E+0	1.0E+0					
2	0.0E+0	5.0E−1	2*B1				
3	0.0E+0			B1			
4	0.0E+0		B2	B2			
5	P3+P4				fails	fails	
6							

"To" state

Figure 19.18 Entering Data into Table.

All of these values can be formulated in a fashion similar to a spreadsheet with a few exceptions. The exceptions are that symbolic algebra can only involve the first two columns as the arguments. (For example, B2 would be the value in the "Base" column at row 2, and 2*P1 would be twice the value in the "Prob" column at row 1.) This is in accordance with the linear format needed to run the simulator. In addition, the "Base" values are treated as constants during the simulation, so they can modify the values in the transition matrix or in the "Prob" column. The "Prob" formulas vary with the simulation time. Invalid data are indicated upon running the simulator. Note again that at least one rate and one "Prob" value must be greater than zero for the simulator to start.

The table entries correspond to the diagram attributes as shown in Fig. 19.19.

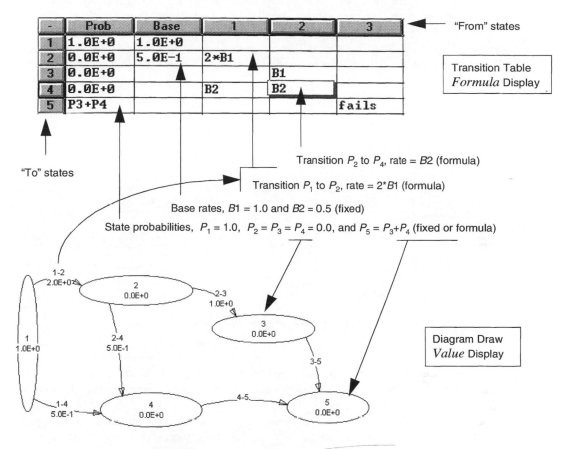

Figure 19.19 Correspondence between Table and Diagram.

Formulas can be built into the "Prob" cells or transition cells, according to the rules in Table 19.1.

TABLE 19.1 CARMS Formula Operators

Operation	Meaning	Formula Examples
* + − /	Standard operations	$2*B1$, $B1+B2$
^	Raise to power	$2^\wedge$
:	Summation	$P_1{:}P_3$
( )	Parentheses	$2*(B1+B2/2)$
T0	Time parameter	
exp ( )	Exponentiate	$exp(-B1*T0)$
abs ( )	Absolute value	$abs(P1)$
ln ( )	Natural log	

19.4.5 Step-by-Step Example

In a hypothetical example, the reliability of a computer system is dependent on the reliability of the main computer and its concurrently operating backup, as well as on the reliability of the memory (reliability block diagram shown below). Figure 19.20 shows the completed state diagram of the fault-tolerant computer. The circles labeled 1 through 5 are the "Prob" states corresponding to the first column in the **Transition Table**. These correspond to the various failure modes as shown in the state diagram.[2]

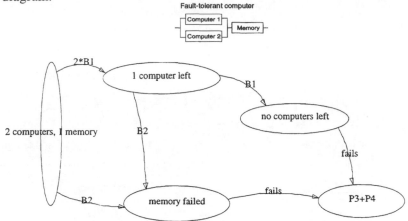

Figure 19.20 Example State Diagram.

The states were formed by clicking and dragging at the various screen positions while in the **Diagram Draw** view. After describing each of the states with the **Name** command, initial conditions were applied. Data were entered through the **Data** command in the diagram. The last state entered, state number 5, is a derived state that sums P_3 and P_4. This state describes the probability of failure of the system (no computers or memory left) at any one time.

The transition arrows were formed by clicking at the beginning, midpoint, and end-point of all the valid failure mode transitions. Failure rates for the transitions were then entered through the **Data** command. Since the transition to state P_5 is derived, a description of "fails" is entered for the transitions $P_3 \to P_5$ and $P_4 \to P_5$.

After completing the state diagram, we can view the **Transition Table**. Base rates 1 and 2 corresponding to the computer and memory failure rates are input directly into the **Transition Table**, just as with a spreadsheet. The completed table appears in Figure 19.21. One can also view the names of the "Prob" and "Base" entries by moving the cursor cell to the desired position. Alternatively, one can use the **Names** view to display these directly on the screen, or the report generation commands to collect into a file.

---

[2] The figures shown were exported directly from CARMS as vector drawings.

	Prob	Base	1	2	3	4	5
1	1.0E+0	1.0E+0					
2	0.0E+0	5.0E-1	2*B1				
3	0.0E+0			B1			
4	0.0E+0		B2	B2			
5	P3+P4				fails	fails	
6							
7							
8							
9							
10							

Figure 19.21 Table before Simulation in Formula Display Mode.

Next, we invoke the **Simulation Control** view. If after CARMS checks that initial conditions are satisfied and no conflicts are observed with the diagram, the simulation can be started by clicking the **Go** command. As a demo, we input a time of three years (the scale can be changed through the **Labels** commands). The result of the simulation is shown in Figure 19.22 for state 1 (decreasing values) and state 5 (increasing values).

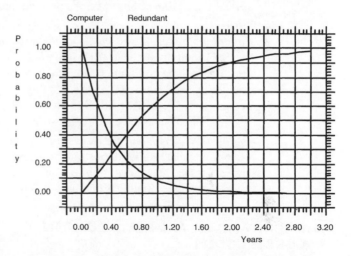

Figure 19.22 Simulation Display.

After finishing the simulation, we return to the **Transition Table**, which is updated as shown in Figure 19.23. The **Value** display is on.

	Prob	Base	1	2	3	4	5
1	5.5E-4	1.0E+0					
2	2.1E-2	5.0E-1	2.0E+0				
3	5.2E-1			1.0E+0			
4	4.6E-1		5.0E-1	5.0E-1			
5	9.8E-1				fails	fails	
6							
7							
8							
9							
10							

Figure 19.23 Table after Simulation in Value Display Mode.

The "Prob" column and the time values are the only visible modifications to the table. By using the command **Back** or **Data Reset**, probability and time values from the previous simulation can be reloaded.

19.5 ALGORITHM SELECTION

Two numerical solution algorithms are provided with the CARMS package. As with any numerical solution, accuracy and precision are dependent on the specific problem being addressed. Certain algorithms may be best suited to a range of problems. Markov modeling is no exception to this rule. As an example, we give two classes of reliability and maintainability problems and the "best" solution algorithm for each. "Best" here implies a qualitative measure of the fastest, most accurate and precise, and most stable solution for the problem at hand. The general guidelines are:

Reliability evaluation with transition rates restricted to a limited range of values. Runge-Kutta (RK) is the "best" method of solution for this class of problems, for numerical integration stability is not a problem and high accuracy can be obtained as a result.

Maintainability problems where failure rates are much smaller than repair rates. The Backwards-Difference (BD) integration method is a good choice for this problem, for the time constants for the failure versus the repair process are orders-of-magnitude apart. This can lead to stability problems or nonconvergence if the RK method is used. The BD method possesses higher stability in solving these so-called stiff problems, but at the expense of lower accuracy.

Nonlinear models featuring rates that depend on probabilities. There are no rules concerning what will work best in these cases, because of the wide range of possibilities for the transition formulas. For some applications the BD method may be faster. (Currently, nonlinear models don't work on this version.)

19.6 MARKOV MODEL AND STATE DIAGRAM CONSTRUCTION

The first step in the use of state diagrams is to determine the number of variables required to specify the system uniquely. This is identical to the number of degrees of freedom within the system, or, to put it another way, one for each distinct state of the system. However, there may not be a unique set of state variables for the system. The number in the set may depend on the degree of identification required in the final solution (how much the user wishes to view), so that extraneous states can be eliminated. For example, if we have a parallel system consisting of two elements, we may wish to identify these elements separately and assign different states to element **1** working in isolation or element **2** working in isolation. Otherwise, these can be combined if identical failure rates for the two elements are assumed.

The strongest requirement is that the states selected and the state equations derived be independent. Under certain conditions, there may be more state equations than degrees of freedom. In these cases, it should be possible to combine these equations in terms of linear combinations to obtain the independent set.

Once the general state diagram showing the transition failure rates has been established, the next step is to derive the state equations.

We let $P_0(t), \ldots P_N(t)$ denote the probability that the system is in state $S_0(t), \ldots$ $S_N(t)$ at time t. First consider the simplest system of only one element. The state diagram for this system is given by

$$S_0 \xrightarrow{\ \lambda\ } S_1$$

The probability $P_0(t+h)$ that the element is in state S_0 at $t + h$ is the probability that it was in state S_0 at time t and no change took place in the short time interval $(t, t+h)$. Thus

$$P_0(t+h) = P_0(t) [1 - \lambda h + o(h)] \tag{19.3}$$

Rewriting Eq. (19.3), we have

$$\frac{P_0(t+h) - P_0(t)}{h} = -\frac{\lambda h P_0(t)}{h} + \frac{o(h)}{h} \tag{19.4}$$

Taking the limit as $h \to 0$, we obtain

$$\lim_{h \to 0} \frac{P_0(t+h) - P_0(t)}{h} = \frac{d}{dt} P_0(t) = P'_0(t) \tag{19.5}$$

and

$$\lim_{h \to 0} \frac{o(h)}{h} = 0 \tag{19.6}$$

Then,

$$P'_0(t) = -\lambda P_0(t) \tag{19.7}$$

Correspondingly for state S_1, the probability that the element is in this state at time $(t+h)$ is the sum of the following probabilities:

1. The probability that the element is in state S_1 at time t.
2. The probability that the element is in state S_0 at time t and a change takes place during the time interval $(t, t+h)$.

Thus,

$$P_1(t + h) = P_1(t) + P_0(t) [\lambda h + o(h)] \tag{19.8}$$

Rewriting this equation as in the previous case and taking the limit as h approaches 0, we obtain

$$P'_1(t) = -\lambda P_0(t) \tag{19.9}$$

The two state equations derived above together with the initial conditions are called the state equations of the system. In our case, the equations are

$$P'_0(t) = -\lambda P_0(t) \qquad P_0(0) = 1$$

$$P'_1(t) = \lambda P_0(t) \qquad P_1(0) = 0 \tag{19.10}$$

For more complex systems a similar derivation will apply.

The basic rules guiding the construction of a state diagram are simple to apply. However, a good understanding of the system being considered is necessary. Specifically, the state diagram is constructed as follows:

1. Begin at the left with a state (circle) identified as S_1 (or as probability P_1). All equipment is initially good in this state.
2. Study the consequences of failing each element (any single-ended part, circuit, or channel defined as a single failure) in each of its failure modes. Group as a common consequence any that result in removing the same or equivalent circuitry from operation.
3. Assign new states (circles) and identify as S_2, S_3, S_4, and so on, for the unique consequences of step 2.
4. Connect arrows from S_1 to each of the new states, and note on each arrow the failure rate or rates of the element or elements whose failure determined transition to the new state.
5. Repeat steps 2, 3, and 4 for each of the new states failing only the elements still operational in that state. Continuously look out for cases where the failures may cause transition to one of the states formerly defined.
6. Continue the process until the initial equipment is totally unserviceable.

19.7 SPECIAL FUNCTIONS

CARMS has several advanced functions to allow it to interact with other programs. A dynamic link library (DLL found on the distribution disk) and dynamic data exchange (DDE) interface enable CARMS to act as a simulation server. Windows Ada expert system (WAES) uses this functionality to interact with CARMS.

The application programming interface (API) to CARMS is specified in the following listing. If you have a Windows-compatible programming environment and the need to link functionality of your own application to CARMS, these functions may prove useful. Ada language specifications are shown, but any DLL language can be adopted (Visual Basic, C), and so on. The CARMS DLL and two specification files for Ada and C are found in the DLL subdirectory on the distribution disk.

The function Link opens the link to the CARMS server. This must be invoked once before any transactions take place. The parameter Window is a window handle from the client application. If Link returns TRUE, an operational link results.

```
CARMS Application Programming Interface
-- Link current application to CARMS. --
function Link(Window: in HWND) return BOOLEAN;
-- Get the probability Value in the state numbered State. --
procedure Get_Prob(State: in INTEGER; Value: out FLOAT; Result: out BOOL-
                   EAN);
-- Run for simulation Time, resulting time returned in Final. --
procedure Run_Time(Time: in FLOAT; Final: out FLOAT; Result: out BOOLEAN);
```

```
-- Load CARMS file called Name. --
procedure Load_File(Name: in STRING);
-- Clears the current model from CARMS. --
procedure Clear_All;
-- Resets the simulation to new starting Time, Final acknowledges the
                    time. --
procedure Reset_Time(Time: in FLOAT; Final: out FLOAT; Result: out BOOL-
                    EAN);
-- Initializes the data to value before last simulation. --
procedure Init_Data;
-- Sets all probability values to zero. --
procedure Zero_Data;
-- Saves the current probability results to file Name. --
procedure Results(Name: in STRING);
-- Positions current cell pointer to base Row. --
procedure Pos_Base(Row: in INTEGER);
-- Positions current cell pointer to probability Row. --
procedure Pos_Prob(Row: in INTEGER);
-- Sets the Value at the current cell pointer. Row returns the cell set. -
        -
procedure Set_Value(Value: in FLOAT; Row: out INTEGER; Result: out BOOL-
                    EAN);
-- Recalculates all formula dependencies. --
procedure Recalc;
-- Write a string to the CARMS console. --
procedure Write(Text: in STRING);
-- Read the name of the current file loaded in CARMS. --
procedure Read(Text: out STRING; Result: out BOOLEAN);
-- Go to probability cell with name given by Text, the Row is returned. --
procedure Find_Prob(Text: in STRING; Row: out INTEGER; Result: out BOOL-
                    EAN);
-- Go to base cell with name given by Text, the Row is returned. --
procedure Find_Base(Text: in STRING; Row: out INTEGER; Result: out BOOL-
                    EAN);
-- Interpret data or formula given by Text at current cell pointer. --
procedure Interpret(Text: in STRING);
-- Position a transition arrow cell to destination row given by Row. --
procedure Pos_To(Row: in INTEGER);
-- Position a transition arrow cell to source column given by Col. --
procedure Pos_From(Col: in INTEGER);
-- Fills a state at cell Row with solid color (works on diagram) --
procedure Fill_Prob(Row: in INTEGER);
-- Tells CARMS to link to AES. --
procedure Link_AES;
-- Rearranges the states in the diagram on a row-by-row basis. --
procedure Pos_Model;
-- Calculates steady-state probabilities. --
procedure Steady_State;
```

20

CARMS Model Library

This chapter lists a representative set of Markov models that can be evaluated through CARMS. The sequence is to start with the simplest models and work through to more complicated system models near the end of the list. All state diagrams were imported directly from CARMS using the Windows clipboard, with the name of the CARMS Markov model file to the right.

The jeep example is from the first chapter. The goal is to determine the probability of reaching a destination after a certain number of miles, either with or without a spare tire. The two state diagrams in Figure 20.1 illustrate the two configurations. The ending states correspond to a stalled trip. The aliases Flat and SpareFlat are the failure rate for each tire in expected failures per mile. The aliases represent alternate names for the CARMS base rates B1 and B2.

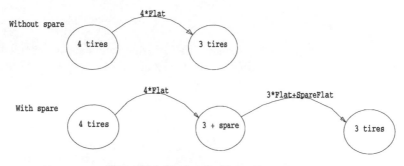

Figure 20.1 The Jeep Problem Jeep.mm.

20.1 SINGLE COMPONENTS

Single implies a nonredundantly configured component. If the component fails, and yet is necessary to continued operation, the system is considered to have failed until it is repaired.

Figure 20.2 is the single-element, single-thread model: the simplest model possible. P_1 is the good state, P_2 is the failed state, and B1 is the failure rate. (See 7.1.1.)

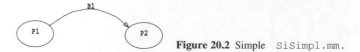

Figure 20.2 Simple SiSimpl.mm.

Figure 20.3 is the single-element, multiple-failure mode model. Two failure modes are given by intermediate states. Final state is a summing state of intermediate states, and "failure mode" indicates a virtual transition to the summing state. B1 and B2 are the failure rates for the two modes. (See 6.8.3.)

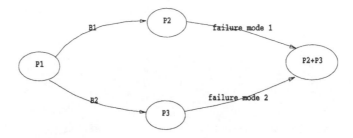

Figure 20.3 Multiple Failure Modes SiMFMode.mm.

The initial probabilities for the mixed population (see Figure 20.4) are specified for two populations. B1 and B2 are the failure rates for the two populations. (See 7.2.6.)

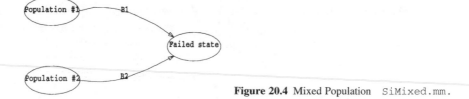

Figure 20.4 Mixed Population SiMixed.mm.

Figure 20.5 shows a system with an intermediate state in a degraded or marginal mode. B1 is the rate of entering the marginal state; B3 and B2 are the failure rates for the good and marginal modes, respectively. (See 7.1.3.)

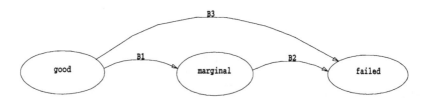

Figure 20.5 Degraded (Marginal) Mode SiDegr.mm.

Figure 20.6 presents an example of a system with simple maintenance. B1 and B2 are the failure rate and repair rate, respectively. (See 11.7.)

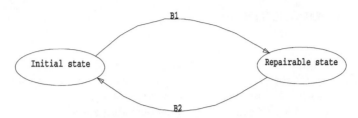

Figure 20.6 Simple Repair `SiRep.mm`.

The model shown in Figure 20.7 is an example of repairable and unrepairable failure modes. `B2` and `B1` are the failure rate and repair rate, respectively. `B3` is the failure rate to the unrepairable state.

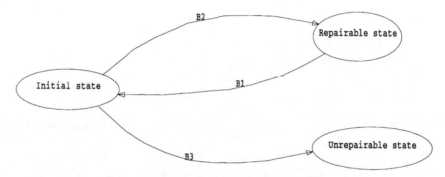

Figure 20.7 Repairable/Nonrepairable `SiRNR.mm`.

The model shown in Figure 20.8 is an example of a fault/error handling model (FEHM) with incomplete coverage and several classes of faults and errors. Initially, no faults or errors occur. `B1` is the benign fault/error rate. `B2` is the benign recovery rate. (A benign fault recovers to a stable state, and a benign error recovers to an active error.) `B3` is the active error production rate. `B4` is the error propagation rate. The `coverage` or `B5` is the proportion of errors that can be recovered from (i.e., the error detectability). `B6` is the fault detection rate.

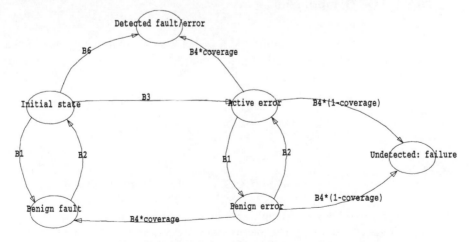

Figure 20.8 Fault/error Handling Model `SiFEHM.mm`.

20.2 SERIAL COMPONENTS

This section illustrates how to treat serial components. In general, if components are connected in series they are deemed to be necessary. Thereafter, if failures from any one of these components occur, then the system has failed.

Figure 20.9 is an example of adding the failure rates (B1 and B2) of two serially connected components. This is a generalization of the single-component example.

Figure 20.9 Two Series Components
Ser2.mm.

Figure 20.10 is an example of a system with *N* identical parts. Any part failing will fail the system. B1 is the failure rate.

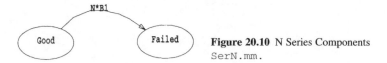

Figure 20.10 N Series Components
SerN.mm.

20.3 PARALLEL COMPONENTS

Initially, a parallel redundant system has all of its components active and operational. A failure in one of these components reduces the number of active components by one. A failed state is entered when the number drops below a certain threshold.

20.3.1 Two Components

Figure 20.11 is an example of a two-component parallel-operation state diagram. Each component has an identical failure rate, B1. P_1 is both active, P_2 is one active, and P_3 is the failed state. (See 7.1.4.)

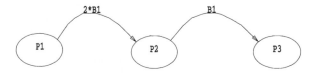

Figure 20.11 Same Failure Rates   Pa2Simpl.mm.

Figure 20.12 is an example state diagram of two parallel components with different failure rates (B1 and B2). The intermediate state Mode 1 is entered if the first component fails and Mode 2 if the other component fails.

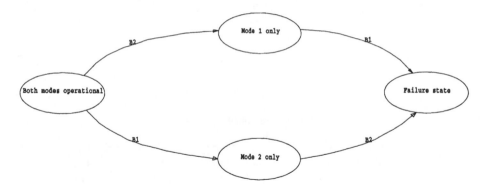

Figure 20.12 Different Failure Rates   `Pa2Diff.mm`.

The model shown in Figure 20.13 is an example of a two-element parallel load-sharing system. Each element carries half the load. Under half-load conditions, the failure rate is one-quarter the normal rate of `B1`. (See 7.2.5.)

Figure 20.13 Load-sharing   `Pa2LS.mm`.

Figure 20.14 is an example of a parallel redundant configuration with repair. Primary is repaired while spare is in operation. Two repairmen are available. `B1` and `B2` are the failure rate and repair rate, respectively. (See 11.7.)

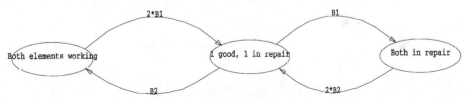

Figure 20.14 Repair with Two Repairmen   `Pa2Rep2.mm`.

Figure 20.15 is nearly the same as the previous model, but only one repairman is available. (See 11.7.)

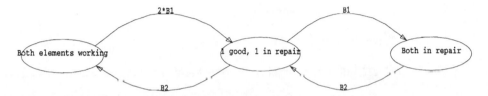

Figure 20.15 Repair with One Repairman   `Pa2Rep1.mm`.

Figure 20.16 is again similar to the previous model, but one element is needed for operation. If the extra element fails, the system is considered failed. (See 11.7.)

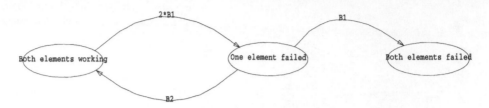

Figure 20.16 Repair (One Component Needed for Operation) `Pa2Reps.mm`.

Figure 20.17 is an example of two-stage repair, with at least one element needed for operation. Primary is repaired while spare is in operation. `B1` and `B2` are the failure rate and repair rate, respectively. `B3` is the debugging or fault-isolation rate. (See 11.7.)

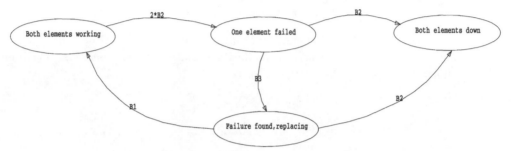

Figure 20.17 Two-Stage Repair `Pa2R2St.mm`.

Figure 20.18 is an example of a parallel model with incomplete coverage. `B1` is the failure rate of a component. A fraction (`1-coverage`) of the failures can lead to an unsafe mode. Note that as `coverage` goes to 1.0, the model becomes a pure parallel configuration.

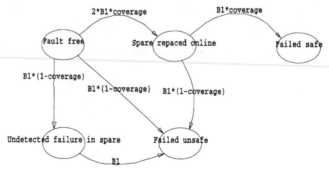

Figure 20.18 Coverage Model `Pa2RCov.mm`.

20.3.2 Three Components

Figure 20.19 is an example of a triple parallel redundant system. (See 11.7.)

Figure 20.19 Parallel `Pa3.mm`.

Figure 20.20 is an example of a triple parallel system with a recovery process. υ denotes the recovery rate (recoveries/hour) and λ is the failure rate. States P_2 and P_5 are the recovery-mode states. If another failure occurs while the subsystem is in the recovery state, then the system is assumed to fail (the conservative approach) [Butler 92]. These transitions will be to states P_3 and P_6.

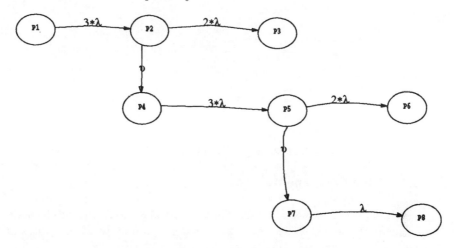

Figure 20.20 SURE Model `Pa3SURE.mm`.

Figure 20.21 is an example of a three-element parallel system with degraded nodes. `B1` and `B2` are the degradation rate and failure rate, respectively.

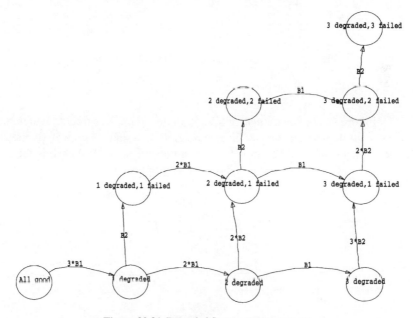

Figure 20.21 Degraded States `Pa3Degr.mm`.

Figure 20.22 is a three-element Markov model. Each element has its own failure rate and repair rate.

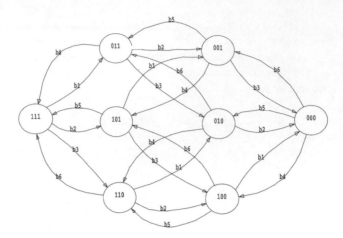

Figure 20.22 Repair (Unequal Failure and Maintenance) `Pa3FR.mm`.

20.3.3 Nine Components

Figure 20.23 is a generalization of the *N*-parallel model to nine elements. This is part of a memory module model where we would like to find the average amount of memory available as a function of time.

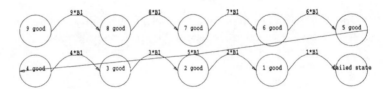

Figure 20.23 Memory Model `Pa9Mem.mm`.

20.3.4 Special

Figure 20.24 is a model for a three-dimensional hypercube, which is a parallel processing configuration with eight nodes. A failed state occurs if diametrically opposed nodes fail. From the diagram below, assuming **a** is a node, then **b** is the near-neighbor, **c** is the second neighbor, and **d** is diametrically opposed.

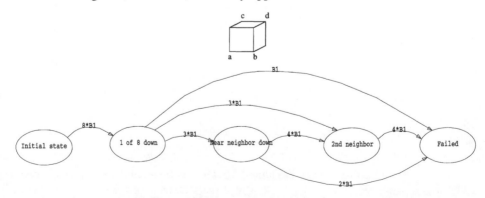

Figure 20.24 3-D Hypercube `Pa3Cube.mm`.

20.4 MAJORITY VOTERS

In general, majority voters need a minimum number of operational components to continue operation. This is due to a majority of votes needed to switch in valid components.

The model presented in Figure 20.25 is a classical majority voting system. At least two operational elements are needed to vote; otherwise the system fails. B1 is the failure rate. The classical voter is more reliable at short times but is more prone to fail at long times. (See 7.1.5.)

Figure 20.25 Triplex-Duplex `MV32.mm`.

Shown in Figure 20.26 is an alternative majority voting system. There are at least two elements operational to vote on, but the system is reduced to one element after the first failure. This is more reliable for long missions. (See 7.1.5.)

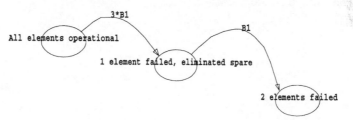

Figure 20.26 Triplex-Simplex `MV31.mm`.

Figure 20.27 is a majority voter where the spare switches in after the first failure. (See 7.2.3.)

Figure 20.27 Triplex-Simplex with Spare `MV31Sp.mm`.

20.5 STANDBY

Standby systems are characterized by spare components that stay inactive until they are needed. In general, this increases the lifetime over that of a continuously operating component.

20.5.1 Two Components

Figure 20.28 is a redundant system model featuring a component under standby operation mode. We assume no failure of standby when in storage (not operational) mode. B1 and B2 are the failure rates of the primary and standby components, respectively. See Section 7.2 for B1=B2.

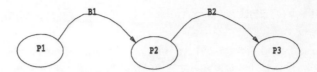

Figure 20.28 Same Failure Rates, Zero Standby Failure Rate   St2.mm.

Figure 20.29 is a model of a single spare replacement capability with a finite switching rate. This model includes a failure rate, B1, and a component switching rate, B2. (See 11.7.)

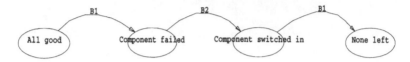

Figure 20.29 Switch Rate   St2Sw1.mm.

Figure 20.30 is a model of a component with a standby, where the nonoperating (storage) element can fail. Primary and standby have the same operational failure rates, B1. The storage failure rate is B2.

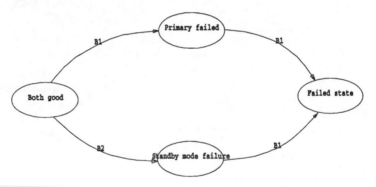

Figure 20.30 Finite Storage (Standby) Failure Rate   St2Stor.mm.

Figure 20.31 shows a standby system, where the switch can fail in two modes. B1 is the failure rate of the component; B2 and B3 are the switch failure rate and the false switching rate, respectively. Primary and standby have the same operational failure rates.

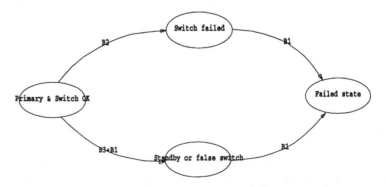

Figure 20.31 Switch Failure Having Two Modes   St2Sw2.mm.

Figure 20.32 presents an example of a standby configuration that includes the effects on the system reliability of the failure detector (monitor), switch, and a non–zero standby failure rate. The detector and switch combination will fail in one of two modes: (1) In a state where the failure detection ability is disabled, and (2) in a state where false switching to the next element in sequence will occur. B1 is the operational failure rate, B2 is the monitor failure rate, B3 is the false switching rate, and B4 is the failure rate in standby condition.

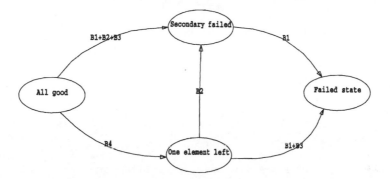

Figure 20.32 Monitor and Standby Failure Rate St2MoSt.mm.

Figure 20.33 depicts a single standby system with a failure monitor that has the potential of failing in a safe or unsafe mode. The monitor will automatically switch the system to a safe mode if it detects an unsafe failure unless it fails itself. B1 is the safe failure rate, B2 is the unsafe failure rate, B3 is the false switching rate of the monitor, and B4 is the failure rate of the monitor.

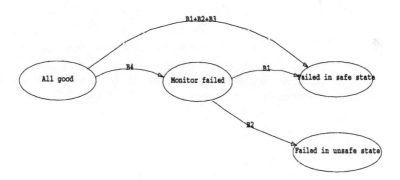

Figure 20.33 Safe/Unsafe Failure Modes St2SNS.mm.

Figure 20.34 models a system with a single standby with a monitor present. The monitor can fail in two ways, false switch and stuck. The rates are as follows: 1B is the backup failure rate; 1A is the primary failure rate; 1AN is the primary failure not detected; 1AD is the primary failure detected; 1MA is the monitor can not switch; 1MB is the false monitor switch; and 1BST is the standby failure rate. A simplified system model with coverage is also included.

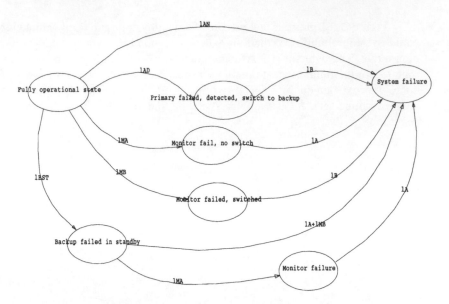

Figure 20.34 Multiple Monitor Failure Modes `St2MMF.mm`.

20.5.2 Three Components

Figure 20.35 models a component with two standby units. The standby units can fail while not in use. B1 is the operating failure rate, and B2 is the storage (standby) failure rate. (See 7.2.1.)

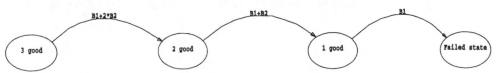

Figure 20.35 Nonzero Standby Failure Rate `St3NZ.mm`.

This model of two standby units in Figure 20.36 illustrates a finite switching rate and includes a failure rate, B1, and a component switching rate, B2. (See 11.7.)

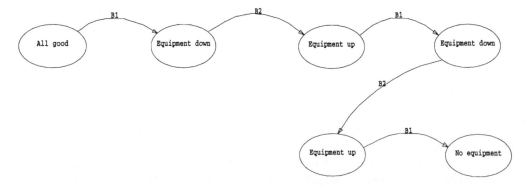

Figure 20.36 Switch Rate `St3Sw.mm`.

Figure 20.37 presents a model consisting of one active operational element with an attached monitor and two standby units. The first standby also contains a monitor, while the second standby is the last stage, without the monitor. B1 is the failure rate, B2 is the monitor failure rate, and B3 is the false switching rate.

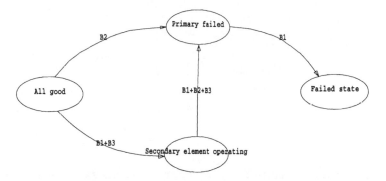

Figure 20.37 Monitor Failure Rate   St3Mon.mm.

20.6 SUBSYSTEM ASSEMBLIES

Figure 20.38 is an example of a dual parallel gyro failure model. B1 is the gyro failure rate, B2 is the monitor disable rate, and B3 is the false switch rate. When the monitor fails, the two gyros still operate at full gain, but when the primary fails, the monitor cannot adjust the gain, so that the remaining gyro runs at half gain.

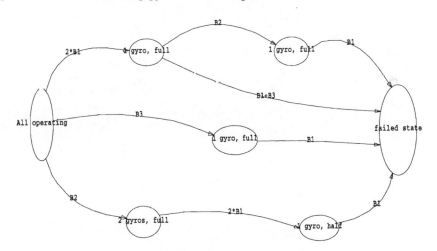

Figure 20.38 Gyro   SaGyro.mm.

Figure 20.39 is a model of a fault-tolerant diode configuration. A single diode or rectifier may not meet the reliability needs of an application. A simple trick is to arrange the diodes in a quad configuration that adds a form of parallel redundancy to the circuit and thus can improve the redundancy. The two possible failure modes for a diode are to short circuit or to open circuit. Failure rates for the two modes (assuming identical diodes) are

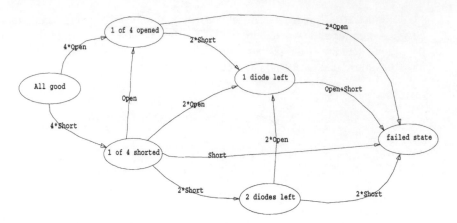

Figure 20.39 Quad Diode 1 `SaDiode1.mm`.

given by the base names `Open` and `Short`. Assuming all possibilities of failure modes, the state diagram above can be derived.

Figure 20.40 is an alternative quad diode configuration. This one is more robust in case of a greater prevalence of open-circuit failure modes, whereas the previous configuration is better equipped to handle more frequent short circuits.

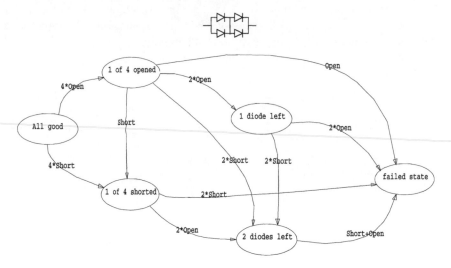

Figure 20.40 Quad Diode 2 `SaDiode2.mm`.

Figure 20.41 presents a Markov model for a capsule separation register independent assembly from the NASA Voyager project design [Hargrave 67]. The terms MV, RC, and B3 represent failure rates for a majority voter, a redundant component (simplex-duplex with spare), and a single-thread component. The entire Voyager system was designed in the 1960s and at last report is still sending messages as it moves out of our solar system. Even though the system models consisted of thousands of states, proper partitioning allowed a successful analysis.

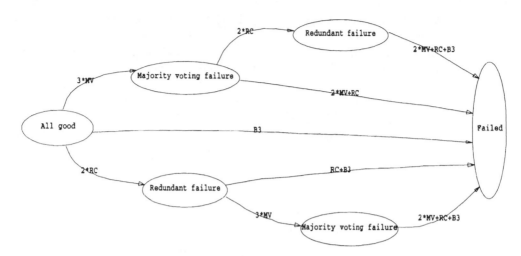

Figure 20.41 Voyager Assembly `SaVoyag.mm`.

Figure 20.42 models a subsystem of a gyro.

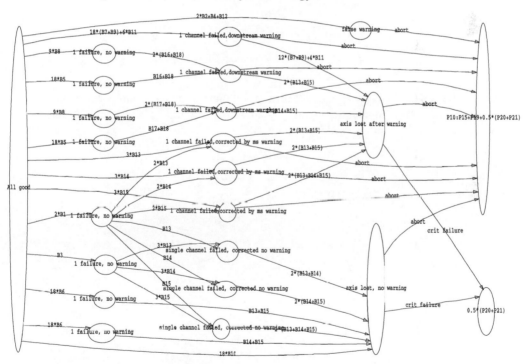

Figure 20.42 Pitch Subsystem `SaPitch.mm`.

20.7 SYSTEMS

Figure 20.43 is a model for the reliability prediction of a multicomponent system. Three subsystems of parallel components are arranged to demonstrate how algebra simplifies the analysis. The three rows consist of dual-redundant components. These groups are independent of each other. A failure occurs if any one of these groups fails to provide at least one operational component. The reliability of the system is given by the multiplication of the reliabilities of the individual groups. The system failure probability is the complement of the reliability. Initially, the first column has probability 1.0.

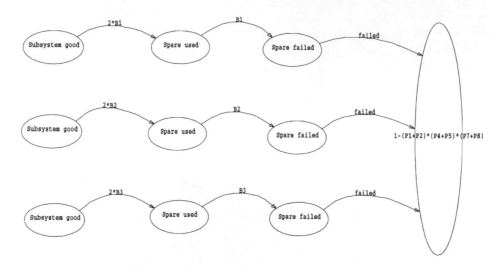

Figure 20.43 3 by 2 Parallel Configuration `Sy3x2.mm`.

Figure 20.44 presents a model for fault-tolerant computer reliability prediction. The computer has a backup, but the memory is nonredundant and so has a single point of failure. This same example is used in Chapter 18.

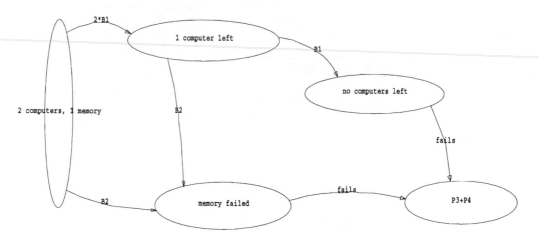

Figure 20.44 Two Computers, One Memory Block `Sy2C1M.mm`.

Figure 20.45 models part of the NASA advanced information processing system (AIPS) I/O network. This example was derived from [Reibman 91].

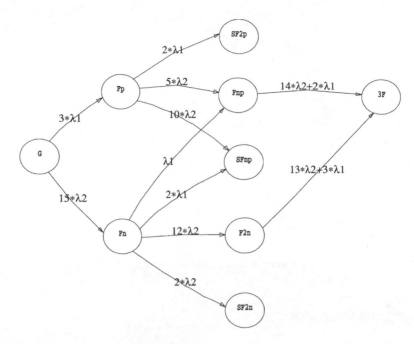

Figure 20.45 AIPS `SyAIPS.mm`.

Figure 20.46 presents a model of a fiber distributed data interface (FDDI) dual-ring, two-concentrator network. The diagram was derived from [Shooman 91].

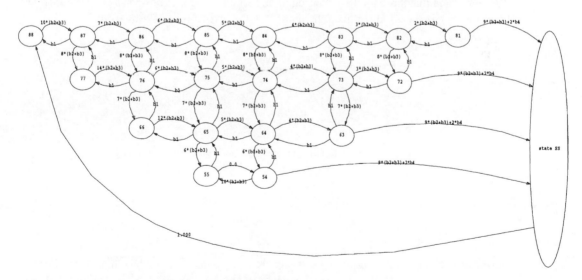

Figure 20.46 FDDI `SyFDDI.mm`.

Figure 20.47 is a model for a combined hardware and software system.

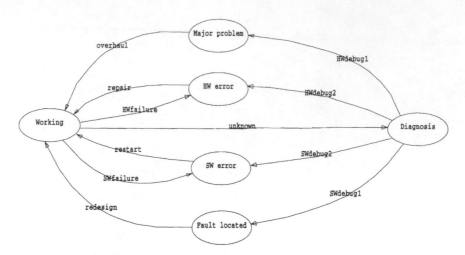

Figure 20.47 Software/Hardware Model   SySoft.mm.

20.8 PERFORMANCE MODELS

Performance or queueing models can be handled by CARMS if the arrival and service rates are exponentially distributed.

   Figure 20.48 represents a queueing model. The system has three jobs and one CPU and two I/O devices available for servicing and throughput, respectively. The marking 3 , 0 indicates that three jobs are waiting to be serviced and that none has been completed. Base rate b1 is the CPU service rate, and b2 is the arrival rate of jobs from I/O.

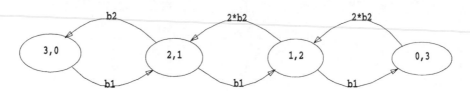

Figure 20.48 CPU-I/O Queueing Model   PerCPUIO.mm.

20.9 CHAIN MODELS

A Markov chain model requires outgoing transitions to sum to less than one (Figure 20.49). Fig. 20.49 depicts how a typical Markov chain is constructed. This diagram does not model any real design, but shows that each set of outgoing transition probabilities obeys the sum rule.

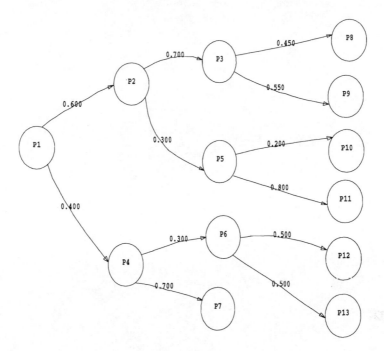

Figure 20.49 Chaining Model `chain.mm`.

21

CARMS Reference

21.1 KEYBOARD AND MOUSE

The following shortcut keys apply:

Function	Normal	Alt
F1	Help system	Clear all data
F2	Edit cell	Save file
F3	Edit name	Load file
F4	Go to Simulation Control	Exit
F5	Reset Probs to zero	Show Probs
F6	Reset time to zero	Show Bases
F7	Go to Diagram Draw	Go to Main Menu
F8	Go to Transition Table	Run Batch
F9	Load old data	Recalc
F10	View conflicts	Validity check

Mouse motion is duplicated by left, right, up, and down cursor keys. The left button key is equivalent to *<Enter>*. To drag, hold the *<Enter>* key or space bar while positioning the cursor. Use *<PageUp>* and *<PageDown>* to scroll the screen up and down. Use *<Tab>* and *<Backspace>* to scroll the screen left and right.

All dialog buttons can be accessed by pressing the key associated with the button. For example, when drawing states, the **State** mode can be entered by pressing 's'.

21.2 COMMANDS

Commands available through CARMS can be accessed by keys, menu selection, or dialog button presses.

The major groupings are:

File	File manipulation
View	Model building/solution
Options	Global commands and settings
Report	Utilities

Main Menu	Diagram Draw	Transiton Table	Simulation Control
File	*File*	*File*	*File*
New	Export	Export	Export
Open	Print	Print	Save Results
Save	Preferences	Exit	Save Graph
Save As	Exit		Print
Save Results		*Commands*	Exit
Recall	*Commands*	Edit Cell	
Link Expert	State	Edit name	*Commands*
Edit Rulebase	Arrow	Recalc	Go
Exit	Erase	List Probs	Update
	Move	List Bases	Back
View	Zoom	List Heads	Pick
Diagram	Copy	List Tails	Mask
Table	Name		Halt
Simulation	Data	*Settings*	
Names	Info	Autocalc	*Settings*
Probs	Draw	Formula	Delta
Bases	Recalc	Set Column	Accuracy
			Solution
Options			RK BD
Time Reset	*Settings*		Step
Data Zero	Scale		Chain
Data Reset	Text Font		Cycles
Labels	Formula Font		Intervals
Title	Formula		Tasking
X,Y-axis	Value		
Run Batch	Text		
Matrix Invert			
Save Config			
Report			
Conflicts			
Validity			
List Cells			
Help			
About			

21.3 FILE

The menu commands for file handling include:

New

Clears the CARMS workspace. Erases all *Transition Table/Diagram Draw* objects.

related: *Erase, Data Zero*

Open

Opens a CARMS file.   Loads state diagram data from disk file via the database loader or the Expert System. Initially, the last used (or default) path is shown. The user can then choose the files from the window by moving the cursor and pressing *<Enter>*. Wild-card symbols such as '*' or '?' will select the matching files. If the CARMS file is not a valid one, an error message will appear. File names can have any extension such as ".db" and ".pro".

To use the Expert System as a front end, it must be manually invoked first via the *Link Expert* menu command. During database loading, the expert system may prompt for data. After the expert system is finished loading, it will stay in the background unless it is deliberately closed by invoking the *Link Expert* command once again.

To change working directories, use the File|Properties command from the Windows Program Manager menu.

related: *Save, Link Expert, Recall*

Save As

Saves CARMS state diagram data to another named disk file.

related: *Open, Export, Save As, Save Results, Save*

Save

Saves CARMS state diagram data to the previously named disk file. The saved file is text and is accessible by Prolog-style interpreters. Use the *Save* command before a simulation is attempted, for the simulation time and "Prob" values are saved according to the last simulation run. As an alternative, use Save Results to store intermediate results.

related: *Open, Export, Save As, Save Results, Save Config*

Save Results

Saves the "Prob" column of values and simulation time to a disk file.

related: *Save*

Recall

Recalls the last file opened or saved.

related: *Open*

Edit Rulebase

Invokes a text editor. To change the default editor, modify the `DAINA.INI` file by changing "`Editor=Notepad.exe`" to "`Editor=(favorite text editor)`".

Link Expert

Starts and creates a DDE link to the expert system. If the expert system is running, this command will terminate its execution. The path for the expert system is located in the `DAINA.INI` file under:

```
[WAES]

Path=C:\CARMS
```

Exit

Exits CARMS to Windows permanently if in *Main Menu*, otherwise exits the current dialog window (via the button labeled "Exit" or "-").

21.4 OPTIONS

Global settings include:

Time Reset

Resets the elapsed time of the simulation to zero. The simulation time indicates the running time after the last simulation.

related: **Data Zero, Data Reset, Back**

Data Zero

Resets the "Prob" column to zeros. The values set to zero are only those that have been entered as numerals. Formulas or text strings are not affected.

related: **Time Reset, Back**

Data Reset

Loads the "Prob" values assigned to the state diagram before the simulator was last accessed. This also reloads the old simulation time. If values previous to the last simulation are desired, reload the data through **Open**. In **Simulation Control** mode, this command is the same as **Back**.

related: **Open, Data Zero, Back**

Labels

System title and x-y axis

Title	The title and configuration labels identify the state diagram.
Y-axis	Change the Y-axis scaling units. Default Y-scale is "Probability."
X-axis	Change time scale units for the **Simulation Control**. Default value is in seconds.

Methods

Use the CARMS expert system to run sensitivity analysis or to model transformations.

Run Batch

Run the simulation without invoking the graphics. From the Windows command line this would be:

> "CARMS input.ext time output.ext"

where

input.ext	Name of input CARMS file (a '+' in front starts the ES)
time	Simulation time
output.ext	Name of results file

related: **Go**

Matrix Invert

Calculates the steady-state values for the state diagram. This corresponds to infinite time. The results are valid only if a closed system (with feedback and no trapping states) is chosen.

related: **Simulation, Go**

Save Config

Saves simulation cycles, graph intervals, solution method, and other parameters to a generic text-based configuration file.

21.5 REPORT

Utilities for generating CARMS reports include:

Conflicts

Shows any conflicts or inconsistencies that may arise between the values entered in the **Transition Table** and the states and transitions displayed in the **Diagram Draw** view.

The **Conflicts** command is supplied because the **Transition Table** does not provide graphical positioning for states. (These will not appear on the **Diagram Draw** view if entered from the table.) It is intended to aid in data input and model building.

related: **Diagram, Table**

Validity

Checks that data are sufficient to run simulation. If data are not valid, the current invalid transitions are displayed on screen in a shorthand notation and the number of invalid states and arrows is counted. Possible error modes are listed as:

Improper termination of transition arrow. Either the transition arrow arrives at an uninitialized state or it is propagated from an uninitialized state.

Values in the transition table are too large for the simulator to work properly.

Negative values exist in the transition table.

related: **Simulation, Conflicts**

List Cells

Lists states, bases, and transitions.

Brief. Displays the current valid transitions on screen in a shorthand notation and counts the number of states and arrows.

Detailed. Transfers current transition table data and names to a disk file or to the printer in an outline format. Pop-up window lets the user choose the data fields to transfer. The option "Compact" stores the report in a compact format by eliminating certain line feeds. The following example shows typical output with all the options loaded.

EXAMPLE

```
LISTING OF PROB TERMS
P1 Initial state 1.00000000000000E+00
P2 Final state 0.00000000000000E+00

LISTING OF BASE TERMS
B1 Failure Rate 1.00000000000000E+00

LISTING OF TRANSITION TERMS
P1 to P2 From: Initial state To: Final state B1
```

```
0.00000000000000E+00
Time = 0.0E+0 Seconds
```

related: *Validity*

21.6 VIEW

Selects from the CARMS window to view. See *Diagram, Table, Simulation,* and *Names* sections for specific commands. Universal commands include:

Export

Exports a Windows Metafile to the Windows Clipboard for use by another drawing, CAD, or other Windows program. The exported drawing will be of the present *View*.

Print

Prints the *Transition Table, Diagram Draw,* or *Simulation Control* graph to a file or to the default printer. To change the default printer to another port, see the Windows user's manual.

21.7 DIAGRAM DRAW OR DIAGRAM

Goes to the state diagram (*Diagram Draw* view) for model building or data input. *Diagram Draw* uses mouse and keyboard input to graphically construct a state diagram. Keyboard translation for all mouse commands is available. States constructed via the *Transition Table* view (but not placed) are shown in the upper left corner.

Zoom

Toggles the zoom in and out. Default setting is zoom in. Toggling the zoom will always left justify and top justify the diagram. To move the diagram around the viewing screen, use the scroll bars.

related: *Scale*

State

Changes to state creation mode. A state is created by dragging and releasing the mouse to the desired size and then labeling with a state number. To *Name* and enter *Data* into the state, the respective modes must be invoked.

To form a state: Click on the control button labeled **State**. Position the cursor at the desired center point, press the left mouse button (or *<Enter>*) to anchor the state, and drag until a circle appears. The size of the state will be set when the mouse button is released. A dialog box will then appear that prompts for the state label number. The state numbers typically are entered in ascending order. Press the escape button at any time to abort the command. The default name of the state (a "P" followed by the state number) or the default value (0.0) will appear if a name, formula, or value has not been previously entered into the state. Press the **Draw** control button to refresh the screen.

The left button also acts as a quick probe to the name of a state or to the source and destination of a transition arrow if it is clicked once without dragging.

See also the keyboard equivalent section.

related: ***Arrow, Copy***

Arrow

Changes to transition creation mode. A transition arrow is created by dragging and releasing the mouse from the source or "tail" state to the desired midpoint, and then clicking on the destination or "head" state. To enter data into the transition, the **Data** mode must be invoked.

To draw a transition arrow: Click the **Arrow** button. Position the cursor on an originating (from) state, click the left button to set the tail of the arrow, and start dragging the mouse. Next, position the cursor at a suitable midpoint and release the button. To set the arrowhead position, reposition and click the mouse button again on a terminating (to) state (arrow is drawn). The connecting states and a default value of 0.0 will appear at the midpoint. Pressing escape or drawing to a nonexistent state will cancel the transition.

See also the keyboard equivalent section.

related: ***State, Copy***

Copy

Copies a state, transition, or region. If the mouse is dragged on a state, only that state is copied. If the mouse is dragged to enclose a region, then all states and arrows within the enclosed region are copied.

related: ***Move***

Move

Moves the anchor position of a state or arrow to another screen coordinate. If a state is to be moved, the mouse depress probes the position to determine if a state exists there. As the mouse is dragged, the state and any connected transition arrows are moved along with it. If an arrow is to be moved, the mouse press must be in the vicinity of the arrow midpoint. In this case, however, connected states are not moved.

Blocking a region will move everything within the enclosing box.

related: *Copy*

Info

Probes the contents of a state or transition arrow. Clicking will probe the location of the current cursor position. If either a state or midpoint of a transition arrow is located in the vicinity, the contents of that cell will be displayed in the message bars.

related: *Name*

Scale

Changes the scale of the state diagram. The scale number must be between 1 and 4 (default=1 is greatest magnification).

related: *Zoom*

Data

Inputs data, formula, or text into a labeled state or transition arrow. This information is then automatically transmitted to the *Transition Table*. The data are allocated to the cell pointing to the state label for a state, or to the transition cell for a transition arrow, respectively.

related: *Name, Conflicts*

Erase

Clears states or transition arrows, depending on where the cursor is located. The first *<Enter>* command will probe the state or arrow at the cursor location, and if something is found in its vicinity, a second *<Enter>* command is necessary to verify. Note that if a state is cleared, the transition arrows accompanying that state are not erased. Entering the state again will gather up the unconnected and hanging arrows.

related: *New*

Name

Designates a name for a given state. A name for a state is limited to 100 characters. To find whether a name has been assigned to a state, click on a state or arrow. If a name has been assigned to the state or "To" → "From" locations, it will appear in the message box.

related: *Info*

Draw

Updates and redraws the current state diagram, and clears any drawing fragments. To speed the data entry process, the screen is not refreshed during *Data* and *Name* entries. For another way to redraw the screen, double click on a blank area of the window.

related: *Recalc*

Value

Displays the value contents of states and transition arrows on the screen.

related: *Formula, Text*

Formula

Toggles the formula display.

On the *Transition Table*, if the *Formula* flag is on, all cell values are replaced with their formula counterparts.

On the *Diagram Draw* window, the formula contents of states and transition arrows will be displayed.

related: *Value, Text*

Preferences

Shows the default display configuration for the *Diagram Draw* view.

Length. Truncates the text to display on the diagram to a maximum number of characters.

Arrow Size. Changes the size of arrowheads in the state diagram.

Arrow Dash. Changes the ASCII-represented connecting character between states (for example, 1-2 to 1>2).

related: **Fonts**

Fonts

Text: Changes the fonts for the state contents.
Formula: Changes the fonts for transition contents.

related: **Preferences**

Step

Steps through a Petri net.

21.8 TRANSITION TABLE OR TABLE

Goes to the **Transition Table**, which is the spreadsheet-like data input tool. The tabular state diagram is arranged according to a source-to-destination defined grid. Diagrams that are constructed with the **Diagram Draw** tool are automatically represented in the table. This is less true in the other direction, as the graphics positioning is not done by the table.

Recalc

Recalculates the transition table by updating formulas. The order of calculation is column by row, starting with the "Prob" column and working downward and right. For this reason, it is important that all of the parameters in a formula have been arranged in the right sequence. Formulas constructed of other defined formulas are disallowed.

related: **Autocalc**

Set Col

Fixes the "Prob" and "Base" columns in place so they will not move during horizontal table scrolling.

Autocalc

Automatically updates formula dependencies in the **Transition Table** when entering data.

related: **Recalc**

Edit Cell

Edits the contents of the cell at the cursor location. Press *<Esc>* to escape from an edit without making changes.

related: **Data, Edit Name**

List Heads

Lists the destination transition arrows for a particular "Prob" state. Alternatively, one can click on the button corresponding to a row identifier.

related: **List Tails**

List Tails

Lists the source transition arrows for a particular "Prob" state. Alternatively, one can click on the button corresponding to a column identifier.

related: **List Heads**

List Bases

Displays the "Base" states in the **Transition Table** state list box. Alternatively, one can click on the button labeled "Base."

related: **List Probs**

List Probs

Displays the "Prob" states in the **Transition Table** state list box. Alternatively, one can click on the button labeled "Prob."

related: **List Bases**

Edit Name

Edits the name of the cell at the cursor location. Press *<Esc>* to escape from edit without making changes. Only cells corresponding to "Prob" or "Base" columns can be edited.

related: **Data, Edit Cell**

21.9 SIMULATION CONTROL OR SIMULATION

Simulation Control interactively displays the results of a CARMS evaluation. Commands are available to control or view the time-dependent simulation. If invalid data are entered or are incorrectly set up through the **Diagram Draw, Transition Table,** or File **Open,** then error messages are displayed (see **Validity** in Section 21.5). Pressing **Go** starts the simulation by displaying a time prompt. The simulation may be stopped by pressing **Halt** during the calculation. Simulation parameters can be changed through the **Settings** submenu.

see also: **Data Reset, Run Batch**

Go

Starts the simulation with the entered simulation time. When toggling between **Transition Table** and **Simulation Control,** the results of the previous simulation will always be displayed. If the data are changed and invalid parameters are entered, error messages will be displayed in the **Main Menu**.

related: **Back, Time Reset**

Back

Resets the total time and "Prob" values to the values from the previous simulation run. For example, when toggling between **Transition Table** and **Simulation Control,** the results of the last simulation will always be displayed. If there is any doubt as to whether the displayed graph is up-to-date with the most recent simulation **Pick** values, use the **Update** command.

related: **Simulation, Go**

Mask

Toggles the display mask on and off. Initially the display mask is off, which allows all the "Prob" plots to be displayed. Toggling the mask on only allows the "Prob" value at the top of the list box to be displayed. Use this command with **Pick** to quickly change the graphs displayed or sent to a file.

related: **Pick**

Pick

Allows the user to display selected "Prob" graphs from the list box. To toggle graphs on and off, double click at the cursor location and click on **Update.**

related: **Mask**

Update

Redraws the display with the last simulation values. This is typically used after **Pick** or **Mask.**

related: **Go**

Halt

Stops the simulation before completion. The **Tasking** setting must be checked on for this to have any effect.

related: **Go**

Accuracy

Changes the relative accuracy of the simulation. Greater numbers (larger tolerance) give lower accuracy but result in faster calculation rates. Accuracy selection is enabled only if the adaptive quality control mode (Delta=0.0) is chosen.

related: **Delta**

Cycles

Controls the maximum number of iterations in the simulation run. This command is included to provide a time-out limit during the simulation process. Typically, a value of 100,000 (default value) will be enough for the majority of simulations. However, if the simulation is exploratory, cutting this number down will limit the total calculation time to gain a faster response. Setting **Cycles** to zero will cause the simulation to be free-running. Cycle values should be numbers between 0 and 10^9. Accuracy is not affected by the choice, but resulting simulation times may not match the expected time if the cycle number is reached before the simulation is completed.

Delta

Allows the user to manually adjust the simulation integration increment. If a (default) delta of 0.0 is chosen, then the adaptive quality control mode is invoked. Otherwise, the accuracy of solution will be dependent on the delta time-step chosen.

related: **Accuracy**

Intervals

Changes the number of time intervals per simulation run. This affects both the display and saving the graph results to a file. The default value is 20, and the number can range between 1 and 60.

related: **Save Graph, Save Config**

Solution

Toggles the numerical integration solution method between the:

RK	Runge-Kutta algorithm.
BD	Backwards-difference algorithm.
Chain	Markov chain using discrete time step algorithm.

Tasking

Turns on the tasking mode so that CARMS will respond to keyboard commands and can be halted during the calculation. If the tasking mode is on, the running time will increase somewhat.

related: *Halt*

Save Graph

Saves the time-dependent simulation results to a space-delimited data file. The probability values saved to disk are identical to those states that have been picked for display during a simulation run. The data are organized by columns, with the first column giving the intermediate simulation time and the remaining columns listing the probability values for the row at that time.

related: *Save Results*

21.10 NAMES

Prob

Displays the "Prob" column names in a pop-up window (Alt-F5). The window can be moved and scrolled. The allocated names can be entered within the *Diagram Draw* or *Transition Table* views.

related: *Name, Edit Name*

Base

Displays the "Base" column names in a pop-up window (Alt-F6). The window can be moved and scrolled. The allocated names are entered through the *Transition Table* view.

related: *Edit Name*

21.11 MISCELLANEOUS

Help

Shows the Windows help screen. If an error message is shown when this command is invoked, the help file was not found in the same directory as the program. Follow the instructions to navigate to the CARMS.HLP file. Mode-sensitive help is available in the **Diagram Draw** view.

About

Shows the copyright notification and available memory in Windows.

21.12 DEFINITIONS

Arrowhead: The destination or head of the transition is designated by the arrowhead. The source or tail is designated by the curve's origin.

Contents: The text identifier shows the state name, formula, or value depending on the current display.

Expert System: The expert system acts as an auxiliary front end of CARMS. It reads the data file, interprets commands for model building, and transforms the data to a form suitable for CARMS. The expert system language is a subset of the Prolog language. To invoke the expert system by itself, run the file or click on the program icon labeled WAES.EXE. Commands for WAES include File Load, Interpret, and Clear.

Label: The state label gives the Prob state number, which is used in the arrow labeling and the Transition Table.

State: An oval signifies a probability state. The term S refers to the state itself, while the term P refers to the probability value. Therefore, in shorthand P_2 refers to the probability in state 2.

Transition: The midpoint of the transition arc displays the transition vertices. The first number is the originating state number, followed by the dash and then the destination state number.

22

Definitions and Acronyms

22.1 RELIABILITY DEFINITIONS

Mission Reliability: The ability of an item to perform its required functions for the duration of the specified mission profile. (MIL-STD-721C).

22.2 TIME DEFINITIONS

Clock Time: Elapsed time for the program execution, including wait time, during which the computer is operating.

Execution Time: CPU time while executing a program.

Calendar Time: Chronological time during which the computer is operating.

Failure Time: Accumulated elapsed time at which failure occurs.

Utilization: Proportion of time a resource is used.

Computer Utilization: Fraction of time the computer is executing.

Up Time: Time interval from system repair to next system failure (MUT).

Down Time: Time interval from system failure to next system repair (MDT).

Cycle Time: Time interval from one system failure to the next system failure. The cycle time is the sum of MUT and MDT (MCT).

Time to First Failure: Time interval from system initiation to the first system failure (MTFF).

Time to Failure: Time interval from an instant when the system is working, chosen randomly, to the next system failure. The randomly chosen instant is assumed to be a long time from system initiation (MTTF).

22.3 MAINTAINABILITY DEFINITIONS

Maintainability: The measure of the ability of an item to be returned or restored to a specified condition when maintenance is performed by personnel with specified skill levels, using prescribed procedures and resources, at each prescribed level of maintenance and repair (MIL-STD-721B).

Mean Time To Repair (MTTR): The total cumulative maintenance time divided by the total corrective maintenance actions during a given period of time (MIL-STD-721B).

Corrective Maintenance: The actions performed, as a result of failure, to restore an item to a specified condition (MIL-STD-721B).

Preventive Maintenance: The actions performed in an attempt to retain an item in a specified condition by providing systematic inspection, detection, and prevention of incipient failure (MIL-STD-721B).

22.4 AVAILABILITY DEFINITIONS

Availability may be defined as a measure of the degree to which an item is in an operable and committable state at the start of the mission when the mission is called for at unknown (random) time (MIL-STD-721C). As a probability measure, it is the expected fraction of time during which the system or component is functioning within the acceptable limits.

Mathematically, it is defined as: Availability = MUT/MCT.

22.5 ACRONYMS

AES	Ada Expert System
AI	Artificial Intelligence
AIPS	Advanced Information Processing System
API	Application Programming Interface
ATE	Automatic Test Equipment
BD	Backwards Difference
BIT	Built-In-Test
CAD	Computer-Aided Design
CAE	Computer-Aided Engineering
CARMS	Computer-Aided Rate Modeling and Simulation
CASE	Computer-Aided Software Engineering
CDR	Critical Design Review
CPU	Central Processing Unit
CR	Carriage Return
DBMS	Database Management System
DDE	Dynamic Data Exchange
DF	Direction Finder
DFT	Design For Test

DLL	Dynamic Link Library
DMA	Direct Memory Access
ECCS	Engineering of Complex Computer Systems
FBD	Functional Block Diagram
FDDI	Fiber Distributed Data Interface
FD/FI	Fault Detection/Fault Isolation
FDIR	Fault Detection, Isolation, and Reconfiguration
FEHM	Fault/Error Handling Model
FFD	Functional Flow Diagram
FMEA	Failure Mode and Effects Analysis
FMECA	Failure Mode, Effect, and Criticality Analysis
FOM	Figure of Merit
FT	Fault-tolerance
FTA	Fault Tree Analysis
FTD	Fault Tree Diagram
GSE	Ground Support Equipment
GSPN	Generalized Stochastic Petri Net
GUI	Graphical User Interface
HLSDL	High-Level Software Description Language
H/W	Hardware
IFF	Identification Friend or Foe
IFR	Instrument Flight Rules
ILS	Instrument Landing System
I/O	Input/Output
IRS	Interface Requirements Specification
LCC	Life-Cycle Cost
LRM	Line Replaceable Module
LRU	Line Replaceable Unit
MCSP	Mission Completion Success Probability
MCT	Mean Cycle Time
MDT	Mean Down Time
MIL-HDBK	Military Handbook
MIL-STD	Military Standard
MLDT	Mean Logistics Delay Time
MM	Markov Model
MRT	Mean Restore Time
MTBCF	Mean Time Between Critical Failures
MTBF	Mean Time Between Failures
MTBM	Mean Time Between Maintenance
MTTF	Mean Time To Failure
MTTR	Mean Time To Repair
MUT	Mean Up Time
MVA	Mean Value Analysis
NHPP	Nonhomogeneous Poisson Process
NMR	N-Modular Redundancy
PN	Petri Net
RAM	Reliability, Availability, Maintainability
RBD	Reliability Block Diagram

RK	Runge-Kutta
RMA	Reliability, Maintainability, Availability
RM&S	Reliability, Maintainability, and Supportability
SE	System Effectiveness
SOR	System Operational Requirements
SPN	Stochastic Petri Net
STD	State Transition Diagram
S/W	Software
TACAN	Tactical Air Navigation
TM	Test and Maintenance
TMR	Triple Modular Redundancy
UHF	Ultra High Frequency
VFR	Visual Flight Rules
VHDL	VHSIC Hardware Description Language
WAES	Windows Ada Expert System
WSEIAC	Weapon System Effectiveness Industry Advisory Committee

22.6 EPILOGUE

The techniques and the computer programs described in this book do not eliminate the need for experienced systems and reliability engineers. They only provide tools that allow the designer to consider more potential systems in the allotted time and thus help to improve reliability and reduce the system cost.

References

[Anderson 85a]. Anderson, T., et al., "Software Fault Tolerance: An Evaluation," *IEEE Transactions on Software Engineering*, SE-11, December 1985.

[Anderson 85b]. Anderson, T., et al., "An Evaluation of Software Fault Tolerance in a Practical System," *IEEE FTCS-15*, 1985.

[Barber 65]. Barber, D. F., et al., "Weapon System Effectiveness Industry Advisory Committee," AFSC-TR-65-2, Vol. 3, 1965.

[Barborak 93]. Barborak, M., and Malek, M., "The Consensus Problem in Fault-Tolerant Computing," *ACM Computing Surveys*, Vol. 25, 1993, p. 171.

[Barlow 65]. Barlow, R. E., and Proshan, F., *Mathematical Theory of Reliability*, John Wiley & Sons, 1965.

[Bavuso 87]. Bavuso, S. J., et al., "Analysis of Typical Fault-Tolerant Architectures Using HARP," *IEEE Transactions on Reliability*, Vol. R-36, No. 2, June 1987.

[Bergquist 67]. Bergquist, C. H., Cohen, C. L., and Lahn, T. G., *Investigation and Demonstration of Techniques for Practical Applications of Redundancy for Flight Controls*, AFFDL-TR-67-61, 1967.

[Bouricius 71]. Bouricius, W. G., "Reliability Modeling for Fault-Tolerant Computers," *IEEE Transactions on Computers*, Vol. 20, No. 11, November 1971.

[Brocklehurst 92]. Brocklehurst, S., and Littlewood, B., "New Ways to Get Accurate Reliability Measures," *IEEE Software*, July 1992.

[Butler 92]. Butler, R., "The SURE Approach to Reliability Analysis," *IEEE Transactions on Reliability*, Vol. R-41, No. 2, June 1992.

[Butler 86]. Butler, R. W., "An Abstract Language for Specifying Markov Reliability Models," *IEEE Transactions on Reliability*, Vol. 35, 1986, p. 595.

[Butler 93]. Butler, R. W., and Finelli, G. B., "The Infeasibility of Quantifying the Reliability of Life-Critical Real-Time Software," *IEEE Transactions on Software Engineering*, Vol. 19, No. 1, January 1993.

245

[Caroli 91]. Caroli, J. A., *A Survey of Reliability, Maintainability, Supportability, and Testability Software Tools,* Rome Laboratory, Air Force Systems Command, Griffiss Air Force Base, RL-TR- 91-87.

[Cha 87]. Cha, S. D., et al., "An Empirical Study of Software Error Detection Using Self-Checks," *IEEE FTCS-17,* 1987.

[Cox 65]. Cox, D. R., and Miller, H. D., *The Theory of Stochastic Processes,* John Wiley & Sons, 1965.

[Cox 62]. Cox, D. R., *Renewal Theory,* Methuen, 1962.

[Eckhardt 85]. Eckhardt, D. E., and Lee, L. D., "A Theoretical Basis for the Analysis of Multiversion Software Subject to Coincident Errors," *IEEE Transactions on Software Engineering*, SE-11, December 1985.

[English 68]. English, J. M., *Cost Effectiveness. The Economic Evaluation of Engineered Systems,* John Wiley & Sons, 1968.

[Feller 57]. Feller, W., *An Introduction to Probability Theory and Its Applications,* Vol. I, John Wiley & Sons, 1957.

[Gnedenko 63]. Gnedenko, B. V., *The Theory of Probability,* Chelsea Publishing Co., 1963.

[Goel 91]. Goel, A. L., and Mansour, N., *Software Engineering for Fault Tolerant Systems*, RL-TR-91-15, March 1991 [AD-A235 459].

[Hac 91]. Hac, A., "Using a Software Reliability Model to Design a Telecommunications Software Architecture," *IEEE Transactions on Reliability*, Vol. 40, No. 4, October 1991.

[Hamming 73]. Hamming, R. W., *Numerical Analysis for Scientists and Engineers,* Dover, 1973.

[Hargrave 67]. Hargrave, L. E., *Application of Redundancy Study*, Voyager Project, NASA CR-89703 (N67-40411), Jet Propulsion Laboratory, July 1967.

[Hecht 86a]. Hecht, H., and Hecht, M., "Software Reliability in the System Context," *IEEE Transactions on Software Engineering*, SE-12, January 1986.

[Hecht 86b]. Hecht, H., "Fault-tolerant Software for Real-Time Applications," *ACM Computing Surveys*, Vol. 8, No. 4, 1986.

[Heimann 86]. Heimann, D. I., et al., "Dependability Modeling for Computer Systems." *Proceedings Reliability and Maintainability Symposium*, 1991, p. 120.

[Howard 64]. Howard, R. A., "System Analysis of Semi-Markov Models," *IEEE Transactions on Military Electronics*, April 1964.

[Huslende 81]. Huslende, R., "A Combined Evaluation of Performance and Reliability for Degradable Systems," *Performance Evaluation Review*, Vol. 10, pp. 157–164, 1981.

[Jalotte 86]. Jalotte, P., and Campbell, R. H., "Atomic Actions for Fault-Tolerance Using Communicating Sequential Processes," *IEEE Transactions on Software Engineering*, SE-12, No. 1, 1986.

[Johnson 82]. Johnson, M. S., "Some Requirements for Architectural Support of Software Debugging," *ACM SIGPLAN*, Vol. 17, No. 4, April 1982, pp. 140–148.

[Johnson 88]. Johnson, A. M., Jr., and Malek, M., "Survey of Software Tools for Evaluating Reliability, Availability, and Serviceability," *ACM Computing Surveys,* Vol. 20, No. 4, December 1988, p. 227.

[Johnson 89]. Johnson, B. W., *Design and Analysis of Fault Tolerant Digital Systems,* Addison-Wesley, 1989.

[Kanoun 93]. Kanoun, K., et al., "SoRel: A Tool for Reliability Growth Analysis and Prediction from Statistical Failure Data," *IEEE FTCS-23*, 1993, p. 648.

[Knight 86]. Knight, J. C., and Levenson, N. G., "An Empirical Study of Failure Probabilities in Multi-Version Software," *IEEE FTCS-16*, 1986.

[Kumar 86]. Kumar, V. K. P., et al., "Distributed Program Reliability Analysis," *IEEE Transactions*, SE-12, No. 1, 1986.

[Lala 91]. Lala, J. H., et al., "A Design Approach for Ultrareliable Real-Time Systems," *Computer*, May 1991, p. 12.

[Laprie 87]. Laprie, J., et al., "Hardware and Software Fault Tolerance: Definition and Analysis of Architectural Solutions," IEEE FTCS-17, 1987.

[Levendel 89]. Levendel, Y., "Defects and Reliability Analysis of Large Software Systems: Field Experience," *IEEE FTCS-1989*, pp. 238–243.

[Lewis 89]. Lewis, P. A. W., and Orav, E. J., *Simulation Methodology for Statisticians, Operations Analysts and Engineers*, Vol. I, Wadsworth & Brooks, 1989.

[Littlewood 87]. Littlewood, B., and Miller, D. R., "A Conceptual Model of a Multi-Version Software," *IEEE FTCS-17*, 1987.

[Lyu 93]. Lyu, M. R., et al., "A Systematic and Comprehensive Tool for Software Reliability Modeling and Measurement," *IEEE FTCS-23,* 1993, p. 648.

[Musa 87]. Musa, J. D., et al., *Software Reliability,* McGraw-Hill Book Co., 1987.

[Nicol 92]. Nicol, D. M., and Palumbo, D. M., "Reliability Analysis of Complex Models Using Sure Bounds," NASA Contractor Report 191445, 1992.

[Nicol 93]. Nicol, "REST: A Parallelized System for Reliability Estimation," *1993 Proceedings Reliability and Maintainability Symposium*, 1993, p. 436.

[NRC 86]. *Isolation of Faults in Air Force Weapons and Support Systems*, National Research Council, July 1986, [AD A176 713].

[O'Connor 91]. O'Connor, P. D. T., *Practical Reliability Engineering,* 3rd ed., John Wiley & Sons, 1991.

[Palumbo 92]. Palumbo, D. L., "Using Failure Modes and Effects Simulation as a Means of Reliability Analysis," *AIAA, DAS 1992*, pp. 102–107.

[Peterson 77]. Peterson, J. L., "Petri Nets," *ACM Computing Surveys*, 1977, p. 223.

[Pitarys 88]. Pitarys, M. J., *Debugging Distributed Ada Software*, in [AGARD 88].

[Probert 82]. Probert, Robert L., "Optimal Insertion of Software Probes in Well-Delimited Programs," *IEEE Transactions on Software Engineering*, Vol. SE-8, No. 1, January 1982, pp. 34–42.

[Pukite 89a]. Pukite, J., Pukite, P. R., and Berman, C. L., *Fail-Safe Fault-Tolerant Electronics*, Phase I, DAINA, June 1989, Air Force Avionics Laboratory, WRDC-TR-89-1074, [AD B133 477].

[Pukite 89b]. Pukite, J., and Secord E. A., *Mission Reliability Analysis (MIREM) Engineering Workstation*, DAINA, Air Force Human Resource Laboratory, AFHRL-TR-89-47 [AD-B144 711].

[Pukite 89c]. Pukite, J., Kernal, M. J., and Pukite, S. J., *Intelligent Built-In-Test Module (IBITM)*, Final Report, DAINA, March 1989, prepared for Naval Air Systems Command [AD-B165 350].

[Pukite 92]. Pukite, P. R., Pukite, J., and Barnhart, D. S., "Expert System for Redundancy and Reconfiguration Management," *IEEE NAECON 92 Conference Proceedings,* Vol. 1, pp. 233–240.

[Reibman 91]. Reibman, A. L., et al., "Reliability Modeling: An Overview for System Designers," *IEEE Computer,* April 1991, p. 49.

[Reifer 79]. Reifer, D. J., "Software Failure Modes and Effects Analysis," *IEEE Transactions on Reliability,* Vol. R-28, No. 3, August 1979, pp. 249–257.

[Scott 87]. Scott, R. K., et al., "Fault-Tolerant Software Reliability Modeling," *IEEE Transactions on Software Engineering,* SE-13, No. 5, 1987.

[Sheldon 92]. Sheldon, F. T., et al., "Reliability Measurement: From Theory to Practice," *IEEE Software,* Vol. 9, No. 4, July 1992.

[Shimeall 91]. Shimeall, T. J., and Levenson, N. G., "An Empirical Comparison of Software Fault-Tolerance and Fault-Elimination," *IEEE Transactions on Software Engineering,* Vol. 17, February 1991 (based on Naval Postgraduate School Report NPS-52-89-047, available as [AD-A214 184]).

[Shooman 91]. Shooman, M., *1991 Proceedings of the Reliability, Maintainability Symposium,* p. 135.

[Simcox 88]. Simcox, L. N., *Software Fault Tolerance,* Royal Signals and Radar Establishment, RSRE-MEMO-4237, June 1988 [AD-A205 180].

[Sumita 86]. Sumita, U., and Masuda, Y., "Analysis of Software Availability/Reliability Under the Influence of Hardware Failures," *IEEE Transactions on Software Engineering,* SE-12, No. 1, 1986.

[Tang 93]. Tang, D., and Iyer, R. K., "Dependability Measurement and Modeling of a Multicomputer System," *IEEE Transactions on Computers,* Vol. 42, No. 1, January 1993.

[Tsai 90]. Tsai, J. J. P., et al., "A Noninvasive Architecture to Monitor Real-Time Distributed Systems," *IEEE Computer,* Vol. 23, No. 3, March 1990.

[Van Karsen 86]. Van Karsen, K. E., *Computer Hardware/Software Monitor,* Army Electronic Proving Ground, September 1986, [AD A179 777].

[Vick 90]. Vick, C. R., et al., *Software Fault Tolerance Design,* System Optimization Technology, RADC-TR-89-325, January 1990 [AD-B142 391].

[Weinstock 93]. Weinstock, C. B., and Schneider, F. B., "Dependable Software Technology Exchange," Software Engineering Institute Rep. No. CMU/SEI-93-SR-4.

[White 91a]. White, A. L., and Palumbo, D. L., *Model Reduction by Trimming for a Class of Semi-Markov Reliability Models and the Corresponding Error Bound,* NASA Technical Paper 3089.

[White 91b]. White, A. L., "An Error Bound for Instantaneous Coverage," *Proceedings Reliability and Maintainability Symposium,* 1991.

[White 92]. White, A. L., "Reliability Prediction for a Class of Highly Reliable Digital Systems," *Proceedings Reliability and Maintainability Symposium,* 1992.

Index

About the Authors

Dr. Paul Pukite has co-authored 30 refereed papers in various basic and applied research topics dealing with advanced electronics system design and software engineering. His projects have included developing new yield analysis techniques for semiconductor manufacturing, using digital signal processors (DSP) to perform a wide range of computationally intensive statistical analysis tasks that have normally been relegated to supercomputers, and architecting the Ada expert system and support software that formed the basis of the Redundancy and Reconfiguration Manager (RRM) developed for the Air Force Pave Pillar Integrated Test Bed at Wright-Patterson AFB. He was also the principal architect and developer of the CARMS reliability analysis program (described in this book) used in designing complex fault-tolerant, fail-safe systems. Presently, he is a project engineer at United Defense, architecting a real-time simulation system for ground-based vehicles.

EDUCATION AND PROFESSIONAL ACTIVITIES: B.Sc. in Electrical Engineering with High Distinction from University of Minnesota in 1982; M.Sc. in Electrical Engineering from University of Minnesota in 1984; Ph.D. in Electrical Engineering from University of Minnesota in 1988. His thesis work investigated basic physical processes related to GaAs molecular beam epitaxy and other semiconductor fabrication techniques. He furthered this research via a postdoctoral appointment at the IBM T.J. Watson Research Center, by investigating novel silicon-based molecular beam epitaxy concepts.

Mr. Jan Pukite has been actively involved in military and commercial system design for over 30 years. His experience includes process and flight control system analysis and design, fault-tolerant system design, analysis and simulation of complex electronic systems, wargaming, design of very large-scale integrated circuits, design of CAD systems, software development, and microcomputer applications. His early experience at Allis-Chalmers included analytical design and computer simulation of control systems. As a project engineer at General Motors AC Electronics Division, he conducted design analysis and design reviews of inertial guidance and bombing and navigation systems (IGC &

BNS) and recommended design changes. While at Honeywell, Mr. Pukite served as principal investigator in many DOD-funded research and development studies, dealing with fault-tolerant system design, system optimization, and system simulation. In 1966 he received Honeywell's Outstanding Engineer and Scientist Award for his original contributions in system analysis and optimization areas. During his assignment in Honeywell's Research and Development Division, he was involved in large-scale wargaming simulation studies used to design and to evaluate unmanned, electronic-sensor-based, border security systems. Later he organized and supervised a new department responsible for design automation and scientific computing support at Honeywell's Solid State Electronics Center. While at Honeywell's Avionics Division, he organized and managed a systems development group (CAMAID — Computer Aided Manufacturing and Integrated Design) to implement computer applications within a design and manufacturing environment. In 1984 he founded DAINA to engage in advanced technology research and development.

EDUCATION AND PROFESSIONAL ACTIVITIES: BSEE (with honors) from University of Wisconsin in 1957. He has completed course requirements for MSEE, with emphasis on optimal control engineering, and has received additional training in system effectiveness, reliability, and maintainability engineering. Mr. Pukite is a member of the IEEE Computer Society.

Printed and bound by CPI Group (UK) Ltd, Croydon, CR0 4YY